Hamlet:
Model Essays
for Students

by

Brendan Munnelly

*"We are what we pretend to be,
so we must be careful
what we pretend to be."*
Kurt Vonnegut,
Mother Night

*To My Dear Catherine,
The Best Daughter Ever.*

ISBN-10: 1980540519
ISBN-13: 978-1980540519
Copyright © 2018 Brendan Munnelly. All Rights Reserved.

First Printing: 2018.

No portion of this book may be copied, retransmitted, reposted, duplicated, or otherwise used without the express written approval of the author, except by reviewers who may quote brief excerpts in connection with a review.

Disclaimer and Terms of Use: No information contained in this book should be considered as financial, tax, or legal advice. Your reliance upon information and content obtained by you at or through this publication is solely at your own risk. The author assumes no liability or responsibility for damage or injury to you, other persons, or property arising from any use of any product, information, idea, or instruction contained in the content or services provided to you through this book. Reliance upon information contained in this material is solely at the reader's own risk.

No skulls were thrown about in the making of this book.

Typeset in PT Sans and PT Serif from Google Fonts.
Cover image from pexels.com.

Published by Amazon Digital Services LLC.

Book website: **www.essaykit.com**
Twitter: **www.twitter.com/essaykit**
Facebook: **www.facebook.com/essaykit**

ABOUT THE AUTHOR
BRENDAN MUNNELLY has written and co-written over a dozen books on computing in education that have sold more than 100,000 copies in five languages and earned multiple five-star Amazon reviews from students and teachers alike. This is his first book on Shakespeare and Hamlet rather than hardware and software.

Contents

1 - The Character of Hamlet..1

Hamlet: Born a prince, parented by a jester, haunted by a ghost, destined to kill a king rather than become one, and remembered as the title character of a play he did not want to be in.

    1.1 – Introduction..2

    1.2 – Revenge and forgiveness: *"Alas, poor Ghost!"*..........................5

    1.3 – Madness: *"Losing his wits … here in Denmark"*........................9

    1.4 – Acceptance or action: *"To be or not to be"*..................................12

    1.5 – Tragic hero, Oedipal son, PTSD sufferer: *"Who's there?"*......16

    1.6 – Conclusion: *"Remember me"*..20

2 - The Character of Claudius..25

His *"ambition"* (3.3) for Denmark's throne leads Claudius to commit one murder only to find he must plot a second to cover up the first. In the end, just like the brother he murdered, and by the same means of his own poison, Claudius is *"Of life, of crown, of queen at once dispatched"* (1.5).

    2.1 – Introduction..26

    2.2 – Kingship: *"Witchcraft of his wit"*...29

    2.3 – Queen Gertrude: *"Our sometime sister"*..............................33

    2.4 – Prince Hamlet: *"Mighty opposites"*......................................36

    2.5 – Tragic hero: *"Some vicious mole of nature"*.......................39

    2.6 – Conclusion: *"He is justly served"*..42

3 - The Character of Gertrude 45

After old King Hamlet's death, Gertrude quickly remarries in the hope her queenly life will continue as before and her son will accept his uncle as a substitute father. But her choice of husband dooms her life and the lives of everyone around her.

   3.1 – Introduction 46
   3.2 – The wedding: *"Taken to wife"* 49
   3.3 – The royal couple: *"I shall obey you"* 52
   3.4 – Hamlet: *"Why seems it so particular with thee?"* 56
   3.5 – Ophelia: *"Your good beauties"* 59
   3.6 – Conclusion: *"I am poisoned"* 62

4 - The Character of Ophelia 67

Her submission to her manipulative father costs Ophelia her sanity and leaves her with only one route of escape. Her *"self-slaughter"* (1.2) is Ophelia's revenge against everyone who dismissed, silenced and humiliated her.

   4.1 – Introduction 68
   4.2 – Sister and daughter: *"A green girl"* 71
   4.3 – Seductress and snitch: *"Where is thy father?"* 75
   4.4 – Traumatized truth-teller: *"Pray you, mark me"* 78
   4.5 – Death: *"Fell into a weeping brook"* 82
   4.6 – Conclusion: *"That's for remembrance"* 85

5 - The Relationship of Hamlet and the Ghost 89

By surrendering Denmark to the son of the man he murdered, a dying Hamlet grants to the doomed-to-walk-the-night Ghost of his *"dear father"* (2.2) the forgiveness his suffering soul needed more than the revenge he demanded: *"Rest, rest, perturbed spirit!"* (1.5).

　5.1 – Introduction..90

　5.2 – The Ghost: *"Questionable shape"*....................................93

　5.3 – King Claudius: *"A brother's murder"*..............................97

　5.4 – Queen Gertrude: *"Leave her to heaven"*......................100

　5.5 – Madness: *"Taint not thy mind"*......................................103

　5.6 – Conclusion: *"Rest, rest, perturbed spirit!"*...................107

6 - The Relationship of Hamlet and Claudius 111

Two men at war with each other—and themselves. Claudius is haunted by the murder he has committed (*"O heavy burden!"*, 3.1). Hamlet by the one he hasn't yet (*"Am I a coward?"*, 2.2). The prince enjoys play-acting in theater. His uncle excels at play-acting in politics.

　6.1 – Introduction..112

　6.2 – The imposter king and the player prince: *"Who's there?"*....115

　6.3 – The reverse revelation: *"The play's the thing"*............119

　6.4 – The two delayers: *"I stand in pause"*............................122

　6.5 – The queen in the middle: *"My heart is cleft in twain"*............126

　6.6 – Conclusion: *"As kill a king"*...129

7 - The Relationship of Hamlet and Gertrude..........................133

A haunted-by-the-past (*"Must I remember?"*, 1.2) Prince Hamlet seeks the truth about his father's death. A live-in-the-present (*"all that is I see"*, 3.4) Queen Gertrude seeks to protect her second husband and throne. To secure his already-thwarted inheritance from the birth of a rival heir, Hamlet attempts to separate Queen Gertrude from his usurping uncle.

    7.1 – Introduction..134

    7.2 – The prisoner of Elsinore:
"Stay with us. Go not to Wittenberg"..................................137

    7.3 – The Player Queen:
"The lady doth protest too much, methinks"....................141

    7.4 – The closet scene: *"Cruel only to be kind"*......................144

    7.5 – Departure and return: *"Hamlet, Hamlet!*......................148

    7.6 – Conclusion: *"Wretched Queen, adieu"*..........................151

8 - The Relationship of Hamlet and Ophelia..........................155

Their relationship begins in uncertainty, descends into mutual deceit and rejection, and ends with their double surrender to death: she to the *"weeping brook"* (4.7), he to Claudius' *"he shall not choose but fall"* (4.7) rigged fencing duel

    8.1 – Introduction..156

    8.2 – Hamlet's wooing: *"I do not know what to think"*.......159

    8.3 – Ophelia's guilt: *"Mad for thy love?"*.................................163

    8.4 – The double deception: *"No more marriages"*.............166

    8.5 – Two truth-tellers: *"Dangerous conjectures"*..................170

    8.6 – Conclusion: *"All trivial fond records"*.............................173

9 - The Relationship of Hamlet and Horatio 177

Their companionship evokes the advice offered to Laertes: *"Those friends thou hast, and their adoption tried, / Grapple them unto thy soul with hoops of steel"* (1.3). Horatio is Hamlet's trusted confidant in life and vows to remain the keeper of his memory after the prince's death.

- 9.1 – Introduction..178
- 9.2 – Meeting Horatio: *"What brings you from Wittenberg?"*...........181
- 9.3 – The Ghost: *"More things in heaven and earth"*.........................185
- 9.4 – The Murder of Gonzago: *"Observe mine uncle"*.......................188
- 9.5 – The pirate rescue: *"Thieves of mercy"*...191
- 9.6 – Conclusion: *"All this I can truly deliver"*..195

10 - The Relationship of Claudius and Gertrude 199

Claudius wanted something (the role of king) he did not have; Gertrude had something (the status of queen) she wanted to hold onto. Ultimately, the *"mirth in funeral"* (1.2) union of Hamlet's *"uncle-father and aunt-mother"* (2.2) ends when both die from the same poison Gertrude's second husband used to murder her first.

- 10.1 – Introduction..200
- 10.2 – The wedding: *"With mirth in funeral and with dirge in marriage"*..................203
- 10.3 – The royal couple: *"I could not but by her"*................................206
- 10.4 – The prince: *"My uncle-father and aunt-mother"*......................209
- 10.5 – The descent: *"When sorrows come ..."*..212
- 10.6 – Conclusion: *"Is thy union here?"*...216

11 - The Themes of *Hamlet* 221

A king murdered, an inhertance stolen, a family divided: Elsinore's older generation destroys its younger when two brothers—one living, one undead—battle in a *"cursed spite"* (1.5) over a crown and queen. The play ends in a *"feast"* of *"Death"* when the characters' *"deep plots"* all rebound back on their *"inventors' heads"* (5.2).

- 11.1 – Introduction 222
- 11.2 – Appearance versus reality: *"Who's there?"* 225
- 11.3 – Revenge and remembrance: *"Where is thy father?"* 228
- 11.4 – Madness: *"Taint not thy mind"* 232
- 11.5 – Corruption, decay and death: *"An unweeded garden"* 235
- 11.6 – Conclusion: *"The fall of a sparrow"* 239

12 - The Theme of Revenge 243

Two bereaved sons journey from vengeance, through obsession and anger, to forgiveness. An opportunist claims an empty throne. And the revenge sought by the Ghost of old King Hamlet on his brother in act one becomes in act five the revenge of old King Fortinbras on old King Hamlet.

- 12.1 – Introduction 244
- 12.2 – Hamlet and his ghost-father: *"Thy dread command"* 247
- 12.3 – Hamlet and his aunt-mother: *"Up, sword ... My mother stays"* 251
- 12.4 – Laertes: *"I'll be your foil"* 254
- 12.5 – Young Fortinbras: *"Lands lost by his father"* 258
- 12.6 – Conclusion: *"Exchange forgiveness with me"* 261

13: The Theme of Appearance Versus Reality 267

'Seems' and 'is' are as maddeningly far apart as Rosencrantz and Guildenstern are comically similar. Hamlet is a play-long triple pun on the verb 'to act': to take action, to behave deceitfully, and to perform in theater.

- 13.1 – Introduction 268
- 13.2 – Claudius: *"He that plays the king"* 271
- 13.3 – Polonius: *"Seeing, unseen"* 275
- 13.4 – Hamlet: *"I know not seems"* 278
- 13.5 – Gertrude: *"Paint ... an inch thick"* 281
- 13.6 – Conclusion: *"Who's there?"* 285

14 - The Theme of Madness 289

Is Hamlet ever really insane? If he is not, why is he pretending to be? Is the prince's behavior the cause of Ophelia's traumatic breakdown and suicide? As for Hamlet's personality, how can we reconcile his scholarly, artistic temperament with his near-sociopathic disregard of others?

- 14.1 – Introduction 290
- 14.2 – Hamlet's performance: *"An antic disposition"* 293
- 14.3 – Hamlet's psychology: *"A kind of joy"* 296
- 14.4 – Oedipal complex?: *"Incestuous sheets"* 301
- 14.5 – Ophelia's trauma: *"Divided from herself"* 305
- 14.6 – Conclusion: *"Cudgel thy brains no more"* 309

1

The Character of Hamlet

"My lord, what is your cause of distemper?"

Hamlet: Born a prince, parented by a jester, haunted by a ghost, destined to kill a king rather than become one, and remembered as the title character of a story he did not want to be in. There are many parallels between the dramatic character and his creator. But why would a playwright create a fictionalized version of himself only to inflict on him such *"a calamity of ... life"* (3.1)?

1.1 – Introduction

Prince Hamlet, the so-called 'melancholy Dane', is also the only title character of a Shakespearean tragedy with a sense of humor. In the play's final 5.2 scene, after many *"purposes mistook"*, the *"providence"* to which the prince ultimately surrenders his fate grants him the opportunity to *"win at the odds"*: his antagonist, exposed and justly punished (Claudius); his soul, forgiven (Laertes); and his life remembered and story told (Horatio).

Sample 1-1
The first sample introduction argues that Hamlet the character doesn't want to be in *Hamlet* the play. Unfortunately, as a dramatic figure, the prince cannot escape the role and storyline Shakespeare has created for him.

Prince Hamlet is the title character of a play he does not want to be in. Although often labeled as a young man who cannot make up his mind, the prince's mind is made up at the very beginning of the play that bears his name: he wishes to leave Elsinore castle and resume the life he loved at Wittenberg University. When that is denied, such is the *"sea of troubles"* (3.1) Hamlet confronts that by the play's second scene the theater-loving prince wishes he could write himself out of the drama in which Shakespeare has cast him: *"How weary"* that the *"Everlasting"* has fixed *"His canon 'gainst self-slaughter"* (1.2).

To borrow the words of his antagonist King Claudius, the prince's losses come *"not as single spies but in battalions"* (4.5): the father he idolized, dead (*"I shall not look upon his like again"*, 1.2); respect for his hastily remarried mother gone too (*"A beast would have mourned longer"*, 1.2); his succession hopes crushed (*"I lack advancement"*, 3.2); and his old school friends and love interest manipulated against him (*"It hath made me mad"*, 3.1).

Moreover, through the character of the Ghost, Shakespeare sets the prince a dilemma to which there seems no solution: how can Hamlet remove his uncle from his father's throne and mother's side without himself becoming another Claudius—a usurping villain in this life and a soul damned in the next?

Were Hamlet a conventional, problem-solving heroic figure, we can imagine he would depose Claudius, marry Ophelia and reign with her over Denmark happily ever after. But *"providence"* (5.2) in the form of Shakespeare cast him in a more tragic role: to kill a king and be killed for it, and to inherit not a royal throne but a soldier's funeral.

Sample 1-2

Is Prince Hamlet really William Shakespeare? There are certainly many parallels between the dramatic character and his creator. What is less clear is why a playwright would create a fictionalized version of himself only to inflict on him such *"a calamity of ... life"* (3.1).

Prince Hamlet of Denmark has been described as the only character in Shakespeare's plays who could have written Shakespeare's plays. In the tragic prince, Shakespeare *"hold(s), as 'twere, the mirror up to nature"* (3.2) by creating a fictional figure much in his own likeness. He is an actor (*"I perchance hereafter shall ... To put an antic disposition on"*, 1.5), playwright (*"The play's the thing / Wherein I'll catch the conscience of the King"*, 2.2) and stage director (*"Speak the speech, I pray you, as I pronounced it to you"*, 3.2). The prince is also a letter-writer who corresponds with Ophelia, Horatio, Claudius, Gertrude and the king of England, and who takes pride in his ability to *"write fair"* (5.2).

The prince's love of the theater is apparent in his happiest moment in the play: Rosencrantz's news that a troupe of Players is on its way to Elsinore. As his old school friend later remarks, *"there did seem in him a kind of joy / To hear of it"* (3.1). He greets the Players warmly as old acquaintances (*"Welcome, good friends"*, 2.2), recites from memory a lengthy speech from the mythical figure of Aeneas, and even offers them professional advice (*"Suit the action to the word, the word to the action"*, 3.2). Actors, declares Hamlet, *"are the abstract and brief chronicles of the time. / After your death you were better have a bad epitaph than their ill report while you live"*, 2.2).

One of the reasons the play that bears his name is Shakespeare's longest is that its title character talks such a lot. And when he does, it is with such eloquence, depth, and wit. Yet no one in drama has revealed so little of himself while saying so much. This essay is my personal effort at a task that has challenged others over a span of over four hundred years: to *"pluck out the heart"* of Prince Hamlet's *"mystery"* (3.2).

Sample 1-3
Sample introduction number three focuses on an often neglected but essential aspect of the prince's personality: his sense of humor. Not many title characters of tragic dramas could be described as comedians, but Prince Hamlet is never dull and often hilarious if sometimes cruelly so: *"A whoreson mad fellow"* (5.1), like his boyhood mentor, the court jester Yorick.

Given that he is *"benetted round with villainies"* (5.2) from the play's beginning, it is with good reason that the title character of Shakespeare's *Hamlet* has come to be known as the 'melancholy Dane.' In four short weeks (*"A little month, or ere those shoes were old"*, 1.2), his mother has become also his aunt, having transitioned from doting spouse (*"why, she would hang on him"*, 1.2) to grieving widow (*"Like Niobe, all tears"*, 1.2) and then to her first *"husband's brother's wife"* (3.4). And, after another month, the uncle the prince clearly despises both steals Hamlet's expected kingship and casts himself as his loving step-parent: *"think of us / As of a father"* (1.2).

As for the prince's actual *"dear father"* (2.1), old King Hamlet is at the same time both dead and alive. His passing left his son grief-stricken (*"I shall not look upon his like again"*, 1.2); and his return as a revenge-seeking ghost traps the prince between feelings of inadequacy in this world (*"Am I a coward?"*, 2.2) and fear of damnation in the next.

Although often despondent (*"I have of late ... lost all my mirth"*, 2.2; *"thou wouldst not think how ill all's here about / my heart"*, 5.2), Hamlet is also the only title character of a Shakespearean tragedy with a sense of humor. From his opening line (*"A little more than kin, a little less than kind"*, 1.2) onward, the prince indulges in bawdy puns and with witty scorn rebukes the failings of others. In what is the play's most visually iconic scene, his words to the skull of his boyhood mentor Yorick could serve as Hamlet's own epitaph: *"a fellow of infinite jest, of most excellent fancy"* (5.1). But the story Horatio survives to tell of Denmark's *"sweet Prince"* (5.2) and Ophelia's *"rose and expectancy of our fair state"* (3.1) is not a comedy but a tragedy: of a kingdom stolen, a family divided, and a young man born to set right a crime that *"hath the primal eldest curse upon't, / A brother's murder"* (3.3).

1.2 – Revenge and forgiveness: *"Alas, poor Ghost!"*

We, the audience, twice hear Claudius' confession (*"O heavy burden!"*, 3.1 and *"a brother's murder"*, 3.3) and are so certain of the king's guilt. But what if, like Hamlet, we had not? Moreover, the *"serpent"* (1.5) that a possible *"goblin damned"* (1.4) has asked the prince to assassinate has been duly elected as king by Denmark's nobles. And he is also the husband to whom Hamlet's mother is very happily—if incestuously—married.

Sample 2-1

After hearing the Ghost's command, why doesn't Hamlet simply seek out King Claudius and run him through with his sword? The first sample response offers one answer to the question of Hamlet's famed 'delay.'

"*This is too long*"—Polonius' comment in 2.2 on a speech delivered by one of Elsinore's visiting Players is more than an ironic statement on the lengthy play that contains it. The "*chiefly loved ... passionate speech*" that continues at Hamlet's insistence offers an insight into the dilemma of the "*thinking too precisely on th'event*" (4.4) prince.

In a "*broken voice*" and with "*Tears in his eyes*", the Player describes Hecuba's grief as she witnesses "*hellish Pyrrhus*" savagely butcher her husband Priam in revenge, "*mincing with his sword her husband's limbs.*" In the Player's performance I suggest Hamlet imagines the heartbreak his mother would experience should he make her a widow a second time in four months.

To his Ghost-inspired revenge mission, I suggest the prince has added a second, more poignant quest of his own: to reunite in the afterlife his fractured-by-Claudius family of mother and father. So, just like his antagonist, the prince is "*a man to double business bound.*" For this reason, he delays murdering the king until he can be sure his "*damned and black*" soul will be condemned to hell. As for his mother, Hamlet wishes to rescue her soul ("*Confess yourself to heaven. / Repent what's past. Avoid what is to come*", 3.4).

However, Hamlet's last words to Claudius in 5.2 ("*Follow my mother*") suggest he believes it will be in the company of the prince's villainous uncle rather than his "*dear father murdered*" (2.2) that the "*Wretched queen*" will be eternally united.

Sample 2-2

Hamlet never actually commits to a vow of revenge. Moreover, his eventual killing of Claudius is, in fact, an act of public justice. At the end, what his son grants his father's Ghost is not vengeance but atonement for his sins.

Prince Hamlet vows to take revenge against Claudius for his father's murder but is delayed by his 'tragic flaw'—variously described as hesitancy, indecision, prevarication or over-thinking—until the play's final scene. Contrary to this widely-held view, the prince never swears to avenge old King Hamlet, nor does he ever actually do.

In 1.5, the prince verbally sidesteps the Ghost's demand (*"Revenge"*) and promises only never to forget him (*"Remember me.' / I have sworn't"*). That Hamlet does not murder his country's duly elected monarch without evidence of guilt (*"grounds / More relative than this"*, 2.2) seems less a personality defect (*"some vicious mole of nature"*, 1.4) and more like the prudent judgement of a *"man / That is not passion's slave"* (3.2) and whose *"will is not his own"* (1.3) because as heir to the throne *"on his choice depends / The safety and health of this whole state"* (1.3).

Hamlet the play becomes a revenge tragedy only after Hamlet the character stages a play about revenge that so enrages him with blind fury he kills the wrong man and so succeeds only in creating another revenge-obsessed son like himself. As Hamlet says of Polonius' son to Horatio: *"For by the image of my cause I see / The portraiture of his"* (5.2).

When the prince does kill his uncle with the poison-tipped sword (for his own death) and goblet of poisoned wine (for this mother's), he makes no mention of either the Ghost or Claudius' original crime. And by surrendering Denmark to the son of old King Hamlet's rival, the prince grants his *"dear father"* (2.2) not the revenge he demanded but the atonement to end his soul's suffering in the *"sulfurous and tormenting flames"* (1.5).

Sample 2-3
The prince's blind and impulsive stabbing of Polonius creates a second fatherless son who will, in turn, seek revenge against him.

Where is thy father?" Had Ophelia asked the same question of Hamlet as he does of her in 3.1, would his answer have been any less dishonest? For a *"figure like the King that's dead"* (1.1) has returned from the grave to assert that *"The serpent that did sting thy father's life / Now wears his crown"* (1.5). But Hamlet does not trust the vengeance-demanding Ghost—a possible *"goblin damned"* (1.4)—any more than he does the living characters at Elsinore. He vows only never to forget his dead father rather than avenge him: *"Now to my word: / It is 'Adieu, adieu. Remember me.' / I have sworn't"* (1.5).

After a two-month-long psychological battle of wits between uncle and nephew, Hamlet devises his first action against Claudius: a performance by the visiting Players to *"catch the conscience of the King"* (3.2). The play-within-a-play does indeed send Claudius to his knees to confess his crime, but in his private chapel rather than publicly in front of the court. *"Now I might do him pat"* (3.3), Hamlet declares when he stumbles across the kneeling-in-prayer Claudius. Ironically, it is the prince's demonic desire not just to kill the king's body but also his soul (*"Up, sword, and know thou a more horrid hent"*, 3.3) that saves Claudius' life.

Minutes later, in his mother's closet and still inflamed by the stage-avenger and uncle-killer Lucianus, Hamlet commits the *"rash and bloody deed"* (3.4) of blindly stabbing Polonius through the arras. It is an irreversible turning point in the tragic unfolding of events; it is here that Hamlet's revenge-seeking storyline ends and Laertes' begins. That the play concludes with a *"feast"* of *"death"* (5.2) which sees the two avengers end each other's lives sends a clear warning against the destructive power of revenge.

1.3 – Madness: *"Losing his wits … here in Denmark"*
"Your noble son is mad" (2.2), Polonius tells Denmark's king and queen. But is Hamlet ever really insane? And if he is not, why is the prince pretending to be?

Sample 3-1
After his conversation with the Ghost in 1.5, Hamlet shares with his trusted colleagues Horatio and the guard Marcellus (*"your fingers on your lips, I pray"*) his plan to put on an *"antic disposition"* (1.5) – but never reveals his reason for so doing.

> Hamlet's motive for his put-on *"antic disposition"* (1.5) cannot be to protect his life from Claudius, for the king has no reason to suspect the prince knows the truth about old King Hamlet's murder. If anything, what Claudius calls Hamlet's *"turbulent and dangerous lunacy"* (3.1) makes him more rather than less suspicious of his nephew.
>
> Is it a ploy by Hamlet to disguise a mental fragility that might disqualify the prince from ever succeeding to the throne? From Hamlet's mother, we learn that the prince is prone to manic outbursts (*"a while the fit will work on him"*, 5.1). That Hamlet himself recognizes his judgment can be clouded by explosive rage (*"did put me / Into a towering passion"*, 5.2) is shown by his recruitment of the level-headed Horatio (*"Whose blood and judgement are so well commingle"*, 3.2) to assist him scrutinize Claudius' reaction to *The Murder of Gonzago*.
>
> In Hamlet's mind, was he planning to respond to any future concerns among Denmark's nobles regarding his mental fitness to rule as king by releasing from their oath of secrecy two credible witnesses: Marcellus, a representative of Elsinore's soldiers, and Horatio, a man trusted by them (*"thou art a scholar"*, 1.3)? Each would be able to confirm that the prince had indeed planned to feign eccentric behavior. And that, at his request (*"As you are friends, scholars and soldiers, / Give me one poor request … Consent to

swear", 1.5), they had agreed to keep his intention a secret (*"Propose the oath, my lord"*, 1.5).

However, in a play of *"purposes mistook / Fallen on th'inventors' heads"* (5.2), the reverse happens. The prince comes to be regarded not as an entirely sane man who only occasionally pretended to be otherwise; but as a complete lunatic (*"he that is mad"*, 5.1) who was banished from Denmark in the hope he might *"recover his wits"* (5.1).

Sample 3-2

A second explanation for the *"antic disposition"* (1.5) charade is that it is a forward-thinking plan by the prince to prepare a defense of temporary insanity should he actually assassinate the king. This theory also offers an interpretation of the prince's behavior towards Polonius' daughter, Ophelia.

> One interpretation of Hamlet's unexplained decision to adopt *"an antic disposition"* (1.5) is as follows: the *"Looking before and after"* (4.4) prince is setting in place a defense of temporary insanity should he assassinate King Claudius and face a trial before Denmark's nobles for the capital crime of regicide. This, of course, is the same excuse the prince later offers to Laertes as a defense for his murder of Polonius: *"I here proclaim was madness. / Was't Hamlet wronged Laertes? Never Hamlet ... Who does it, then? His madness"* (5.2).
>
> In this view, the prince shares his intent to feign episodes of insanity with Horatio and the guard Marcellus in 1.5 to assure them of his fitness to rule as a future king capable of protecting the *"safety and health of this whole state"* (1.3). So, in the interim, they should not doubt his sanity or otherwise lose confidence in him, however *"strange or odd soe'er I bear myself"* (1.5).
>
> Ophelia's father-commanded ending of her relationship with Hamlet provides the prince with the final element of his 'antic' ploy: to *"let belief take hold"* (1.1) that Ophelia's rejected love is the cause of *"the madness wherein*

now he raves" (2.2). Hence, Hamlet's disheveled *"doublet all unbraced"* (2.1) visit to her closet, his teasing of Polonius (*"Have you a daughter?"*, 2.2), and his risqué banter at *The Murder of Gonzago* (*"Here's metal more attractive"*, 3.2).

But, on fearing she is responsible for the prince's madness and, with it, his murder of her father, Ophelia herself succumbs to insanity. In summary, I see Hamlet's antic disposition ploy as an example of the disaster-prone *"deep plots"* (5.2) about which the prince later speaks to Horatio.

Sample 3-3

The third sample response argues that the Hamlet's 'antic' behavior provides an emotional outlet for the prince to release his rage and, by so doing, enables him to cling to his sanity.

"How came he mad?", Hamlet inquires about himself to the grave-digging sexton who is unaware it is the prince with whom he is speaking. *"On account of losing his wits"* (5.1) is the unhelpful reply he receives. Shakespeare leaves us guessing why the prince decides to *"put an antic disposition on"* (1.5).

"But break, my heart, for I must hold my tongue", the disinherited prince declares in his first soliloquy of 1.2. When he decides shortly afterward to put on an *"antic disposition"* (1.5), I believe it is at least in part because such a talkative lover of *"words, words, words"* (2.2) recognizes he cannot remain silent for very long.

I do not believe Hamlet's so-called madness is ever anything but an act that he uses as a coping mechanism to protect his sanity against the *"sea of troubles"* (3.1) that engulf him. He taunts and vents his rage at those who serve the king and queen. Polonius, he calls a *"fishmonger"* (2.2); and Rosencrantz he insults as a toadying *"sponge"* (4.2). In effect, he pretends to be mad to prevent himself from collapsing into actual insanity.

Horatio twice questions Hamlet's rashness: firstly, his desire to speak with the Ghost, and later to enter the fencing duel. But his trusted friend never doubts the prince's sanity. Certainly, Hamlet's sharp awareness of others' duplicity never deserts him.

When Claudius' remarks about his nephew that neither *"th'exterior nor the inward man / Resembles that it was"* (2.2), we are reminded that Elsinore is a place where there may be two possible answers to the question posed in the play's opening line: *"Who's there?"* While Hamlet's pretense mirrors Claudius falsity, the key difference is that the king impersonates someone he is not; the prince, in his mental turmoil (*"my weakness and my melancholy"*, 2.2), impersonates himself. For his outward feigned insanity both conceals and yet reveals his genuine inner anguish. Later, on board ship to England, Hamlet will commit his second act of self-impersonation: he will use his father's signature and seal as if he were the rightful King of Denmark which, of course, he actually is.

1.4 – Acceptance or action: *"To be or not to be"*

The content of the famous speech of 3.1 is less Elsinore Hamlet than Wittenberg Hamlet, such as might be spoken at a university debate. Nowhere does the speech contain the word 'I.' And, whatever the aristocratic Hamlet's problems, *"to grunt and sweat under a weary life"* isn't one of them. One further point: the opening question of *"To be or not to be"* is so phrased that it does not include a question mark.

Sample 4-1
Even after he has made up his mind to follow a course of action, Hamlet continues to analyze the dilemma that confronts him. Here is the first sample response on his *"To be or not to be"* speech.

"To be or not to be" (3.1)—it is significant that Hamlet delivers the famous speech that begins with these words after he has already committed to a course of action: of using the visiting Players to *"catch the conscience of the King"* (3.2). It tells us that the *"thinking too precisely on th'event"* (4.4) prince has still not resolved the eternal question: what is the right thing to do?

For Hamlet at this juncture, the alternative to life is not suicide, an option he has already soliloquized and dismissed because of God's *"canon 'gainst self-slaughter"* (1.2). Now the alternative to his *"calamity of ... life"* (3.1) is the suicide mission of following the Ghost's command and as a result facing likely execution for the crime of regicide.

Both the classical and Christian worldviews each offer conflicting guidance. The Players remind us of how the Greek warrior Pyrrhus savagely took revenge for his father's death. But the prince's confidant, Horatio, *"more an antique Roman than a Dane"* (5.2), provides a contrary example of Stoic endurance: *"As one, in suffering all, that suffers nothing"* (3.2). For Christians, vengeance belonged only to God, but as Hamlet later asks Horatio, might a Christian not also *"in perfect conscience"* take a life to prevent *"further evil"* (5.2)?

More generally, the prince's dilemma is between acceptance and action: should we endure the world as it is with all its *"sling and arrows"* and or take on *"a sea of troubles"* (3.1) by seeking to remake the world more to our liking? Hamlet, a Renaissance man of reason, cannot reason his way to a solution. He *"cudgels"* his *"brains"* in vain (5.1) for he is trapped in a tragic storyline in which, as Claudius later expresses it, *"he shall not choose but fall"* (4.7).

Sample 4-2
Sample analysis number two argues that the universal and timeless appeal of Hamlet's most famous speech rests on the fact that its concerns impact everyone, in every circumstance, in every era.

Commonly regarded as the most famous speech in the English language, Hamlet's *"To be or not to be"* soliloquy of 3.1 isn't really a soliloquy at all. It is, in fact, an extended aside, uttered while other characters are on stage but is unheard by them.

And although spoken by the prince, it does not refer to his personal circumstances. For what does an aristocrat know what it means *"to grunt and sweat under a weary life"*? Death is described as *"The undiscovered country from whose bourn / No traveler returns"*, yet Hamlet has spoken with a ghost. Nor can the prince plausibly complain about *"the law's delay"* when shortly afterward his royal status helps him evade punishment for Polonius' murder. Central to the speech's appeal is Hamlet's generalization of his particular dilemma—between taking, and not taking, revenge—into a universal and timeless choice that can trouble every *"fellow ... crawling between earth and heaven"* (3.1).

Is it *"nobler in the mind"* to endure the *"whips and scorns"* of our current circumstances? Or should we *"take arms against a sea of troubles"* by seeking to change the world for the better? For doing so may imperil more than our lives; it may also damn our souls if we are tempted into committing a wrong to achieve a rightful goal: *"Thus conscience does make cowards of us all ... And enterprises ... lose the name of action."*

It is a speech with an opening question so phrased that it does not include a question mark; that nowhere contains the word "I"; that ends without a conclusion; and that is followed by an unheard request for prayer to Ophelia who, as we know but Hamlet does not, isn't really praying at all.

Sample 4-3
The third sample response links the speech's two options of *"To be"* and *"not to be"* with sentiments expressed through the voices of other characters in the play.

Which is better—to live uselessly or die uselessly? That's the bleakest reading of Hamlet's *"To be or not to be"* speech of 3.1. In this *"calamity … of life"*, what does it matter whether we *"fly to others that we know not of?"* rather than *"bear those ills we have"* when all human choices lead to the same destination: the grave?

The *"To be"* option of living defensively is expressed in Rosencrantz's words that *"the single and peculiar life is bound / With all the strength and armour of the mind / To keep itself from noyance"* (3.3). In a similar vein, Laertes cautions his sister Ophelia that *"Best safety lies in fear"* (1.3). But a life spent fearfully behind the *"the pales and forts of reason"* (1.4) and *"Out of the shot and danger of desire"* (1.3) seems little elevated above the existence of a *"beast"* whose *"chief good and market of his time"* is merely *"to sleep and feed"* (4.4).

That Hamlet phrases the contrary *"not to be"* option as *"to take arms against a sea of troubles"* is a recognition that our challenges can appear so overwhelming that opposing them seems as hopeless as attempting to defeat the ocean. And even if one succeeds after *"Exposing what is mortal and unsure / To all that fortune, death, and danger dare"* (4.4), all human endeavor seems futile, for *"To what base uses we may return"* (5.1).

Hamlet ends his speech with an unheard request to Ophelia (*"in thy orisons / Be all my sins remembered"*, 3.1) reflecting that the prince has already made his choice: to follow the dangerous path of *"not to be"* and with it his own destruction.

1.5 – Tragic hero, Oedipal son, PTSD sufferer: *"Who's there?"*

Is Prince Hamlet a tragic hero as the term was understood in classical Greek drama? If so, what is his 'fatal flaw'? And how would psychologists diagnose Denmark's prince?

Sample 5-1

Is Hamlet a tragic hero? The answer seems to be: 'not really.' The prince is at least as much a victim of other characters' tragically flawed choices as he is of his own *"rash and bloody deed"* (3.4): his murder of Ophelia's father, Polonius.

> Claudius, Gertrude, Laertes and Polonius all resemble tragic heroes from classical Greek drama: high-born figures who doom themselves and others by yielding to a tragic flaw (*"some vicious mole of nature"*, 1.2). Their flaws are: a brother's jealously (*"mine own ambition"*, 3.3); opportunistic self-delusion (*"hoodman-blind"*, 3.4), impulsive vengeance (*"Let come what comes, only I'll be revenged,"* 4.5) and cynical meddlesomeness (*"Thou find'st to be too busy is some danger"*, 3.4).
>
> But if Prince Hamlet is a tragic hero, what is his flaw? It is hardly procrastination, for no character delays longer than the throne-winning Young Fortinbras. And Hamlet's murder of Polonius is rightly described by the queen as a *"rash ... deed"* (3.3). The stabbing in the back of a kneeling-in-prayer Claudius might have avoided further tragedy, but it would hardly have been heroic.
>
> In Greek tragedy, the term for a fatal flaw is *hamartia*, a word derived from archery meaning 'missing the mark.' That Hamlet's through-a-curtain stabbing of Polonius is literally a 'stab in the dark' reflects the play's concern with the difficulty of taking correct action in a world where we lack certain knowledge. As Claudius reflects: *"But 'tis not so above. / There is no shuffling / There the action lies / In his true nature"* (3.3).

> Although his stabbing of Polonius sets the play on its downward course to the final catastrophe, Hamlet is at least as much a victim of other characters' tragically flawed choices as he is of his own *"rash and bloody deed"* (3.4).
>
> Hamlet the character is both a wrong-doer and a *"benetted round with villainies"* (5.2) victim of other's choices. *Hamlet* the play can be viewed a warning both against revenge and against revenge plays. For what prompts the prince's rash killing (*"Dead for a ducat"*, 3.4) is a play he himself stages about revenge (*"a knavish piece of work ... writ in choice Italian"*, 3.2).

Sample 5-2

Not knowing he was adopted, title character of Sophocles' *Oedipus Rex,* married Jocasta, with neither groom nor bride realizing they were, in fact, son and mother. When both afterward discovered the truth, he blinded himself in shame and she hanged herself with bedsheets.

In the 1890s, psychologist Sigmund Freud misapplied the term 'Oedipal complex' to describe a psychological development stage in which sons sexually lust after their mothers. Assuming that Freud's theorized 'Oedipal complex' actually exists, is there anything to suggest the Prince of Denmark suffers from the psycho-sexual condition that the original Oedipus and King of Thebes never did?

> *Hamlet* productions that include a bed in 3.4 and show son and mother kiss full on the lips are inspired by psychologist Sigmund Freud's theory that the prince suffers from a so-called 'Oedipal complex'—and are unsupported by the actual text of Shakespeare's play. But then Freud also believed *Hamlet* was written by Edward de Vere, the 17th Earl of Oxford, and not William Shakespeare.

There is no 'bedroom scene' in Shakespeare's *Hamlet*; 3.4 takes places in Gertrude's closet. Such a room is defined in the Merriam-Webster dictionary as "a monarch's or official's private chamber." And how likely is it the queen would have a second *"royal bed of Denmark"* (1.5) in her closet in addition to the one in her bedroom? Moreover, Hamlet's directions to his mother in this scene—*"Sit you down"* and *"You shall not budge"*—hardly suggest sexual interaction between the two.

In my view, his wish to protect his already-thwarted inheritance is sufficient reason for Hamlet to urge Queen Gertrude: *"go not to mine uncle's bed"* (3.4). For the birth of a rival heir to Hamlet's *"uncle-father and aunt-mother"* (2.2) would provide King Claudius with his own line of hereditary succession and make permanent the prince's exclusion from Denmark's throne.

Hamlet's only fantasy about his parents' marriage is less perverse than poignant. It is not to imagine himself as an incestuous interloper between father and mother; quite the contrary. He longs to reunite in the afterlife the parental relationship still alive in his cherished memory (*"so loving to my mother ... Why, she would hang on him"*, 1.2). Nothing could be less incestuous or 'oedipal' than a son wishing he could restore his father to his mother's side.

Sample 5-3

Prince Hamlet: the artistic, scholarly intellectual—and the callous, near-sociopathic serial killer. Is Post-Traumatic Stress Disorder (PTSD), following his loss in childhood of the court jester and surrogate parent Yorick, an explanation for these dual and seemingly contradictory aspects of the prince's personality?

Is the play's most visually iconic moment—Hamlet's holding of the skull of the long-dead Yorick—also a clue as to why the title character is the person he is? In Hamlet's recollections of the court jester there is a sense of human connection strikingly absent from his family relationships. Yorick seemed not only a substitute for an absent-at-war father (*"he hath borne me on his back a thousand times"*). But a surrogate mother too for a self-absorbed Gertrude (*"those lips that I have kissed I know not how oft"*, 5.1).

It is recognized that a deep grief can cause a person to lose temporarily both their sense of self and connection with the world around them. For example, in *Romeo and Juliet*, the male lead laments to his Horatio-like friend, Benvolio: *"This is not Romeo ... I have lost myself. I am not here."* (1.1). Was Hamlet's loss in childhood of Yorick a traumatic moment when the aged-seven only child was *"from himself be ta'en away"* (5.2)?

Among the more extreme personality-modifying symptoms of Post-Traumatic Stress Disorder (PTSD) may be a long-term retreat from the real world into an imaginary one. Did a traumatized prince afterward find refuge in the make-believe world of theater? Certainly, Hamlet is never less like his 'melancholy Dane' caricature than when in the company of the Players. Indeed, the prince fancies he would enjoy success as a playwright and actor: *"Would not this ... get me a fellowship in a cry of players?"* (3.2).

However, when a person loses the ability to distinguish between the real life and their imaginary one, they may value the humanity of actual people as no greater than that of make-believe characters; in either world, everything is merely a series of *"actions that a man might play"* (1.2). The result can be behaviors that appear almost sociopathic. For example, the prince's sending to execution of his two old school friends so shocks Horatio that he will later absolve Claudius from any blame for it.

1.6 – Conclusion: *"Remember me"*

The play ends with the prince asking Horatio to tell his story, for the *"wounded name"* (5.2) Hamlet leaves behind of *"he that is mad and sent into England"* (5.1) is an incomplete version of his tragic tale: of a prince who, like Yorick, was *"a fellow of infinite jest, of most excellent fancy"* (5.1), but who was destined to kill a king rather than become one. His duty done, Hamlet is granted a soldier's farewell by Young Fortinbras: *"Bear Hamlet like a soldier to the stage … And, for his passage, / The soldiers' music and the rites of war / Speak loudly for him"* (5.2).

Sample 6-1

The first sample conclusion summarizes how the title character's various concerns are brought together in its final scene.

> The Hamlet who escapes Claudius' execution plot returns to Elsinore in 5.1 a changed man, both on the outside and inside. Gone are both his *"inky cloak"* (1.2) and *"antic disposition"* (1.5). And in his graveyard reflections, the prince belatedly recognizes the truth of his mother's observation that *"All that lives must die, / Passing through nature to eternity"* (1.2).
>
> From Laertes, the once self-described *"proud, revengeful, ambitious"* (3.1) prince begs for forgiveness: *"Give me your pardon, sir. I've done you wrong"* (5.2). Admitting he *"hurt my brother"* (5.2), Hamlet unhesitatingly accepts Laertes' challenge of a fencing duel.
>
> The *"divinity that shapes our ends"* (5.2) to which Hamlet has surrendered his fate resolves all the prince's concerns in a few short moments at the play's end. The plotters against him are *"hoist with (their) own petard"* (3.4); Laertes pardons him for his and Polonius' deaths; after his exposure as a murderous criminal (*"The King's to blame"*, 5.2), the villainous Claudius is publicly executed; Horatio will ensure his *"sweet Prince"* (5.2) will not leave behind a *"wounded name"* (5.2); with Hamlet's *"dying voice"* (5.2),

Young Fortinbras will protect the *"safety and health of this whole state"* (3.1); and, finally, if at the cost of his life, Hamlet is granted his original wish: to leave the *"prison"* (2.2) of Denmark. *"The rest is silence"* (5.2).

As for the destination of the prince's soul, we can imagine that question being debated by the grave-digging sexton who began his work on the day when the prince was born and Denmark's new King Fortinbras lost his father in a fatal duel with old King Hamlet.

Sample 6-2

Sample conclusion number two focuses on how the fates of old King Hamlet and Prince Hamlet mirror one another. The important difference lies in how they wish to be remembered: the father demanded revenge; the son wishes only for his story to be told.

The play ends with the Prince Hamlet's fate echoing that of old King Hamlet. His father's death was a secret murder disguised as an accidental snake-bite, a *"forged process"* with which *"the whole ear of Denmark"* was *"rankly abused"* (1.5). Similarly, as Claudius assures the blinded-by-vengeance Laertes, Prince Hamlet's demise in front of the assembled court will appear so unsuspicious that *"no wind of blame shall breathe"* and "*even his mother shall ... call it accident*" (4.7).

Unlike the original crime in the palace orchard, the rigged fencing duel is exposed publicly to the court, and the last members of the Hamlet and Polonius families perish in the *"feast"* of *"death"* (5.2) that greets Norway's Young Fortinbras, who arrives fortuitously to occupy Denmark's empty throne.

With the fast-acting poison in his body, Prince Hamlet ends the play much as old King Hamlet began it: as a ghost, suspended between this world and the next, fearing his life will be forgotten and the truth forever hidden: *"Remember me"* (1.5), asked the father; *"Report me and my cause aright"* (5.2), pleads the son.

Whereas the Ghost demanded remembrance in the form of revenge (*"If thou didst ever thy dear father love"*, 1.5), all Prince Hamlet asks of Horatio (*"If thou didst ever hold me in thy heart"*, 5.2) is that his story be told to the *"unknowing world"* (5.2). As for his final words *"The rest is silence"*, the legacy of Shakespeare's Prince Hamlet continues to be the very opposite. He remains the most written-about figure in all of literature. For still we wonder: *"Who's there?"* (1.1).

Sample 6-3

Previously, Hamlet was like an actor rebelling against the script of a play in which he has been reluctantly cast. Now he accepts Providence as the playwright of his fate. All he need do is be ready to act his assigned part when the moment comes.

On his return Elsinore, Gertrude's *"my too much changed son"* (2.2) has undergone a second transformation. He has left behind his *"antic disposition"* (1.5), his Polonius-like struggle to *"find / Where truth is hid"* (2.2) and his Claudius-style stratagems of deception and *"a little shuffling"* (4.7).

The *"providence"* (5.2) to which Hamlet attributes his escape from execution in England he now believes will provide the circumstances for him to complete the task in Denmark for which *"my fate cries out"* (1.4): *"To quit (Claudius) with this arm"* (5.2). But as his letter to Claudius (*"I am set naked on your kingdom"*, 4.7) and conversation with Horatio reveal, he feels no need to devise failure-prone *"deep plots"* (5.2); all the prince need do is be prepared, for *"the readiness is all"* (5.2).

Claudius' final murderous ploy of the rigged fencing duel and poisoned wine goblet ends with his public exposure to the court (*"The King, the King's to blame"*) and the deaths of four characters: Hamlet, Gertrude, Laertes and lastly the king himself. With deadly symbolism, Hamlet by two methods kills the *"arrant knave"* (1.5) whose poison claimed the lives of both his parents and who had twice schemed to murder him. To the arriving Young Fortinbras, he grants his *"dying voice"* (5.2) as Denmark's next king.

Before his body is carried *"High on a stage be placed to the view"* (5.2), Hamlet's last request is to Horatio: to *"tell my story ... more and less."* That the prince believes an *"audience to this act"* will *"look pale and tremble"* (5.2) suggests the title of the tale Horatio will tell and perhaps the Players may perform: 'The Tragedy of Hamlet, Prince of Denmark.'

2

The Character of Claudius

"High and mighty ... One may smile, and smile, and be a villain."

His *"ambition"* (3.3) for Denmark's throne leads Claudius to commit one murder only to find he must plot a second to cover up the first. His final villainous scheme rebounds when it leads to the death of the woman he loved (*"It is the poisoned cup; it is too late"*, 5.2) and, moments later, his own. So, in the end, just like the brother he murdered, and by the same means of his own poison, Claudius is *"Of life, of crown, of queen at once dispatched"* (1.5).

2.1 – Introduction
King Claudius is Prince Hamlet's Machiavellian antagonist whose corrupt ambition is the *"something rotten"* (1.4) in the state of Denmark. Appropriately for the villain of the play, his name is never spoken aloud by any other character.

Sample 1.1
This first sample response introduces Claudius as an essentially tragic figure whose 'fatal flaw' of unrestrained ambition brings about the downfall of himself, his family and his country.

> That the full title of Shakespeare's play is *The Tragedy of Hamlet, Prince of Denmark* suggests its protagonist is someone who plays the part of a 'tragic hero'—a high-born figure who, through some flaw or defect in his character, dooms his own life and destroys lives of everyone around him. I will argue that, to an extent greater than the play's title character or any of the others, his antagonist King Claudius fulfills this dramatic role of a tragic figure.
>
> Prince Hamlet may be impulsively violent, Queen Gertrude opportunistically self-deluding, Rosencrantz and Guildenstern mercenary, Laertes too easy to manipulate and his sister Ophelia too eager to please; but King Claudius brings about—and entirely deserves—his own downfall.
>
> Claudius' corrupting vice or *"vicious mole of nature"* (1.4) is his lust for political power. However, Claudius cannot be accused of ever deceiving himself. On his knees in his private chapel, he is unflinchingly honest about his power-hungry nature. He admits he cannot seek divine forgiveness because so doing would demand he surrender the rewards of his crime: *"My crown, mine own ambition, and my queen"* (3.3). In terms of classical Greek tragedy, this is his moment of *anagnorisis* when Claudius recognizes and accepts his character and fate.

In this essay, I will analyze the character of King Claudius under the following headings: his position as monarch; his relationships with Queen Gertrude and Prince Hamlet; and his dramatic role as an essentially tragic figure whose jealous ambition brings about the downfall of himself, his family and his country.

Sample 1.2

The second sample introduction characterizes the play's antagonist King Claudius as an envious brother who yielded to a criminal desire to steal his brother's life wife and throne.

Appropriately for the villain of the play *Hamlet*, Claudius' name is never spoken aloud by any other character. His secret *"brother's murder"* (3.3) of Prince Hamlet's father, his *"within a month"* (1.2) marriage to his *"sometime sister"* (1.2) Queen Gertrude and his election shortly afterward as Denmark's king provide the starting point to the play's storyline.

After thirty years his late brother's shadow, Claudius now possesses both the throne and queen old of King Hamlet. But the usurper's triumph is short-lived; it begins and ends with the pomp, ceremony, cannon-firing and carousing of act one. As the drama unfolds, Claudius' villainy sets in motion a series of events that brings calamity to everyone around him. In the words of the title character's confidant, Horatio, *Hamlet* the play is a story of *"purposes mistook / Fallen on th'inventors' heads"* (5.2).

But Claudius is no one-dimensional villain; only a man deeply haunted by his conscience would admit to himself how "*this cursed hand*" is tainted *"with brother's blood"* (3.3). And while his marriage to Hamlet's mother is motivated primarily by his desire to share her throne, there also is throughout the play ample evidence that he does indeed love Queen Gertrude (*"I could not but by her"*, 4.7)—and that his devotion is returned by Hamlet's mother.

In this essay, I will argue that Claudius is flawed figure who is morally corrupted by his desire for power. And I will describe how his reign as king is continually overshadowed by the unlawful means through which he achieved the throne until, at the end, he is *"justly served"* by a *"poison tempered by himself"* (5.2).

Sample 1.3

Sample introduction number three highlights the references in *Hamlet* to the Biblical stories of the first couple, Adam and Eve, and two of their sons, Cain and Abel.

In depicting the character of King Claudius in *Hamlet*, Shakespeare draws on two stories from the first book of the Bible with which his London audience would have been familiar: the fall of Adam and Eve; and the motivated-by-jealousy murder of one of their sons by another.

When the Ghost reveals to Prince Hamlet that *"The serpent that did sting thy father's life / Now wears his crown"* (1.5), I believe the playwright is inviting us to compare Claudius with Satan, who appeared in the Garden of Eden in the form of a snake. In his first soliloquy, Hamlet despairs that the Denmark previously ruled by his late father (*"so excellent a king"*) has under Claudius descended into a fallen kingdom, *"an unweeded garden / That grows to seed"* (1.2). Later, Claudius will plot the prince's execution using Rosencrantz and Guildenstern as his *"adders fanged"* (3.4) accomplices.

In his private chapel, a conscience-stricken Claudius acknowledges that his *brother's murder ... hath the primal eldest curse upon't"* (3.3). This is a reference to the tale of Cain and Abel, two sons of the Bible's first couple. Motivated by envy, the elder son Cain killed his younger brother, Abel. In the play's graveyard scene, Hamlet will imagine a skull to be *"Cain's jawbone, that did the first murder!"* (5.1).

In the era of the play, it would have been typical for the firstborn son to succeed to his father's position. Was Claudius, as Cain was to Abel, an elder brother to the prince's father, old King Hamlet? If so, why was he passed over for Denmark's kingship? Whatever the reason, it is not difficult to imagine Claudius' resentment, accumulating over three decades, tempting him to repeat Cain's brother-murdering crime.

2.2 – Kingship: *"Witchcraft of his wit"*

This second section focuses on Claudius' succession to Denmark's throne and his skills as a manipulative politician. The Ghost's remark about *"the witchcraft of his wit"* (1.5) accurately describes Claudius' strategic mind and charismatic manner.

But the *"arrant knave"* (1.5) is compelled to expend almost all his attention and energy grappling with the consequences that follow, directly and indirectly, from his pre-play poisoning of old King Hamlet. Claudius' criminal past continually overshadows his kingly reign.

Sample 2.1

The first sample response addresses the question: how did Claudius become king? Ophelia's description of old King Hamler's son as the *"rose and expectancy of our fair state"* (3.1) suggests the prince was regarded as the likely heir to Denmark's throne. Yet it was Claudius who won the support of Denmark's nobles in the pre-play election and gained the crown.

One possible answer lies in the contrasting attitudes of uncle and nephew towards their country's courtiers and nobles: the scheming politician Claudius is deferential; Hamlet the scholar is contemptuous.

Claudius admits his nephew is admired by *"the distracted multitude"* (4.3) and enjoys the *"great love the general gender"* (4.7). Moreover, the Elsinore castle guards feel a stronger bond with Hamlet than they do with him. It is to the prince they and Horatio report the Ghost's appearance, *"As needful in our loves, fitting our duty"* (1.1). Their later willingness to swear a vow of secrecy on Hamlet's sword (*"Propose the oath, my lord"*, 1.5) would have been regarded as a treasonous act; such loyalty was due only to a reigning king. So how was Claudius, in Hamlet's words, able to *"Pop ... between th'election and my hopes"* (5.2) to win Denmark's throne in preference to the prince?

In my view, Hamlet's contemptuous attitude towards the two nobles Polonius and Osrick reveals why he was unlikely to win the support of the aristocrats with the power to elect old King Hamlet's successor. The prince teases Polonius in every scene they share together. As for the wealthy, *"spacious in the possession of dirt"* landowner Osrick, Hamlet dismisses him as *"a beast"* who is a *"lord of beasts"* (5.2).

In contrast, Claudius is deferential towards those Hamlet disdains. In the opening court scene, he thanks them for their *"better wisdoms"* (1.2) in supporting his marriage to Gertrude and election as king. Later, after Polonius' murder by Prince Hamlet, he says to his wife and queen: *"Come, Gertrude, we'll call up our wisest friends; / And let them know, both what we mean to do"* (4.1).

And in the play's final moments, after he has been stabbed by Hamlet with Laertes' poison-tipped sword, it is to the nobles that the king again turns for support: *"O, yet defend me, friends; I am but hurt"* (5.2). But other than shout out *"Treason! Treason!"*, they make no move to assist the man they elected only six months previously to protect *"The safety and health of this whole state"* (1.3).

Sample 2.2
The second sample response offers the examples of the opening court scene and his later conversion of Laertes from insurgent to accomplice as evidence of Claudius' Machiavellian skills.

Claudius is a figure who seems to come directly from the pages of Machiavelli's *The Prince*, an Italian handbook for political rulers published almost a century before *Hamlet*. Indeed, his character can be viewed as a dramatic vehicle for exploring the philosophy of Machiavellian kingship: that a successful ruler does not allow moral scruples stand between him and whatever needs to be done to win and hold onto power. Shakespeare was aware of Machiavelli's cynical opinions and cited him by name in two earlier plays, *Henry VI Part III* and *The Merry Wives of Windsor*.

Two scenes in particular show Claudius displaying the mastery of rhetoric and manipulation that are the hallmarks of a Machiavellian ruler. In the 1.2 court scene, he alters his speaking style when addressing different topics. For example, he is formal when dealing with his kingship and marriage (*"In equal scale weighing delight and dole"*), but gracious when responding to a personal request (*"Take thy fair hour, Laertes. Time be thine, / And thy best graces spend it at thy will"*).

Later in 4.5, even at the point of Laertes' sword after a rebellious mob has overpowered his personal guards, Claudius cunningly turns the situation to his advantage. After Gertrude absolves her husband of any role in Polonius' death (*"But not by him"*), he praises Laertes' fencing skills (*"'twould be a sight indeed / If one could match you"*, 4.7) for the purpose of manipulating him into a rigged fencing duel with Hamlet. Ironically, the final victim of Claudius' craftiness is himself: the *"envenomed"* (5.2) sword and *"chalice for the nonce"* (4.7) he intended for the prince become the means by which he loses his own life.

Sample 2.3
Sample response number three asks the question: does Claudius in any way redeem himself by using his ill-gotten kingly power for the good of Denmark? The answer would seem to be 'No.'

If we are to feel empathy for the villainous Claudius, it can only be because of some positive aspects of his character that may balance—even if they can never justify—his evil actions. For example, does Claudius use wisely, and in Denmark's interests rather than his own, the royal power he gained through *"a brother's murder"* (3.3)?

Only in the opening court scene, when he sends ambassadors to the Norwegian king in response to the threat of invasion, do we see Claudius focused on his country's welfare. But even on that occasion, the king is dealing with a problem of his own creation. As he admits, it was his accession to the throne that led Norway's Young Fortinbras to believe *"Our state to be disjoint and out of frame"* on the basis that Claudius was likely to be a less formidable adversary than his *"late dear brother"* (1.2).

Later in 2.2, when Polonius announces that the ambassadors have *"joyfully returned"*, and, as *"the fruit to that great feast"*, he has uncovered *"the very cause of Hamlet's lunacy"*, the king is less interested in the news from Norway than in the mental state of Hamlet: *"O, speak of that! / That do I long to hear."* In my opinion, Claudius' reply reveals that the safety of his kingdom's borders is his second priority. His primary obsession is with the threat to his position posed by the *"turbulent and dangerous lunacy"* (3.1) of his nephew.

In summary, Claudius is compelled to expend almost all his attention and energy grappling with the consequences that follow, directly and indirectly, from his pre-play crime in the palace orchard. His criminal past continually overshadows his kingly reign.

2.3 – Queen Gertrude: *"Our sometime sister"*
Why did the Claudius propose to Gertrude? Why did she say 'I do'? And how should we best describe their royal marriage?

Sample 3.1
What led Claudius and Gertrude to the altar? This first sample response explores the motivations for their marriage.

Was the marriage of Claudius and Queen Gertrude the culmination of an adulterous love affair that began before old King Hamlet's death?

In *The Murder of Gonzago,* so adapted as to *"catch the conscience of the King"* (2.2), Hamlet presents the seduction of the Player Queen (*"you shall see anon how the murderer gets the love of Gonzago's wife"*) as following rather than preceding the murder of the sleeping Player King (*"A poisons him i'th'garden for his estate"*, 3.2). And Hamlet's farewell words to Claudius include no accusation of adultery: *"thou incestuous, murderous, damned Dane"* (5.2).

Instead, I see Claudius' marriage to Gertrude as the second step in a three-part, throne-winning strategy. With his brother disposed of, step one was complete. Next was to propose marriage to the widowed, *"all tears"* (1.2) queen in the shrewd expectation of how she would respond: with an immediate 'I do' to a union that held out for her the opportunity of retaining the queenly role she had for three decades enjoyed. I suggest the scene from *The Murder of Gonzago* depicting how *"The Poisoner woos the Queen with gifts"* (3.2) supports this interpretation of events.

Only one step for Claudius remained: to present himself to the nobles as the candidate for kingship who offered Denmark the prospect of continuity and stability. With the reigning queen now as his wife and with her support, it is easy to understand why this final step successfully led Claudius to the throne he coveted.

Sample 3.2
The second sample response argues that the marriage of Claudius and Gertrude is largely a practical arrangement that advanced both their interests. It eased his path to Denmark's throne and enabled her to continue to live the life of a queen.

The royal relationship we see on stage between King Claudius and Queen Gertrude is far removed from the unrestrained sensuality that old King Hamlet's Ghost luridly imagines. It more resembles that of a middle-aged, married couple which, of course, Claudius and Gertrude actually are.

In my view, the marriage of the couple Hamlet scornfully refers to as *"my uncle-father and aunt-mother"* (2.2) represented a union of mutual self-interest rather than a bond of passion. It was an arrangement that furthered both their practical interests; his political, hers social. He wanted something (the role of king) he did not have; she had something (the status of queen) she wanted to hold onto.

Nevertheless, I can also see genuine affection in their relationship. For an otherwise cold-hearted schemer, Claudius' description of his Gertrude is touchingly sentimental: *"My virtue or my plague, be it either which— She's so conjunctive to my life and soul, / That, as the star moves not but in his sphere, / I could not but by her"* (4.7).

Despite Hamlet's bitter comment about *"Frailty thy name is woman!"* (1.2), Gertrude remains steadfastly loyal to her second husband. And although she promises her son to shun Claudius' bed (*"Be thou assured"*), we see no evidence that the queen heeds what she later describes in an aside as the *"guilt"* in her *"sick soul"* (4.5). At the end in 5.2, one small act of defiance of her husband (*"Gertrude, do not drink"*) by the heretofore obedient queen (*"I will, my lord; I pray you, pardon me"*) leads to his exposure as a murderous villain (*"the King's to blame"*) and then to his final comeuppance.

Sample 3.3
The third sample response suggests that Gertrude is loved by Claudius—but only as far as a man of Claudius' character is capable of love. At the end of the play, he jeopardizes Gertrude's life rather than risk exposing his poison plot against Prince Hamlet.

Both on the first and final occasions we see King Claudius on stage, he is accompanied by his wife, Queen Gertrude, the woman Ophelia addresses as *"the beauteous majesty of Denmark"* (4.5). In the opening court scene, the royal couple presents a united and stately front to the assembled courtiers; in the final scene, however, he jeopardizes her life to protect his secret *"exploit"* (4.7) against her son.

When in 3.1 Claudius wishes her to leave so he may speak alone with Polonius and Ophelia, he does not order her away but requests her politely: *"Sweet Gertrude, leave us too."* Her response is equally graceful: *"I shall obey you."* Claudius feels close enough to his queen to share his burdens: *"O Gertrude, Gertrude, / When sorrows come, they come not single spies / But in battalions"* (4.5).

In 4.5, Claudius had to restrain his queen after she leapt from her throne to protect her husband from the sword-wielding Laertes: *"Let him go, Gertrude."* But only days later, Claudius fails to return her loyalty and save her life. When in 5.2 Gertrude reaches for the poisoned wine, Claudius does not jump up and sweep the goblet from her lips; to do so would be to reveal his murderous plot against Prince Hamlet. All his scheming nature will allow him to do is utter a half-hearted and fatally ineffective *"Gertrude, do not drink"* (5.2).

The usurping king wastes no time mourning his wife's death but turns to the nobles for help: *"O, yet defend me, friends."* To the very end, Claudius is focused on holding onto what he values more than the love of any woman: the crown of Denmark.

2.4 – Prince Hamlet: *"Mighty opposites"*

The relationship between the *"mighty opposites"* (5.2) Claudius and Hamlet begins with mutual dislike and suspicion, escalates into a psychological battle, and ends with both their deaths.

Sample 4.1

This first sample response describes how Prince Hamlet responds to Claudius' impersonation of a legitimate monarch by putting on a masquerade of his own: *"an antic disposition"* (1.5).

If old King Hamlet stood between Claudius and the throne, his son Prince Hamlet is his potential obstacle to retaining it. Although Gertrude's new husband urges the prince *"to think of us / As of a father"* (1.2), it is only to be expected that Hamlet would be suspicious of the man who benefited most from his father's sudden death. And entirely natural too that Claudius would want to keep a watchful gaze (*"the cheer and comfort of our eye"*, 1.2) on his nephew.

But even the wily Claudius could not have foreseen that Hamlet would respond to his kingship with a *"turbulent and dangerous lunacy"* (3.1). So unnerved is the king that Rosencrantz, Guildenstern and Ophelia are recruited to *"sift"* the prince to discover what *"aught, to us unknown, afflicts him thus"* (2.2). But their spying efforts are quickly exposed and scornfully repelled by Hamlet.

Next, Hamlet stages a performance by the visiting Players that publicly reenacts a seemingly perfect crime that left behind neither witnesses nor evidence: Claudius' secret poisoning of old King Hamlet. How did the prince know? The fatal stabbing of the king's closest ally, Polonius, the rebellion of Laertes and the drowning of Ophelia all follow in a downward series of events that spiral out of Claudius' control. Even dispatching Hamlet to execution in England backfires when the prince engineers his escape and then mocks the king with a letter that begins with the taunting salutation *"High and Mighty"* (4.7).

Prince Hamlet is Claudius' nemesis, the character he can never fully control and through whom the usurping king receives his ultimate comeuppance.

Sample 4.2
As a result of their shared relationship with Queen Gertrude, both Claudius and Hamlet's 'delay' openly striking against each other.

Although *Hamlet* is most celebrated for the inner conflict of its title character, the external conflict we see enacted on stage is between King Claudius and Prince Hamlet.

What inhibits uncle and nephew from striking openly against each other is the relationship they share with Queen Gertrude. As Claudius says to Laertes of Hamlet: *"The queen his mother / Lives almost by his looks"* (4.7). From the prince's perspective, he can see in the First Player's enactment of Hecuba's grief in 2.2 the heartbreak his mother would experience should he kill Claudius and make her a widow a second time in four months.

There are also political considerations. Just as Hecuba's husband King Priam was the rightful ruler of Troy (*"their lord's murder"*, 2.2), King Claudius was elected legitimately by the country's nobles. Conversely, King Claudius must take account of the prince's popularity, for he enjoys the *"great love the general gender"* (4.7). Both uncle and nephew *"stand in pause"* (3.3) until, following Hamlet's stabbing of Polonius, Claudius exiles his nephew from Denmark in a secret plan for his execution.

However, much as his father's Ghost returned from the dead, the prince reappears from his death sentence in England. In the end, the conflict between uncle and nephew ends with defeat for both: Horatio's *"sweet Prince"* Hamlet is the last to die; and Claudius, the villain who had *"Thrown out his angle for my proper life"* (5.2), is the last to be killed.

Sample 4.3
Sample response number three places the conflict between Claudius and Hamlet in the context of the rivalry between two brothers over the crown of Denmark and the hand of Queen Gertrude.

The central conflict that drives the storyline of *Hamlet* is the struggle between two brothers—one living, one undead—over a crown and queen. Trapped between the murderous ambition of his uncle and the vengeful fury of his father is Prince Hamlet.

Horatio's opening tale in act one (*"At least the whisper goes so"*, 1.1) was of a duel fought directly between two combatants, Denmark's old King Hamlet and Norway's old King Fortinbras. The story he promises to *"truly deliver"* (5.2) at the play's end is of a conflict between two Danish kings who fought each other through two surrogates, Hamlet and Laertes, both of whose lives it destroyed.

I suggest the phrasing of Laertes' declaration in the final scene that *"The King, the King's to blame"* (5.2) invites us to conclude that not one but two kings are responsible for the tragedy that has unfolded. Claudius is the obvious candidate for blame; he is exposed as responsible, if indirectly, for Gertrude's and Laertes' deaths, and vicariously for the prince's. But what of old King Hamlet, *"the King that's dead"* (1.2)? What if instead of revenge the Ghost had asked for prayers to end the suffering of two souls: his in the *"fires"* (1.5) of purgatory; and his brother's on Denmark's throne, *"limed"* and *"struggling to be free"* (3.3)?

In its warning against revenge, the Biblical story of Cain and Abel states: *"If anyone kills Cain, vengeance shall be taken on him sevenfold"* (Genesis 4:15). Excluding old King Hamlet and King Claudius, seven is, of course, the number of victims who die in the chain of *"purposes mistook"* (5.2) events that result from the *"cursed spite"* (1.5) between the two brothers of the Hamlet family over a crown and queen.

2.5 – Tragic hero: *"Some vicious mole of nature"*

This section describes how Claudius' jealousy-driven pursuit of Denmark's throne brings about his own downfall and that of everyone around him.

Sample 5.1
In his role as a tragic hero, Denmark's usurping king would not have been out of place in a play performed in ancient Greece.

Of all the characters in *Hamlet*, I believe Claudius most closely resembles a tragic hero as the term would have been understood in classical Greek theater of two thousand years ago. He has, by his own frank admission, turned his soul *"black as death"* in his amoral pursuit of *"My crown, mine own ambition, and my queen"* (3.3).

The resentment we can imagine Claudius felt from living so long in the shadow of old King Hamlet is expressed by the prince's comment how *"those that would make mouths at him while / my father lived"* are now willing to *"give twenty, forty, fifty, a hundred ducats apiece for his picture"* (2.2).

But Claudius' usurpation of his brother does not bring security or stability to Denmark. His election is followed by an invasion threat that demands frenzied defense preparations *"whose sore task / Does not divide the Sunday from the week"* (1.1). And that crisis is in turn followed by a Laertes-led, life-threatening popular uprising (*"Save yourself, my lord ... The doors are broke"*, 4.5).

Nor does his winning of the crown and queen bring Claudius contentment. After hearing Polonius' remark to Ophelia about how with *"pious action we do sugar o'er the devil himself"* (3.1), Claudius admits in an aside: *"How smart a lash that speech doth give my conscience! ... O heavy burden!"* (3.1).

Ultimately, Denmark itself falls victim to Claudius' unrestrained ambition when, at the play's end, it loses its independence to the rival kingdom of Norway.

Sample 5.2
Sample response number two places King Claudius firmly in the tradition of Greek dramatic tragedy. It includes three terms from the field of dramatic analysis: *hamartia, peripeteia* and *anagnorisis.*

As a dramatic character, King Claudius would be instantly familiar to the theater audiences of ancient Greece as a 'tragic hero'—a person of noble birth whose choices affect not only his own life but also carry the potential to bring about either the salvation or ruin of his family and country.

Over two thousand years ago in his *Poetics*, Aristotle identified the main elements of a tragic drama. Three of them are: *hamarita*—a fatal flaw or weakness in an otherwise good and capable person (in Claudius' case, his unrestrained ambition); *perpeteia*—a decision that brings consequences opposite to what the character intended (his murder of old King Hamlet and, perhaps too, his decision to block Prince Hamlet's wish to leave Elsinore); and *anagnorisis*—the moment of self-awareness (his frank acknowledgment of his sinfully power-hungry nature in the chapel scene of 3.3). Claudius may be a deceitful manipulator of others, but he is undeniably honest with himself.

In an era when a monarch as regarded as God's representative on earth (*"There's such divinity doth hedge a king"*, 4.5), Shakespeare's audience would have found it entirely credible that the brother-poisoning, *"sometime sister"*-marrying (1.2) and kingdom-stealing villainy of Claudius was followed by a breach in the natural boundary between this world and the next. A *"dreaded sight"* (1.1) in the *"questionable shape"* (1.4) of the assassinated *"majesty of buried Denmark"* (1.1) was released from beyond the grave with the command *"Bear it not"* (1.5). And the rightful heir to Denmark's stolen throne was fated to play the role of *"scourge and minister"* for *"heaven hath pleased it so"* (3.4).

Sample 5.3
Another perspective on Claudius is that his ambition exceeded his abilities. Old King Hamlet ruled Denmark successfully for at least three decades. His usurping brother lasted only about six months.

An alternative view of Claudius is that he not a tragic figure but a pathetic one. As such, his downfall is less the result of some 'fatal flaw' in his character but more the outcome of his inability to command the position to which his jealous ambition drove him: the role of king. In the assessment of the Ghost, his usurping brother is *"a wretch whose natural gifts were poor / To those of mine."* And of the many insults cast at him in 3.4 by Hamlet, perhaps the most telling is *"a king of shreds and patches"*: a fool, a buffoon, a clown.

In act one, Claudius' soldiers are not only demoralized (*"I am ... sick at heart"*, 1.1) and disloyal (*"Marcellus and Bernardo, on their watch ... This to me / In dreadful secrecy impart they did"*, 1.2); they are also in disarray. The first line of *"Who's there?"* is asked by the relieving guard rather than, as is proper, the on-duty one.

Later, the king allows Young Fortinbras' troops march through Denmark to Poland without giving any apparent thought to their return journey. Nor does he seem to recognize the permanent threat posed by old King Fortinbras's decision to fund a standing army (*"three thousand crowns in annual fee"*, 2.2) to replace his nephew's original mercenary gang of *"lawless resolutes"* (1.2). In addition, so unpopular is Claudius with his own people that an angry Laertes has little difficulty in fermenting a castle-storming rebellion that easily overpowers the king's personal bodyguards (*"Where are my Switzers?"*, 4.5).

In summary, *"he that plays the king"* (2.2) delivers *"a bad performance"* (4.7). Old King Hamlet ruled Denmark successfully for at least three decades. His usurping brother lasted only about six months. *"A king of shreds and parches"*, indeed.

2.6 – Conclusion: *"He is justly served"*

The play ends with Claudius' exposure and comeuppance, when he is *"justly served"* by *"a poison tempered by himself"* (5.2).

Sample 6.1

The first sample conclusion argues that King Claudius' killing by Hamlet is not delayed revenge but is instead spontaneous justice.

It is a measure of King Claudius' cunning that in the final scene he has contrived a fencing duel between the two characters who earlier were on the brink of killing him. Exploiting Laertes' grief, Claudius in 4.7 draws the son of the murdered Polonius into his scheme to dispose of Hamlet, with the assurance that not *"even his mother shall uncharge the practice / And call it accident."* However, the king seems to have little confidence in Laertes' ability, either to keep their plot a secret (*"keep close within your chamber"*) or to win the fencing contest (*"If this should fail … I'll have prepared him / A chalice"*). But Claudius' words to his co-conspirator Laertes about Hamlet (*"He shall not choose but fall"*, 4.7) rebound on him in 5.2 when Gertrude's unforeseen reaching for the goblet of poisoned wine is followed by an accidental swapping of fencing swords.

I do not see the prince's killing of King Claudius as the enactment of the Ghost-commanded but long-delayed *"Revenge"* for the *"Murder … most foul, strange and unnatural"* (1.5) of six months before. Instead, I regard it as spontaneously-delivered public justice by Hamlet in response to the king's exposed guilt for the deaths of Gertrude (*"Thy mother's poisoned"*) and the prince himself (*"In thee there is not half an hour of life"*). With deadly symbolism, Prince Hamlet by two methods kills the *"arrant knave"* whose *"leperous distilment"* (1.5) claimed the lives of both his parents and who had twice schemed to murder him. In the words of Laertes, Claudius is *"justly served"* (5.2).

Sample 6.2

Hamlet is often described as a play where everybody dies in the end. But in the end, not everyone is damned to hell. This second response contrasts the redemption achieved by other characters with the unapologetic-to-the-last death of King Claudius.

As is typical of revenge tragedies, the play concludes with the exposure and comeuppance of the villain; in this case, King Claudius.

Of the four bodies that lie dead on-stage at the end of 5.2, three achieve a degree of redemption. Laertes exposes Claudius' twin-plot of the sharpened, poison-tipped sword (*"The treacherous instrument … Unbated and envenomed"*) and the tainted wine goblet (*"Thy mother's poisoned"*). Moreover, he seeks and receives Hamlet's pardon (*"Exchange forgiveness with me, noble Hamlet. / Mine and my father's death come not upon thee, / No thine on me!"*). As for Gertrude, her final words of *"O my dear Hamlet—The drink, the drink! I am poisoned"* are both a damning exposure of her husband and a warning to her son.

Claudius, however, dies as he lived—a duplicitous and unrepentant villain. He makes no effort to purge himself of his sins but attempts instead to explain away Gertrude's fainting as a reaction to the fencing duel (*"She swoons to see them bleed"*). Before a dying Hamlet slays his uncle (*"thou incestuous, murderous, damned Dane"*), the last sight Claudius witnesses is the woman he married killed by the same poison he earlier used to murder his brother and her first husband.

But are Gertrude's unintended reaching for the poisoned goblet and the confused swapping of fencers' swords evidence of the intervention of *"providence"* (5.2) in order that villainy be *"justly served"*? Or has the ending been just another turn of the *"wheel"* of *"fortune"* (2.2) of which the Players spoke?

Sample 6.3

The third sample response argues that Claudius was, both literally and figuratively, a poisoner. His corrupt and corrupting reign was the *"something rotten"* (1.4) sensed by the guard Marcellus.

The storyline of *Hamlet* ends as it begins: with a murder disguised as an accident. In both instances, the perpetrator is the play's villain, Claudius; and in each case, his chosen weapon is the same: poison. The first victim was old King Hamlet; the second is his son, Prince Hamlet.

Claudius successfully attributed the death of the afternoon-napping old King Hamlet to an accidental snake-bite. In the words of the Ghost: *"the whole ear of Denmark ... by a forged process of my death"* was *"Rankly abused"* (1.5). But unlike Claudius' brother-poisoning crime in the palace orchard, his nephew-poisoning ploy of the final 5.2 scene is publicly exposed to the court.

After Claudius' excuse for the queen's fainting (*"She swoons to see them bleed"*) is contradicted by the dying Gertrude (*"The drink, the drink! I am poisoned"*), the conscience-stricken Laertes confesses all (*"I am justly killed with my own treachery"*). With only moments left to live, Hamlet is at last able to bring himself to murder his usurping uncle by forcing him to drink down the *"poison tempered by himself."*

Both literally and metaphorically, Claudius was a poisoner: his *"juice of cursed hebenon"* (1.5) ended forever the Hamlet family dynasty; and his reign of falsity contaminated with distrust and deception the natural human bonds of friendship and romantic love. The two *"Good lads"* (2.2) Rosencrantz and Guildenstern are executed in England. And in Claudius' *"unweeded garden"* (1.2), the unwed couple of Hamlet and Ophelia end the play not together on Denmark's throne but united only in death in Elsinore's graveyard.

3

The Character of Gertrude

"Where is the beauteous Majesty of Denmark?"

After the death of her first husband, old King Hamlet, Gertrude quickly remarries her former brother-in-law in the hope her queenly life at Elsinore will continue as before; her son will accept his uncle as a substitute father; and, in time, Prince Hamlet will marry his love interest, Ophelia. But her choice of the villainous Claudius as second husband dooms her life and the lives of everyone around her.

3.1 – Introduction

As *Hamlet* the play unfolds, Queen Gertrude is drawn deeper and deeper into her second husband's manipulative and murderous schemes. Tragically, when *"the beauteous majesty of Denmark"* (4.5) is at last forced to confront the type of man she married, it is too late for her, her son and Denmark.

Sample 1.1

The first sample response introduces Queen Gertrude as a woman whose desire to retain the role of queen blinds her to the villainous nature of the man she accepted as her second husband.

"Have you eyes?", the prince demands of his mother Queen Gertrude during their confrontation in 3.4 of Shakespeare's *Hamlet*. The relationship between old King Hamlet's widow and her former brother-in-law is a tragic tale of opportunistic self-delusion colluding with murderous ambition. Others in the play put on acts of 'seeming' to conceal their true selves. No one more so than the duplicitous Claudius who fools everyone—except Prince Hamlet (*"One may smile, and smile, and be a villain"*, 1.5). Gertrude fools only one person—herself.

In my view, Queen Gertrude's character flaw is her deliberate blindness to what she must surely suspect: that her second husband Claudius is, in her son's words, a *"murderer and villain"* (3.4). The answer to the question asked of her by the prince (*"What devil was't / That thus hath cozened you at hoodman-blind?"*, 3.4) was, I believe, her desire to continue by means of a second marriage the privileged status she enjoyed for three decades through her first: the position of Denmark's queen.

Tragically for her, Gertrude is forced to confront the truth about Claudius' only when it is too late, and she has drunk the poison he intended for her son. And her wished-for, happily-ever-after fairytale concludes in a violent bloodbath that consumes her entire family.

In this essay, I will give my opinion on the character and actions of Gertrude. In particular, I will explore her decision to remarry so quickly; her conflicted role as wife to Claudius and mother to her only child, Prince Hamlet; and on her relationship with the play's only other female character and her son's love interest, Ophelia.

Sample 1.2

Sample introduction number two summarizes Gertrude's storyline in the play and argues that her choice of second husband dooms her life and the lives of everyone around her.

In Shakespeare's play *Hamlet*, Queen Gertrude is a woman who dooms her family and country by deciding, within *"a little month"* (1.2) of her first husband's death, to marry and share her throne with her *"sometime"* (1.2) brother-in-law, Claudius. Gertrude's choice of second husband sets in motion a downward spiral of *"purposes mistook"* (5.2) events that conclude with the violent destruction of the Hamlet dynasty and Denmark's loss of political independence to the rival kingdom of Norway.

The phases of Gertrude's storyline can be summarized as follows: the new bride and decorously ceremonial monarch (*"Enter Claudius, King of Denmark; Gertrude the Queen; and others"*, 1.2); the attempted peace-maker between son and stepfather (*"Good Hamlet … let thine eye look like a friend on Denmark"*, 1.2); the concerned mother (*"Guildenstern and gentle Rosencrantz … I beseech you instantly to visit / My too much changed son"*, 2.2); the suddenly frightened and briefly self-aware spouse to a magnetic but dangerous man (*"O Hamlet … Thou turn'st mine eyes into my very soul"*, 3.4); the once-hopeful but eventually disappointed family matriarch (*"I hoped thou shouldst have been my Hamlet's wife … sweet maid"*, 5.1); the wife betrayed by a scheming Claudius who loved the throne more than her (*"She swoons to see them bleed"*, 5.2); and finally, the woman in some measure redeemed by her dying words that are both a damning exposure of her villainous second husband and a warning to her son (*"O my dear Hamlet—The drink, the drink! I am poisoned"*, 5.2).

In this essay, I will give my opinions on Gertrude: queen, wife, mother, and, ultimately, tragic victim of her own opportunistic self-delusion.

Sample 1.3
This third sample response contrasts the Shakespeare-created character of Queen Gertrude with England's then reigning monarch.

Audiences at Shakespeare's *Hamlet* would have been struck by the contrast between the fictional queen of Denmark and England's actual queen whose subjects they were. Queen Elizabeth I personally directed every aspect of government and with such success that her reign came to be regarded as England's 'Golden Age.' The on-stage Queen Gertrude, however, displays no interest in her country's welfare. It would be comical to suggest that the female lead in Shakespeare's tragedy oversaw a Gertrudian golden era for Denmark.

A little over a decade before *Hamlet*'s premier performance, with an invasion threatened from Spain, Elizabeth I rallied her soldiers with a rousing speech that passed into her nation's folklore. After rhetorically conceding she had but *"the body of a weak, feeble woman"*, she continued: *"I have the heart and stomach of a king."* And, if necessary, *"I myself will take up arms"* and *"be your general"* against *"any prince of Europe"* who *"should dare to invade the borders of my realm."*

In contrast, Queen Gertrude's demoralized soldiers (*"I am ... sick at heart"*, 1.1; *"something rotten in the state"*, 1.4) of act one receive neither encouragement nor explanation for their frenzied defense preparations *"whose sore task / Does not divide the Sunday from the week"* (1.1). It falls to

Horatio (*"thou art a scholar"*, 1.1) to report how Denmark's borders are threatened by Norway's Young Fortinbras, he *"Of unimproved mettle hot and full"* (1.1).

In the end, Queen Gertrude loses her life to her second husband's villainy and her throne to the son of the man her first husband defeated on the day her own son Prince Hamlet was born.

3.2 – The wedding: *"Taken to wife"*

Why did Claudius and Gertrude become man and wife? In my opinion, Gertrude's relationship with Claudius is tainted with personal ambition. For it enabled her to continue in the role of *"the beauteous majesty of Denmark"* (4.5).

Sample 2.1

The first sample response suggests why, on the evidence of the opening court scene, Gertrude may have been so easily able to justify to herself her throne-retaining decision to wed her former brother-in-law, Claudius.

> Why did the widowed Queen Gertrude accept the proposal of marriage from her former brother-in-law, Claudius? In my view, old King Hamlet's death did not only leave Gertrude without a husband at her side. In a dangerous world, and with her scholarly son the prince absorbed in his studies at Wittenberg University, it also left her country without a king.
>
> The order of words spoken by Claudius in the chapel scene (*"My crown, mine own ambition, and my queen"*, 3.3) suggests Gertrude has been *"taken to wife"* (1.2) by a man motivated primarily by the desire to gain the throne of his late brother, and only to a lesser extent by love for his *"sometime sister"* (1.2).

But self-serving ambition also tainted Gertrude's within *"a little month"* (1.2) wedding. For it enabled her to retain by means of a second marriage what she had for three decades enjoyed through her first: the status of queen.

In the 1.2 court scene, King Claudius appears to be exactly the type of commanding and decisive figure Denmark needs at a time when an invasion is threatened from Norway. The queen's words to her son (*"all that lives must die"*) may sound cold-hearted. But they can also be heard as a reminder to the royal prince of his duty: to set aside his *"inky cloak"* and join in the Danish court's show of unity for their country's sake.

While she can be criticized as motivated by an opportunistic desire to retain her queenly status, I can easily understand why the practically-minded Gertrude (*"More matter, less art"*, 2.2) so completely convinced herself that by answering 'I do' to her brother-in-law she was also acting in Denmark's interests.

Sample 2.2

Was the marriage of Claudius and Gertrude the culmination of an adulterous love affair that began before the death of Prince Hamlet's father? And would Claudius have poisoned Gertrude's first husband were he not confident she would opportunistically accept him afterward as her second (1.2)?

Why did King Claudius and Queen Gertrude wed one another? Was their marriage preceded by an illicit love affair that began before old King Hamlet's death? It is even possible that Gertrude was an accomplice to the murder of her first husband?

An adulterous relationship is never mentioned or hinted at in the king and queen's private conversations, nor when they speak in soliloquy or asides. No other character voices any such suspicion. Gertrude's shocked reaction to Hamlet's accusation (*"As kill a king, and marry with his brother"*, 3.4) strongly suggests Claudius alone was responsible for what the conscience-haunted king will later confess was *"a brother's murder"* (3.3).

Yet, one line from the prince's rant at Ophelia—and, by extension, at all womankind—hangs over the relationship between Denmark's royal couple: *"wise men know well enough / what monsters you make of them"* (3.1). For we may well wonder whether Claudius would have turned his soul *"black as death"* (3.3) by disposing of Gertrude's first husband were he not confident the *"Like Niobe, all tears"* (1.2) widow would accept him afterward as husband number two—and with *"most wicked speed"* (1.2) at that?

In his first soliloquy, the prince struggles to reconcile the fond memory of his parents' marriage (*"why, she would hang on him"*, 1.2) with the painful reality expressed by Gertrude's choice of second husband. I suspect Hamlet's later raging at Ophelia (*"we will have no more marriages"*, 3.1) is rooted in his suspicion that Gertrude's first marriage, which brought the prince into this *"calamity of so long life"* (3.1), was to his mother only the first of two *"As false as dicers' oaths"* (3.4) throne-seeking enterprises.

Sample 2.3

This third sample response argues that, in contrast to England's Queen Elizabeth I, the dramatic character of Queen Gertrude regards the role of queen as a privileged status to be enjoyed rather than a patriotic opportunity to serve.

Old King Hamlet's death left Queen Gertrude as a woman alone on her country's throne; a similar position, in fact, to that occupied by England's Queen Elizabeth I some four decades before *Hamlet*'s first performance.

With the aid of a council of trusted advisors, Elizabeth I raised economic fortunes, restored internal stability, repelled threats from foreign powers, and presided over a flourishing of arts and culture of which Shakespeare's plays were a celebrated example. Although much-pursued by suitors, Elizabeth rebuffed all proposals of marriage. As she told her parliament: "I have already joined myself in marriage to a husband, namely the kingdom of England."

Elizabeth I's popularity was reflected in the affectionate title she earned among her subjects—'Good Queen Bess.' In contrast, so unpopular is the reign of Gertrude and her second husband that a rebellious Laertes has little difficulty in fermenting a commoners' uprising. It is only when they are storming her castle that the queen gives any attention to her subjects, and then it is only to call them *"Danish dogs"* (4.5).

Another distinction between the real-life and fictional queens was that Elizabeth inherited her royal position; she was the daughter and grand-daughter of kings, and was so of royal blood. In contrast, Gertrude acquired her crown through the more tenuous means of marriage. But with old King Hamlet dead, and she lacking any interest in or capacity for governing, the position of old King Hamlet's widow was now in jeopardy.

It must have seemed to Gertrude that accepting the proposal of marriage from her former brother-in-law Claudius held out the attractive prospect of continuing to live and enjoy the only life she had known for thirty years.

3.3 – The royal couple: *"I shall obey you"*

Claudius' loving words about his queen (*"I could not but by her"*, 4.7) reveal another side of an otherwise cold and calculating man. And the rebellious, mob-leading Laertes discovers that Gertrude is no mere trophy wife but is indeed *"the imperial jointress to this warlike state"* (1.2) when he threatens the throne she shares with her husband.

Sample 3.1

The first sample response emphasizes Gertrude's steadfast loyalty to her second husband. It further asserts that Claudius really does love Gertrude—if only as far as his character allows him.

One of the play's great ironies is that the person that Prince Hamlet most bitterly accuses of fickle disloyalty (*"Frailty thy name is woman ... O God, a beast that wants discourse of reason / Would have mourned longer!"*, 1.2) is, in fact, the most loyal character in the entire play.

Up until the very last scene, she remains steadfastly at the side of her second husband. When in 4.5 a rebellious mob led by Polonius' angry son shouts out *"Laertes shall be king!"*, she responds defiantly with: *"O, this is counter, you false Danish dogs!"* She defends her husband from any role in Polonius' murder (*"But not by him"*) and even throws herself on the enraged, sword-wielding Laertes when she fears for the king's safety. This is hardly the behavior of a merely decorous trophy wife; rather they are the actions of a woman who fulfills the king's description of her as the *"imperial jointress to this warlike state"* (1.2).

Her husband Claudius is a man of intricate schemes rather than sweeping passion, a thinker rather than a feeler. I believe he does love Gertrude—if only as far as the limitations of his character allow him. He speaks of her in words that come directly from his heart (*"My virtue or my plague, be it either which / She's so conjunctive to my life and soul ... I could not but by her"*, 4.7) and turns to her for comfort as his troubles mount: *"O Gertrude, Gertrude, / When sorrows come, they come not single spies / But in battalions"* (4.5).

Sample 3.2
As this second sample response illustrates, Gertrude successively won the heart and hand of two brothers: the first, a triumphant warlord; the second, a Machiavellian schemer.

Queen Gertrude is clearly a woman of great personal magnetism. Prince Hamlet's first question to Horatio about the Ghost's demeanor (*"looked he frowningly?"*, 1.2) suggests his father was as aggressive in temperament as he was combative in battle, when *"He smote the sledded Polacks on the ice"* (1.1). Yet the Ghost later speaks to his son about Gertrude as *"a radiant angel"* (1.5), just as the prince recalls how old King Hamlet was *"so loving to my mother / That he might not beteem the winds of heaven / Visit her face too roughly"* (1.2).

As for the otherwise cold-hearted schemer Claudius, he talks of Gertrude to Laertes in sentimental terms: *"My virtue or my plague, be it either which / She's so conjunctive to my life and soul ... I could not but by her"* (4.7).

In the 3.4 closet scene, Gertrude submits to her son's *"scourge and minister"* shaming by agreeing to no longer share her bed with Claudius: *"Be thou assured, if words be made of breath ... What thou hast said to me."* But in none of the subsequent scenes is there evidence to indicate the queen has distanced herself from the king. She will end the play as she began it: sitting by her second husband's side. Indeed, as Claudius and Gertrude appear onstage to oversee the fencing duel between Hamlet and Laertes, the prince remarks to his confidant Horatio of how the royal couple arrive together *"In happy time"* (5.2).

Sample 3.3

King and queen share their ceremonial duties with stately decorum and treat each other with mutual affection and respect. In 4.7, Gertrude provides a listening ear to her husband's litany of troubles (*"O Gertrude, Gertrude, / When sorrows come ..."*) that threaten their shared throne, including *"the people muddied, / Thick and unwholesome in their thoughts and whispers."*

In their royal marriage, Claudius is respectful towards Gertrude in public; and in their private scenes, they are comfortably at ease in each other's company. In 2.2, on hearing Polonius' claim that Ophelia's rejection of his romantic advances is the cause of *"the madness wherein now (Hamlet) raves"*, Claudius immediately seeks out his wife's opinion: *"He tells me, my dear Gertrude, he hath found / The head and source of all your son's distemper ... Do you think 'tis this?"* Later, in 3.1, when Claudius wishes to speak alone with Polonius and Ophelia, he does not order his wife away; instead, he requests politely: *"Sweet Gertrude, leave us too."* She responds with equal consideration: *"I shall obey you."*

In 4.1, Claudius' first reaction to Gertrude's report that her *"Mad as the sea and wind"* son has stabbed Polonius is not concern for his wife's distress but fear for his own safety (*"O heavy deed! / It had been so with us, had we been there"*, 4.1). But such capacity as he does possess for romantic love, Claudius invests it all and fully in Gertrude. For, as he tells Laertes: *"I could not but by her"* (4.7).

Even after all they have been through—Polonius' death and hugger-mugger burial, Hamlet's exile, and Ophelia's madness and suicide—Claudius and Gertrude remain loyally at each other's side. In the end, it is not external events that doom their *"mirth in funeral"* (1.2) relationship, but the dark secret of *"a brother's murder"* (3.3) that hides in the past.

3.4 – Hamlet: *"Why seems it so particular with thee?"*

Her decision to wed Claudius so quickly after old King Hamlet's death creates a barrier between a mother and her son. To Gertrude, it must seem she has gained a second husband and retained her throne at the cost of losing her son to insanity and, for his own safety, to exile from Denmark.

Sample 4.1

Gertrude is saddened by the refusal of the still-grieving and suspicious Prince Hamlet to share her evident happiness at her remarriage. But is it only in the 3.4 closet scene that she fully understands his reasons and grasps the depth of his fury.

In 1.2, Gertrude's tenderness towards her son (*"Good Hamlet"*) is mixed with annoyance at the reluctance of the *"inky cloak"*-wearing prince to celebrate her remarriage with the rest of the court: *"Good Hamlet, cast thy nighted colour off."* Later, in the prince's reaction to the Ghost's accusations (*"O my prophetic soul! My uncle!"*, 1.5), we understand why Hamlet viewed the court's celebrations in such a suspicious light.

His father dead in mysterious circumstances; his mother quickly, happily—and incestuously—remarried; and Denmark's nobles apparently untroubled (*"Your better wisdoms, which have freely gone / With this affair along"*, 1.2): to Hamlet it must seem, in the words of the guard Marcellus, that *"something is rotten in the state of Denmark"* (1.4).

Gertrude acknowledges to Claudius that their *"o'erhasty marriage"* (2.2) is in part the cause the unhappy mental state of *"my too much changed son."* In the 3.4 closet scene, Hamlet rails against Gertrude with such verbal violence (*"would it were not so!—you are my mother"*) that she submits to his shaming (*"No more!"*), seeks his advice (*"What shall I do?"*), and accedes to his demand to no longer share her bed with Claudius (*"Be thou assured"*).

> I sense Gertrude is not sincere in her promise; she is simply terrified of her son (*"Alas, he's mad!"*) who has just murdered Polonius and spoken with an invisible—to her—ghost. After Hamlet departs, dragging away Polonius' *"guts"* and bidding her a nonchalant *"Good night, mother"*, it must seem to Gertrude that she has gained a second husband and retained her throne at the cost of losing her son to insanity and, for his own safety, to exile from Denmark.

Sample 4.2

"Pray you, be round with him" is Polonius advice to Gertrude regarding her son in 3.4. But after running his sword through the hidden eavesdropper (*"Thou wretched, rash, intruding fool, farewell!"*), Hamlet puts the queen on notice who his next victim will be: her *"murderer and a villain"* of a second husband.

> In the court scene of 1.2, Hamlet verbally evades King Claudius' request to *"think of us / As of a father"* with *"I am too much in the sun."* The only allegiance he pledges is to his mother: *"I shall do my best to obey you, madam."* It is the performance of *The Murder of Gonzago* that changes Hamlet's attitude towards the reign of his *"uncle-father and aunt-mother"* (2.2): reluctant acceptance (*"It is not nor it cannot come to good"*, 1.2) gives way to outright rebellion (*"And do such bitter business as the bitter day / Would quake to look on"*, 3.2).
>
> In her closet in 3.4, Gertrude attempts to scold her son for what Polonius calls his *"pranks."* But it is Hamlet who takes on the role of the chastising parent. The prince seeks to separate her from Claudius (*"Go not to thy husband's bed"*) to minimize the Hecuba-like devastation she will feel at her second husband's death. For the prince's words over Polonius' lifeless body make it clear who he intends his next victim to be: *"Thus bad begins and worse remains behind."* Echoing Gertrude's earlier request of him (*"Let not thy mother lose her prayers, Hamlet"*, 1.2), he departs her closet

hoping she will shun Claudius' bed (*"Confess yourself to heaven. / Repent what's past. Avoid what is to come"*) so that as a son he can ask his mother's blessing: *"And when you are desirous to be blessed, / I'll blessing beg of you."*

When the prince reappears from exile in 5.1, Gertrude exclaims *"Hamlet, Hamlet!"* In this double-greeting, I hear both joy from a mother's heart and relief from a guilty soul. After their fraught conversation in 3.4, when she confessed *"Thou turn'st mine eyes into my very soul"*, she must have thought she would never see her *"dear Hamlet"* (3.2) again.

Sample 4.3

Sample response number three stresses the gulf in personality and outlook between queen and prince. Yet, despite all their differences, there are many instances of spontaneous motherly affection displayed by Gertrude towards her son.

Although mother and son, Gertrude and Hamlet are as different as two people can be. He delights in wordplay; she is direct in her speech and is the only character to tell Polonius to come to the point: *"More matter, less art"* (2.2). She seeks to smooth over everything without thinking too deeply; he is continually *"thinking too precisely"* (4.4) about everything.

It is their contrasting attitudes towards the death of old King Hamlet that reveals the greatest difference between the two. Hamlet recalls fondly how his mother *"would hang on"* his late father *"As if increase of appetite had grown / By what it fed on"* (1.2). To Gertrude, however, all memory of her first marriage died with her first husband.

The Ghost who appears in Gertrude's closet in 3.4 is visible to the prince (*"My father, in his habit as he lived!"*) but unseen by the queen (*"To whom do you speak this?"*). Such is the gulf between the haunted-by-the-past Hamlet (*"Do you see nothing there? ... Nor did you nothing hear?"*) and the live-in-the-moment Gertrude (*"Nothing at all; yet all that is I see ... No, nothing but ourselves"*).

However different in character and outlook, mother and son share a common bond of affection. *"Come hither, my dear Hamlet, sit by me"* (3.2), she says to him before *The Murder of Gonzago*. At Ophelia's funeral in 5.1, she speaks of him possessively as *"my Hamlet."* And on his reappearance, she excitedly shouts out his name twice (*"Hamlet, Hamlet!"*); orders Laertes to unhand him when the two men jostle in Ophelia's grave (*"For love of God, forbear him"*); and excuses her son's outburst as only a *"fit"* that will last merely *"awhile."*

3.5 – Ophelia: *"Your good beauties"*

We do not know if Gertrude follows Hamlet's direction to distance herself from Claudius and shun her husband's bed: *"Assume a virtue, if you have it not"* (3.4). But the evolving nature of her relationship with Polonius' daughter suggests something inside her has changed.

Sample 5.1
The first sample suggests that Ophelia's death is a devastating blow for Gertrude. With her are gone the queen's hopes for future grandchildren to carry on the dynasty of the Hamlet family at Elsinore.

Gertrude shares no scene alone with the play's only other female character, Polonius' daughter and Hamlet's love interest, Ophelia. Nevertheless, their few interactions are very revealing of the queen's character development.

Their first meeting is immediately before Ophelia's stage-managed, *"'twere by accident"* (3.1) encounter with the prince, arranged, as Claudius explains to Gertrude, to discover *"If't be th'affliction of his love or no / That thus (Hamlet) suffers for"* (3.1). The romantic worldview of newly-remarried Gertrude is evident in her hope that Ophelia's *"good beauties"* are *"the happy cause / Of Hamlet's wildness."* And that: *"I hope your virtues / Will bring him to his wonted way again, / To both your honours"* (3.1).

Later in act four, Ophelia's descent into madness, her songs of mourning and lost love, and her accusatory offering of rue—a bitter-tasting plant associated with sadness, regret and adultery—clearly trouble Gertrude. Ophelia's mental distress prompts the queen to speak, in her first and only aside, of her *"sick soul"* where *"sin's true nature is"* (4.5).

In 1.2 we saw the queen as a woman quick to move on from the past; as she told her son: *"All that lives must die, / Passing through nature to eternity."* But in 5.1, as she grieves over Ophelia's grave, Gertrude finds her future slipping away from her. There will be no grandchildren at Elsinore to carry the name of Hamlet: *"Sweets to the sweet: farewell! / I hoped thou shouldst have been my Hamlet's wife. / I thought thy bride-bed to have decked, sweet maid, / And not have strewn thy grave"* (5.1).

Sample 5.2

A change in the character of Gertrude, following the madness and death of Polonius' daughter, is suggested by the second sample response. Cheerful, romantic-minded optimism has given way to dread and foreboding.

In the play's first two acts, both Ophelia's brother and father regard her lack of royal birth as an obstacle to marriage with Denmark's crown prince. Of Hamlet, Laertes tells his sister: *"He may not, as unvalued persons do, / Carve for himself; for on his choice depends / The safety and health of this whole state"* (1.3). Later in 2.2, it is unclear whether Ophelia is present on stage to endure the embarrassment of hearing her father Polonius tell the king and queen he regards his daughter as unworthy the prince's affections:

"this I did bespeak: 'Lord Hamlet is a prince, out of thy star / This must not be'" (2.2).

To Gertrude, however, romantic love can conquer all. She tells Ophelia of her hopes *"That your good beauties be the happy cause / Of Hamlet's wildness"* (3.1). Months later in 5.1, at the funeral of Polonius' daughter, Gertrude's graveside eulogy expresses heartfelt sadness: *"I hoped thou shouldst have been my Hamlet's wife."*

Earlier in 4.5, when confronted with Ophelia's madness, Gertrude spoke uncharacteristically of the *"guilt"* in her *"sick soul."* I see her reluctance to meet with a distressed Ophelia (*"I will not speak with her ... What would she have?"*) as typical of the queen's instinct to turn away from uncomfortable realities; in this case, from the sight of a woman driven insane and her heart torn by divided love and loyalties. The queen's cheerful optimism has given way to dread and foreboding, when *"Each toy seems prologue to some great amiss."* I suspect Gertrude is now reflecting ruefully on all the unhappiness that has followed her remarriage when *"the funeral baked-meats / Did coldly furnish forth the marriage tables"* (1.2).

Sample 5.3

No discussion of Gertrude's relationship with Ophelia is complete without exploring the queen's possible role in the drowning of her son's love interest. What motives might Gertrude have had for wanting to end Ophelia's life?

In 4.7, Queen Gertrude reports the drowning of Ophelia in such detail as to suggest she witnessed the event in person. If so, we are left to ponder two questions.

Firstly, why did the queen at least not try to intervene when Ophelia *"Fell in the weeping brook"* and was *"Pulled ... to muddy death."* By Gertrude's own account, there was sufficient time to save the life of the *"poor wretch"* who, clutching a coronet of wildflowers, floated awhile in the water, singing snatches of *"old tunes."* And, secondly, is it even possible that Gertrude was not merely the passive witness to a suicide but the perpetrator of a murder? Did the queen break the brook-side tree branch (*"envious sliver"*) on which Ophelia was standing?

Gertrude's possible motivations for negligence or murder might include: blame for the exile from Denmark of *"my Hamlet"* (5.1); punishment for Ophelia's accusatory flower offerings (*"There's rue for you"*, 4.5); and fear that she was pregnant with Hamlet's child (*"I hope all will be well. We must be patient"*, 4.5), an heir who might make Ophelia a threat to Gertrude's position as queen.

One hint of Gertrude's possible guilt is provided in 4.7 when Claudius, who earlier soliloquized about his *"limed soul"* (3.3), describes her as *"conjunctive"* not just to his *"life"* but also his *"soul."* And that the queen dies onstage in the company of three male murderers, and does by the same means of poison, perhaps suggests that she too is experiencing comeuppance for a crime and is accordingly *"justly served"* (5.2).

3.6 – Conclusion: *"I am poisoned"*

Nowhere is the *"hoodman-blind"* (3.4) naivety of the *"all that is I see"* (3.4) queen more pathetically evident than in the final scene when. She is to be unknowing witness to the assassination of her son disguised as a sporting duel between Laertes and Hamlet—a *"brother's wager"* preceded by a display of reconciliatory *"gentle entertainment"* (5.2).

Ultimately, Gertrude falls victim to the same poison that her second husband used to murder her first. At the play's beginning, it was the offer of marriage from Claudius that enabled her to continue as queen on Denmark's throne. But at the end, Gertrude is literally dethroned when she collapses to the floor as a result of drinking from the tainted wine goblet the same Claudius intended for her son.

Sample 6.1
As this first sample conclusion asserts, Gertrude pays the ultimate price for her tragic self-delusion. She meets her end from the same poison her second husband used to murder her first.

In the court scene of 1.2, Gertrude tried to reconcile her son with her new husband with her request to the prince that he *"look like a friend on Denmark."* After the scuffle between him and Laertes in Ophelia's grave in the final act, she again takes on the role of peace-maker. Before their fencing duel, the two young men join hands following Gertrude's request, communicated through Osrick: *"The Queen desires you to use some gentle entertainment to Laertes before you fall to play"* (5.2).

Far from being a *"terms of honour"* (5.2) duel, the fencing match is, in fact, a 'play-within-a play' conceived by Claudius with the collusion of Laertes: a plot to murder the prince so well disguised that *"no wind of blame shall breathe"* and *"even his mother shall ... call it accident"* (4.7). If the prince loses, he will die of a wound from a sharpened and poisoned-tipped sword; if he wins, a goblet of poisoned wine will be his prize.

But the king's words to his co-conspirator Laertes about Hamlet—*"He shall not choose but fall"* (4.7)— rebound on him in 5.2 when it is Gertrude who reaches for the goblet of poisoned wine. Torn between revealing his murderous, nephew-poisoning plot or saving the life of his queen, all Claudius can do is utter a meek and fatally ineffective: *"Gertrude, do not drink."* The queen's final words of *"O my dear Hamlet—The drink, the drink! I am poisoned"* are a cry for help, a warning to her son and an exposure of her husband. Hamlet's parting words to her (*"Wretched Queen, adieu"*, 5.2) reveal that the prince is unwilling to extend to his mother the forgiveness he received from a repentant Laertes (*"Mine and my father's death come not upon thee"*).

Sample 6.2

Sample conclusion number two focuses on how Hamlet kills Claudius without making mention of vengeance for old King Hamlet. It suggests that it is his mother's rather this father's death from Claudius' poison that finally moves the prince to action.

In a play where so many characters set out to deceive one another, I see Gertrude as a person who deceived only herself. Nowhere is the naivety of the (*"all that is I see"*, 3.4) queen so pathetically apparent than in play's final 5.2 scene. She thinks she is watching a non-lethal fencing duel of honor (*"a brother's wager"*) between Laertes and her *"dear Hamlet."* In reality, she is to be the unknowing spectator to the prince's planned assassination. As the duel progresses, she speaks to him with motherly affection: *"Here, Hamlet ... Come, let me wipe thy face."* Her offer of wine from the poisoned goblet is declined politely by the prince: *"I dare not drink yet, madam. By and by."* Despite Claudius' half-hearted request, she sips from the goblet in a toast to her son (*"The queen carouses to thy fortune"*), collapses to the floor and cries out a warning: *"O my dear Hamlet—The drink, the drink! I am poisoned."*

On his return to Denmark, Gertrude's son introduced himself with the kingly title of *"Hamlet the Dane"* (5.1). It is now at this moment of his mother's literal fall from the throne (*"How does the Queen?"*) that he seizes command of events and acts as Denmark's ruler: *"Ho! Let the door be locked. / Treachery! seek it out."* I think it significant that when Hamlet finally kills Claudius, he does so without making any reference to vengeance for old King Hamlet. It is his mother's rather this father's death from Claudius' poison that moves Prince Hamlet to action. Gertrude pays the ultimate price for her naivety, but not before she is finally forced to confront the reality of her second husband's manipulative character.

Sample 6.3

Why does the queen, in defiance of her husband, drink down the goblet of poisoned wine (*"A chalice for the nonce, whereon but sipping"*, 4.7) Claudius intended for her son? This is the question posed by the third sample response.

In a play where almost every action can be interpreted in multiple ways, Queen Gertrude's behavior with the goblet of poisoned wine in 5.2 leaves us wondering: why does she do that? Is she just yielding to thirst? Or, when she hears Claudius say *"Gertrude, do not drink"*, does she suspect her husband of devising a death-by-poison plot for her son—and is willing to sacrifice herself in his place?

Certainly, it is the first time in the play we see her defy her husband's wishes. The queen who earlier responded to one of the king's requests with a deferential *"I shall obey you"* (3.1) now disobeys his direction with the words: *"I will, my lord. I pray you, pardon me."* Moreover, she follows what seems like a small act of defiance with a truth-revealing exposure that prompts a confession of complicity and guilt from the conscience-stricken Laertes' (*"thy mother's poisoned: / I can no more: the King, the King's to blame"*, 5.2). As she falls from her royal throne of Denmark to the floor, she undermines Claudius' attempt to explain her fainting as a reaction to the fencing duel with this damning accusation against her husband: *"O my dear Hamlet—The drink, the drink! I am poisoned."*

Hamlet's last words to Claudius in 5.2 (*"Follow my mother"*) suggest he believes it will be in the company of the prince's *"incestuous, murderous, damned"* uncle rather than his *"dear father murdered"* (2.2) that Gertrude will be eternally united. It seems a harsh judgment on a woman who in life admitted to him that her *"heart"* was *"cleft in twain"* (3.4) and who, in her death, perhaps earned a measure of redemption by acting as a self-sacrificing mother to her son.

4

The Character of Ophelia

"I cannot choose but weep."

Ophelia struggles to remain true to herself in a maddening world of deception and betrayal. Her submission to her manipulative father, who in turns serves a corrupt king, costs Ophelia her sanity and leaves her with only one route of escape. Her *"self-slaughter"* (1.2) is Ophelia's revenge against everyone who dismissed, silenced and humiliated her.

4.1 – Introduction

Ophelia has become an iconic representation of every powerless and voiceless young woman who is divided between her true self and the role she has been forced to play in order to conform to social expectations.

Sample 1-1

The first sample introduction traces the development of Ophelia's role in *Hamlet*: from her father's *"green girl"* (1.3) to the grave-digger's *"One that was a woman"* (5.1). Her play-long journey from uncertainty, to victim and practitioner of deception, and ultimately to death mirrors that of her suitor and the play's title character, Prince Hamlet.

In this essay, I will argue that, over the course of Shakespeare's *Hamlet*, the character of Ophelia progresses through five phases.

When we first meet her in 1.3, she is the affectionate and gently teasing sister to her departing brother, Laertes (*"No more but so?"*); the unsure recipient of Prince Hamlet's romantic overtures (*"I do not know ... what I should think"*); and the submissive daughter to her cynical-about-love father, Polonius (*"Affection? Pooh!"*), by whom she is commanded to end her relationship with the prince (*"I shall obey, my lord"*).

Secondly, at the bidding of her father and King Claudius, she transforms into a seductress who attempts but fails to lure Hamlet into confessing his past love for her (*"I have remembrances of yours / That I have longed long to redeliver"*, 3.1).

In her third phase, both traumatized and liberated by the death of her controlling father, Ophelia becomes the mad but also defiant woman who will be no longer crushed into silence (*"Pray you, mark"*, 4.5). Through the language of flowers and fragments of ballads, she expresses her feeling of abandonment (*"He is dead and gone"*, 4.5) and sense of futility (*"I cannot choose but weep"*, 4.5).

Following her mental breakdown, she enters her fourth phase: the despairing if visually iconic figure who surrenders to the escape of death in a *"weeping brook ... As one incapable of her own distress"* (4.7).

In her final and fifth phase, she is described by the grave-digging sexton as having lost not only her life but even her female identity: *"One that was a woman ... but rest / her soul she's dead"* (5.1).

Sample 1-2

Sample response number two explores Ophelia's struggle to remain true to oneself in a world of falsity. Her submission to her manipulative father, who in turns serves a corrupt king, in the end costs Ophelia her sanity and leaves her with only one route of escape from the *"heartache / That ... flesh is heir to"* in the *"calamity of ... life"* (3.1).

Ophelia in *Hamlet* does not share the leading role occupied by the female title characters in other Shakespearean dramas such as *Romeo and Juliet* and *Anthony and Cleopatra*. However, her character illustrates one of the play's main themes: the collapse of sanity that results from being crushed by contradictory demands in a world of deception and betrayal.

Moreover, Ophelia's character has over time come to transcend her original role in *Hamlet*. She has become an iconic representation of every powerless and voiceless young woman who is divided between her true self and the role she has been forced to play in order to conform to social expectations.

Ophelia's submissive reply to her father's demand to end her relationship with Prince Hamlet (*"I shall obey, my lord"*, 1.3) mirrors similar compliant responses by other characters in the play: Hamlet to Gertrude (*"I shall in all my best obey you, madam"*, 1.2.), and both Gertrude (*"I shall obey you"*, 1.3) and Guildenstern (*"we both obey ... To be commanded"*, 2.2) to King Claudius. In Ophelia's case, however, obedience is such an integral part of her character that it is only in her later madness that she can give voice to her true feelings.

By surrendering to death in the *"weeping brook"* (4.7), she is at last free from the manipulative world of Elsinore. In a way, her *"self-slaughter"* when her *"too too sullied flesh ... resolve(s) itself into a dew"* (1.2) is Ophelia's revenge against everyone who silenced, dismissed and humiliated her.

Sample 1-3

In 3.2, Prince Hamlet defiantly lashes out at Guildenstern, saying: *"Sblood, do you think I am easier to be played on than a pipe?"* He continues: *"Call me what instrument you will ... yet you cannot play upon me."* Over the first three acts and without consideration for her feelings, Ophelia is used by other characters as an instrument to advance their own interests.

The most striking feature of the character of Ophelia in Shakespeare's *Hamlet* is how she is exploited for their own selfish purposes by everyone around her. She is valued by others only as means to further their intentions.

Prince Hamlet uses her to pretend that her rejection of his love (*"I did repel his letters and denied / His access to me"*, 3.1) is the cause of his put-on *"antic disposition"* (1.5). By her father Polonius, she is exploited to gain favor with Claudius (*"I hold my duty as I hold my soul, / Both to my God and to my gracious King"*, 2.2). Polonius and Claudius manipulate her to investigate the source of Hamlet's 'antic' behavior (*"If't be the affliction of his love or no / That thus he suffers for"*, 3.1).

Prince Hamlet survives Elsinore's duplicitous world by adopting a false mask of his own. His *"antic disposition"* (1.5) is more than a strategy; it is a coping mechanism that provides him with an outlet to vent his rage and despair. In contrast, the submissive Ophelia carries the pain of her continual silencing and humiliation inside her, until, in 4.5, her sanity collapses under its weight. Put simply: Hamlet gets mad; Ophelia goes mad.

In common with Prince Hamlet, Ophelia expresses helplessness about the tragic fate to which she eventually surrenders: *"I cannot choose but weep"* (4.5). Speaking with a similar tone of resignation, the prince later tells his confidant Horatio: *"But thou wouldst not think how ill all's here about my heart. But it is no matter"* (5.2).

In this essay, I will give my opinion on the character of Ophelia and her relationships with the play's other figures. Her name means 'helper', but, in the end, she could not even save herself.

4.2 – Sister and daughter: *"A green girl"*

Indecision is a trait most associated with the character of Prince Hamlet. But in act one, it is Ophelia who is unsure: of the sincerity of Hamlet's romantic interest in her as expressed by his *"almost all the holy vows of heaven"* (1.3). That word 'almost'!

Sample 2-1

Sample response number one highlights the intelligence and eloquence of the young woman we first see in 1.3. She is clearly more than *"Pretty Ophelia"* (4.5), as King Claudius condescendingly describes her. Ophelia's gently teasing ripostes to her brother Laertes mirror the wordplay of the scholarly and pun-loving Prince Hamlet.

The Ophelia we first meet in 1.3 has not yet had her spirit crushed by the world of Elsinore. In her conversation with a departing Laertes, her responses of *"Do you doubt that?"* and *"No more but so?"* suggest agreement with her brother's warnings against the romantic advances of Prince Hamlet. Ophelia declares she will accept Laertes' guidance as a *"lesson"* she will keep *"in my memory locked, / And you yourself shall keep the key of it"* (1.3).

Yet at the same time, her words also display a certain amusement at her brother's sermonizing tone which echoes that of their pompous father, Polonius. Showing both an independent mind and a worldly awareness of male hypocrisy, Ophelia's gently implores Laertes not to emulate those *"ungracious pastors"* who neglect to practice what they preach. Her riposte mirrors the eloquence of the scholarly and pun-loving Prince Hamlet: it contains a subtle biblical reference (*"Enter through the narrow gate"*, Mathew 7:13) and a clever play on the words *"recks"* and *"reckless."* After showing herself more than equal to her brother in conversation, Laertes suddenly remembers his ship is waiting (*"I stay too long"*).

It is with the arrival of Polonius that Ophelia's manner descends into submissiveness. After chiding her for accepting Hamlet's affections (*"Do not believe his vows"*), dismissing her as *"a green girl"* and instructing her to think of herself *"as a baby"*, Polonius orders his daughter to end further contact with Hamlet and never again speak with him. To which she utters in meek compliance: *"I shall obey, my lord."*

Sample 2-2

Shakespeare associates Ophelia's character with flowers from the first moment we see her on stage in 1.3. Later, she will distribute flowers in her 'mad scene' of 4.5. In 4.7, Queen Gertrude will recount how Ophelia clutched a garland of wildflowers as she sunk to her death in a brook. And in 5.1, Laertes will speak of the violets which will spring from her grave.

The metaphor of flowers which is so associated with Ophelia's character appears in 1.3, the first scene in which we see her. In his words of leave-taking to his sister, Laertes characterizes Prince Hamlet's romantic interest in her as *"A violet in the youth ... the perfume ... of a minute ... no more"* (1.3). In response, she teasingly extends his floral analogy by comparing the Paris-bound, pleasure-seeking Laertes with those *"ungracious pastors"* who ignore their own moral preaching to pursue *"the primrose path of dalliance."*

Conceding of Hamlet that *"Perhaps he loves you now,"* Laertes cautions his sister that the prince's romantic choices are governed not by his heart but his royal position: *"He may not ... as unvalued persons do, / Carve for himself"* for he is responsible for *"The safety and health of this whole state."* Ironically, it is the same Laertes who, at the *"riotous head"* (4.5) of a castle-storming mob, will later threaten the crown of Denmark.

Whereas the departing Laertes offers Ophelia brotherly advice regarding Prince Hamlet, her arriving father Polonius is at first inquisitive (*"What is between you? Give me up the truth"*) and then scornful (*"Affection? Pooh! You speak like a green girl"*). Polonius next offers some cynical advice (*"Be somewhat scanter of your maiden presence; / Set your entreatments at a higher rate"*) before commanding her to end their relationship: *"I would not ... Have you so slander any moment ... As to give words or talk with the Lord Hamlet."*

Sample 2-3
In an aside in 2.2, Polonius admits that *"truly in my youth I suffered much extremity for love"* (2.2). But Ophelia's father now takes an entirely cynical and self-interested approach to romance and insists his daughter do the same.

In 1.3, before he receives Polonius' much-quoted speech of fatherly advice (*"And these few precepts in thy memory ..."*), the Elsinore-departing Laertes offers to his sister, Ophelia, some guidance of his own. Concerning her relationship with Prince Hamlet, Laertes cautions Ophelia against giving up her *"heart"* or *"chaste treasure"* to the prince, for his overtures are only *"trifling"* and not *"permanent"* or *"lasting."*

If Ophelia's brother believes that, for royal princes, romantic love must be subordinated to political interests (*"He may not ... as unvalued persons do, / Carve for himself"*), her father Polonius seeks to convince her that it does not exist at all (*"Affection? Pooh!"*). Or does so only in the naïve mind of a *"green girl"* or *"baby"*, two terms he applies dismissively to his daughter.

In response to Ophelia's admission that Hamlet has *"of late made many tenders / Of his affection to me"*, he chastises her that her suitor's attentions are not *"true pay"* or *"sterling"*, but only *"springes to catch woodcocks."*

Polonius' financial interpretation of the words 'tender' and 'dear' (*"Tender yourself more dearly, ... Set your entreatments at a higher rate"*) reveals his cynical attitude towards romance. To Polonius, the only 'tender' of value would be the proposal of a legally-binding marriage contract, something which Hamlet's *"almost all the holy vows of heaven"* falls short of. He is a man who approaches human relationships as self-interested transactions (*"to thine ownself be true"*), to be pursued only for personal advantage and best avoided by the unsophisticated who are *"Unsifted in such perilous circumstance."*

4.3 – Seductress and snitch: *"Where is thy father?"*

Having exposed his two old school friends Rosencrantz and Guildenstern as spies serving the king and queen (*"Were you not sent for? ... Come, come, deal justly with me"*, 2.2), Hamlet naturally reacts with suspicion on suddenly encountering Polonius' daughter. At the end of the so-called 'nunnery scene', a humiliated Ophelia is left holding the *"remembrances"* she intended to return to Hamlet: *"And I, of ladies most deject and wretched"* (3.1).

Sample 3-1

The downward descent of Ophelia's character begins with her agreement to participate in the *"'twere by accident"* encounter with Prince Hamlet in 3.1. At the end of the so-called 'nunnery scene', a humiliated Ophelia is left holding the *"remembrances"* she intended to return to Hamlet: *"And I, of ladies most deject and wretched"* (3.1).

> In 1.3, Ophelia felt unsure of how to receive Hamlet's romantic overtures (*"I do not know ... what I should think"*). Now, in 2.1, she comes to fear her rejection of him has driven insane the prince on whom depends, in her brother's words, *"The safety and health of this whole state."*
>
> The *"doublet all unbraced"* visit of Hamlet to her closet that Ophelia reports to Polonius in 2.1 has left her in a condition of genuine distress: *"I have been so affrighted."* As neither daughter nor father is aware of the prince's put-on *"antic disposition"* (1.5), she worries that Polonius' interpretation of Hamlet's behavior (*"Mad for thy love?"*) may be correct: *"My lord, I do not know. / But truly, I do fear it."*
>
> Under her father's direction, Ophelia participates in the *"'twere by accident"* meeting with Hamlet of 3.1 in order to discover, as Claudius explains to Gertrude, *"If't be th'affliction of his love or no / That thus he suffers for."* But an at first suspicious and then hostile Hamlet subjects her to an abusive and self-contradictory rant—against women, men and himself. Later, at *The Murder of Gonzago*, he will

continue his tirade against Ophelia with vulgar banter about *"country matters"* (3.2).

Following this humiliating exchange, Polonius' murder and Hamlet's exile, the uncertain and distressed Ophelia of the first three acts descends into the mad Ophelia of act four. We next hear of her in the courtier's plea that *"Her moods will needs to be pitied"* (4.5), spoken in response to the dismissive refusal of the play's only other female character, Queen Gertrude, to offer her comfort: *"I will not speak with her ... What would she have?"*

Sample 3-2

Sample response number two highlights how the roles demanded of Ophelia by her father and the king he serves are not only manipulative but also contradictory.

With her brother absent in Paris and lacking a Horatio-like companion in whom to confide, it is to her father Polonius (*"What's the matter ... i'th'name of God?"*) that a clearly upset (*"affrighted"*) Ophelia turns in 2.1 with her report of Hamlet's wordless and disheveled (*"no hat upon his head"*) appearance in her closet.

When Polonius bring news to the king and queen of Hamlet's former relationship with his daughter, it is unclear whether Ophelia is present on stage to endure the embarrassment of having her private correspondence read aloud. Or to hear her father tell the king and queen he regards his daughter as unworthy of her suitor's love: *"this I did bespeak: 'Lord Hamlet is a prince, out of thy star / This must not be'"* (2.2).

After earlier chastising Ophelia for possessing feelings of romantic and sexual desire (*"Think yourself a baby"*, 1.3), Polonius next demands she exploit those same feelings she has aroused in Hamlet to uncover the source of the prince's *"turbulent and dangerous lunacy"* (3.1) which King Claudius fears may contain *"some danger"* (3.1).

> Hamlet's behavior towards Ophelia reflects the successively contradictory roles her father demands of her: firstly, a coy maiden (*"a green girl"*, 1.3); and then, in the so-called 'nunnery scene', an alluring, information-gathering temptress (*"Ophelia, walk you here..."*, 3.1). The prince who once courted Ophelia *"In honorable fashion"* with *"holy vows of heaven"* now insults her as a representative of manipulative womanhood: *"God hath given you one face, and you make yourselves another"* and *"for wise men know well enough what monsters you make of them."* It is a strand of invective he will continue at *The Murder of Gonzago* with his jibe about the brevity of *"woman's love"* (3.2). Afterward, Ophelia will succumb to the madness she mistakenly believed the denial of her love caused in Hamlet.

Sample 3-3

The third sample response suggests that Ophelia's conduct in the 'nunnery scene' of 3.1 reveals she still holds feelings for the prince. Her initial greeting, her production of his *"remembrances"* and the patient silence with which she endures his ranting all point to this interpretation. But when she overhears King Claudius' plan to ship Hamlet away to England *"with speed"*, Ophelia must surely feel any hope of restoring her relationship with the prince is forever lost.

> Why does Ophelia so willingly comply with her father's and Claudius' scheme to *"sift"* (2.2) Hamlet with the staged *"'twere by accident"* encounter of the so-called 'nunnery scene' in 3.1?
>
> In my view, her agreement arises in part from the same submissiveness to Polonius that led her to end her relationship with Hamlet (*"as you did command"*, 2.1) and to surrender to him the prince's love letters (*"in obedience, hath my daughter shown me"*, 2.2). A second reason is that Ophelia, knowing nothing of Hamlet's *"antic disposition"* (1.5) ploy, blames herself for *"the madness in which he now*

raves" (2.2). And, like Queen Gertrude, she hopes her action *"Will bring him to his wonted way again"* (3.1).

A third motivation is suggested by her opening remark to the prince, with its implied lament that she misses him in her life: *"How does your honour for this many a day?"* Next—and unrequested by her father, the king or queen—Ophelia says to her former suitor: *"My lord, I have remembrances of yours / That I have longed long to redeliver. / I pray you now receive them."* In my view, Ophelia is encouraging the prince to recall his past love for her (*"words of so sweet breath composed"*) in the hope that so doing she may also rekindle it.

Despite Hamlet's cruel taunts and his suggestion for her to *"Get thee to a nunnery"*, it is Hamlet's loss of mind (*"noble and most sovereign reason"*) that causes her the most sorrow. For the same madness which Ophelia mistakenly believed was caused by her rejection of him, she now sees as the reason for his rejection of her. Ophelia's grief at Hamlet's apparent loss of sanity (*"O, what a noble mind is here o'erthrown!"*) foreshadows her own 'mad scene' in the next act.

4.4 – Traumatized truth-teller: *"Pray you, mark me"*

Ophelia's descent into insanity is both shocking and yet dramatically inevitable. The world of Elsinore has finally broken her. But her madness is also a liberation that enables Ophelia to find her voice. But, for so long unaccustomed to communicating her true feelings, she must borrow from popular ballads and the symbolism of flowers to express her dilemma.

Sample 4-1

The first sample response focuses on the symbolic meaning of the various flowers distributed by Ophelia. For each offering carries a specific accusatory message for its recipient.

Through fragments of traditional songs, but more vividly through the symbolic language of flowers, in 4.5 the traumatized Ophelia expresses her clear understanding of the dark truths that lie unspoken beneath the surface of the Danish court. Although the play's text does not identify which flowers Ophelia distributes to whom, I believe their symbolic meaning strongly suggests that different flowers are intended for specific characters.

I believe the first recipient of Ophelia's floral gifts is her brother, who has just spoken about her: *"This nothing's more than matter."* She hands him rosemary (*"that's for remembrance"*) and pansies (*"that's for thoughts"*). The other flowers I suggest are offered first to Claudius and then to Gertrude.

To the king, she presents fast-wilting fennel (representing flattery) and then columbines (adultery). To the queen and herself, Ophelia offers the bitter-tasting symbol of sorrow and regret: *"There's rue for you, and here's some for me."* But she adds that Gertrude must wear hers differently: as *"'herb of grace' o' Sundays"* which carries the extra connotation of repentance-seeking for past sins. Next, *"There's a daisy"*, which I suggest Ophelia picks up only to put down again; the innocence and gentleness it represents have no place in what Hamlet called the *"unweeded garden"* (1.2) of Elsinore. And, finally and most poignantly, is the flower symbolizing faithfulness: *"I would give you some violets, but they withered all when my father died."* Ophelia's mood of grief and sadness will shortly descend into the self-annihilating despair of *"self-slaughter"* (1.2).

Sample 4-2
In Ophelia's traumatized mind, the loss of her father and the loss of her lover are incoherently combined; her words turn from one grief to the other and then back again.

The Ophelia we see in her 'mad scene' of 4.5 is traumatized both by her father's death and her lost love for Prince Hamlet. As her parting two lines demonstrate, her thoughts about the two commingle incoherently: firstly, she recalls her absent lover (*"For bonny sweet Robin is all my joy"*); and secondly, she then remembers her late father (*"They say he made a good end"*).

She begins the scene by singing three ballad verses: the first portrays Hamlet as a pilgrim departed on a journey of repentance (*"cockle hat and staff / And his sandal shoon"*); the second is a lament for Polonius (*"He is dead and gone"*); and the third refers to her father's rushed and secret *"hugger-mugger"* burial: *"sweet flowers, / Which bewept to the ground did not go."*

When the king enters and attributes her grief solely to Polonius' death (*"Conceit upon her father"*), she quickly dismisses his interpretation: *"Pray you, let's have no words of this, but when they ask you what it means, say you this."* She next recites sixteen lines of verse that express what has pushed her beyond the bounds of sanity: the maddening contradictions of her situation. In the ballad of a naïve girl who is seduced by the promise of marriage only to be abandoned because she is no longer a virgin, Ophelia sees the impossibility of anything but failure. Her bleak recognition of *"I cannot choose but weep"* anticipates Claudius' later words about Hamlet before the rigged fencing duel: *"He cannot choose but fall"* (4.7). If the prince loses, he will die from a fatal wound; if he wins, a poisoned chalice is his prize. In the end, instead of being *"tumbled"* by a seducer, Ophelia tumbles to *"muddy death"* (4.7) to become a *"cold maid"* (4.7).

Sample 4-3

As Hamlet did through theater with *The Murder of Gonzago*, Ophelia in 4.5 through flowers and ballads exposes Elsinore's dark secrets.

Ophelia's so-called 'mad scene' is, in fact, her exposure of the corrupt Danish court. No longer in the shadow of her now-dead controlling father, in 4.5 she has transformed into a dangerous truth-teller: *"Pray you, mark me."* As a spectator of Hamlet's adapted *The Murder of Gonzago*, she has, to borrow Polonius' words from the nunnery scene, *"heard it all"* (3.1): Denmark is ruled by a king and queen who owe their position to a secret murder followed by politically convenient marriage.

I hear Ophelia's opening question of *"Where is the beauteous majesty of Denmark?"* (4.5) as a reference to Denmark before it became, in the term used by the guard Marcellus, *"rotten"* (1.4). Or perhaps even to old King Hamlet himself, for her words echo Horatio's statement from the very first scene about *"the majesty of buried Denmark"* (1.1).

Her first song, addressed to Gertrude who is alone on stage with Horatio, accuses the queen of failing to distinguish her *"true love"* from *"another one"* and not appropriately mourning her first husband with *"true love showers."* She then challenges her father's *"hugger-mugger"* burial in an unmarked grave (*"At his head a grass-green turf"*). The ballad she sings of sexual seduction is a direct response to Claudius' condescension (*"Pretty Ophelia"*) and can be interpreted as a portrayal of the king as a seducer of Denmark. The fennel and columbines presented to the king and queen carry accusatory messages that highlight the guilt of their recipients. Moreover, her entire performance, with its motifs of death and burial, is both an enactment of the funeral her father never had and a warning of impending doom: for everyone to whom she hands out flowers, including herself, will shortly die.

4.5 – Death: *"Fell into a weeping brook"*

There is a dramatic irony in that the news of Ophelia's drowning is delivered by Queen Gertrude. For it was what Hamlet's mother described as her *"o'erhasty marriage"* (2.2) that darkened the prince's attitude about love. The pre-play wedding of Claudius and Gertrude means that *Hamlet* cannot end with the marriage of the prince and Ophelia. Tragically, it concludes instead with both their deaths. And the question remains: if Ophelia's garments bore her up long enough in the *"weeping brook"* (4.7) for her to sing her snatches of old songs, why did the queen or other eyewitnesses not attempt to rescue her?

Sample 5-1

The first sample response explores how, at least as reported by the queen, Ophelia's drowning contains elements of both accidental death and intentional suicide: she did not deliberately throw herself into the brook; but, once in the water, she made no attempt to save herself. Ophelia did not actively seek to end her life—but she did nothing to prevent her death, either.

> The image of a drowning Ophelia ranks alongside Hamlet's graveside cherishing of Yorick's skull as one of the play's most enduring and iconic images. The scene which has inspired artists is of a fair-skinned young woman, floating in a brook with her face looking upward in a state of despair; as she sings of lost love and holds in her hands a garland of wildflowers, her sodden white dress slowly pulls her down to her death.
>
> Ophelia's demise is reported to the court in 4.7 by the play's only other female character, Queen Gertrude. Her lyrical account of Ophelia as a *"mermaid-like ... creature"* is at odds with what we have known of the queen's character up to this point: her ready acceptance of human mortality (*"'tis common; all that lives must die"*, 1.2); her preference for plain-speaking (*"More matter, with less art"*, 2,2) and her unreflective, live-in-the-moment personality (*"all that is I see"*, 3.4).

Gertrude describes Ophelia's drowning as the result of a figure so incapacitated by madness (*"incapable of her own distress"*) that she lacked the common sense to save herself from a preventable death (*"her garments, heavy with their drink, / Pulled the poor wretch"*). In this view, Ophelia's despairing surrender to the *"weeping brook"* was just another example of the passivity that characterized her life. An alternative interpretation is that it was a deliberate act: a self-drowning that was both an escape from what Hamlet earlier called the *"prison"* (2.2) of Elsinore; and a form of revenge against everyone who silenced, dismissed and humiliated her.

Sample 5-2
Sample response number two focuses on how the play borrows references from popular folklore and classical myth to represent Ophelia's character and fate. The young woman who Hamlet characterized in life as a *"nymph"* (3.1) is described in death by Gertrude as a *"mermaid"* drawn back by nature to the water, *"like a creature native and indued / Unto that element"* (4.7).

"Nymph, in thy orisons / Be all my sins remembered"—in a play that mixes classical with Biblical allusions, Hamlet's sighting of Ophelia after at the end of his *"To be or not to be"* speech in 3.1 prompts him to ask for a Christian prayer from a woman to whom he assigns a term from Greek mythology. Beautiful and free-spirited, nymphs were woodland-dwelling goddesses associated—prophetically, in Ophelia's case—with the element of water.

Gertrude's account in 4.7 of Ophelia's drowning is expressed in poetic language that characterizes her death as the return of her body to the natural world. The queen's description refers as much to Ophelia's clothing and environment as it does to the women herself.

> The brook-side tree she attempted to climb was a willow, often termed a 'weeping willow' because of its association with sadness and lost love; its downcast, water-overhanging branches suggesting tears and depression. In her hand was a coronet of wildflowers: crowflowers, (buttercups, suggesting ingratitude), nettles (sharp and stinging weeds); and daisies (representing innocence). Lastly, there were also long purples *"That liberal shepherds give a grosser name"* (orchids, representing sexual love).
>
> But Ophelia's attempt to hang the wreath on the willow ended when the branch (an *"envious sliver"*) on which she had climbed broke and she *"Fell in the weeping brook."* There, *"her garments, heavy with their drink"*, she floated for a while singing snatches of *"old tunes"*, until the weight of her clothes *"Pulled the poor wretch"* to her *"muddy death."*

Sample 5-3

No discussion of Ophelia's drowning is complete without at least posing the following question: was she murdered? And even if Ophelia was not deliberately pushed into the brook, why was no attempt made to pull her from the water? Did Queen Gertrude personally witness the event? And what motives might the queen have had for wanting to end Ophelia's life?

> Queen Gertrude's account in 4.7 of Ophelia's death is poetic in expression and yet suspiciously detailed in content. It raises three questions. Firstly, did the queen witness the event personally? Secondly, if so, why did she not at least try to intervene? And, lastly, is it even possible that Gertrude was not a witness to a suicide but actually the perpetrator of a murder?
>
> It seems reasonable to assume that the queen is providing a first-hand account rather than relaying news reported to her by a servant. For the same scene demonstrates that the practice at Elsinore is for the king to receive all messages first: we see Claudius presented with

the two letters from the absent Hamlet, although one is addressed to Gertrude: *"This to your majesty, this to the queen. (gives CLAUDIUS letters)."*

Assuming she was present at the *"weeping brook"*, why did Gertrude not attempt to save Ophelia? Did she break the brook-side tree branch (*"envious sliver"*) on which Ophelia was standing? Gertrude's possible motivations for murder might include: blame for the exile of *"my Hamlet"* (5.1); punishment for Ophelia's accusatory flower offerings; and fear that she was pregnant with Hamlet's child, an heir who might make Ophelia a threat to her queenly position.

One hint of Gertrude's possible guilt is provided in 4.7 when Claudius, who earlier soliloquized about his *"limed soul"* (3.3), describes her as *"conjunctive"* not just to his *"life"* but also his *"soul."* And that the queen dies onstage in the company of three male murderers, and does by the same means of poison, perhaps suggests that she too is experiencing comeuppance for a crime and is *"justly served"* (5.2).

4.6 – Conclusion: *"That's for remembrance"*

The who-loved-her-more struggle in Ophelia's open grave between her brother and suitor (*"Why, I will fight with him upon this theme / Until my eyelids will no longer wag"*, 5.1) prompts the rigged fencing duel that ends with both Laertes and Hamlet following Polonius' daughter to their graves. But if she appears omitted from Horatio's summarized account of *"How these things came about"* (5.2), Ophelia is present in the story Shakespeare tells. It is her *"living monument"* (4.7).

Sample 6-1

In the era of the play, suicide was viewed as a crime equivalent to murder; that is, taking one's life was no different from taking the life of another. Also, in Christian doctrine, suicide was regarded as a sin.

In his private chapel soliloquy of 3.3, Claudius reflects on how in the *"corrupted currents of this world"* the *"gilded hand may shove by justice"* and *"Buys out the law."* A poignant example of royal power overriding the rule of law comes in the play's final act.

The taking of one's life was regarded both as a crime against the law and a sin against God. A coroner's suicide verdict had two consequences: in this world, the confiscation of the deceased person's property by the crown; and, in the next, the eternal damnation of their soul. Remarking on how *"her death was doubtful"*, the figure described by Laertes as the *"churlish priest"* states that Ophelia *"should in ground unsanctified been lodged"* and *"Shards, flints, and pebbles should be thrown on her."* But, he then continues, the *"great command o'ersways the order."* In other words, the coroner's verdict of suicide was overruled by King Claudius.

That Ophelia, after accidentally falling into the water, did nothing to save herself but in despair surrendered to her fate does indeed suggest her death was intentional. However, Shakespeare's portrayal of Ophelia's drowning evokes sympathy rather than condemnation. When seeking forgiveness from Laertes for his fatal stabbing of Polonius, Hamlet in 5.2 uses the defense of insanity: *"If Hamlet from himself be ta'en away, / And when he's not himself does wrong Laertes, / Then Hamlet does it not."* If madness can be offered by Hamlet and accepted by Laertes (*"I am satisfied in nature"*) as a defense against homicide, the message the play leaves us with is that madness too should exculpate suicide, and that the taking of one's life is not the act of a criminal but of a victim.

Sample 6-2

The comments regarding Ophelia by the two clownish grave-diggers illustrate how a character's life and death are shaped by a combination of fate and personal choice. Ophelia did not choose to fall into the brook, but she accepted her death by drowning just she chose to accept her life of submissiveness.

Gertrude's poetic description of Ophelia's death in 4.7 is followed in 5.1 by a debate between the two grave-diggers on the circumstances of her drowning. One is the church sexton who regards himself as an expert on *"crowner's quest law"*; the other, a common laborer. Significantly, the sexton who earlier remarked on Prince Hamlet's supposed insanity (*"he that / is mad, and sent into England"*) makes no mention of Ophelia's mental state in commenting on the decision to grant her a *"Christian burial"* and to *"make her grave straight."* That is, in a church graveyard and facing east towards the Holy Land so that, in the words of the priest, she may with other *"peace-parted souls"* await the *"last trumpet"* and the second coming of Christ.

Of the legal verdicts available to the coroner—which include *filo de se* (self-murder), *non compos mentis* (insanity) and accidental death—the sexton adds one entirely of his own creation: *"It must se offendendo, it cannot be else."* In this conclusion he is supported by his colleague: *"Why, 'tis found so."*

While *'se defendendo'* (meaning self-defense) has a legal relevance for homicide (the killing of another), no such corresponding legal term of *'se offendendo'* exists in the case of suicide. For it would mean that Ophelia literally ended her life in order to defend her life. Or, as the sexton phases it: *"she drowned herself in her own defence."* And yet the twisted logic that would portray Ophelia as both victim and criminal, murdered and murderer, accurately captures the two opposing strands of Ophelia's passivity: partly imposed on her by others—but also partly chosen by her.

Sample 6-3

Both Laertes and Hamlet in 5.1 express heartbreak at Ophelia's death. Her brother demands to be buried with her (*"Now pile your dust upon the quick and the dead"*) and Hamlet declares *"I loved Ophelia"*, Yet, after her burial, she is never spoken of again.

When in 5.1 the *"churlish priest"* refuses to provide the deceased Ophelia with more than *"maimed rites"*, an angry Laertes lashes out at him: *"A ministering angel shall my sister be / When thou liest howling"* (5.1). Laertes had already lost his father, who was buried, in Claudius' words, *"hugger-mugger"* (4.5)—that is, without ceremony in an unmarked grave. Now, he cannot contemplate his sister damned to hell for the sin of *"self-slaughter"* (1.2); instead, he imagines her residing angelically above in heaven.

Laertes request of the *"Must there no more be done?"* brings a reply of *"No more be done"* that echoes Ophelia's response to him when he urged her to doubt the sincerity of Hamlet's love for her: *"No more but so?"* (1.3). Similarly, Laertes' anguished plea of *"Lay her i'th'earth, / And from her fair and unpolluted flesh / May violets spring!"* recalls Ophelia's remark in her 'mad scene' of 4.5: *"I would give you some violets, but they withered all when my father died."*

Prince Hamlet's shock on learning of the death of the woman to whom he *"made many tenders / Of his affection"* is followed moments later by an expression of love that is, poignantly, in the past tense: *"I loved Ophelia."* Queen Gertrude's words over her grave (*"I thought thy bride-bed to have decked, sweet maid, / And not have strewed thy grave"*) are the last time she is mentioned or even alluded to in the play. Nowhere in Horatio's summarized account of *"Purposes mistook / Fallen on th'inventor's heads"* is there any suggestion that Polonius' daughter will feature. It seems that *"fair Ophelia"* (3.1), who in life handed out rosemary (*"that's for remembrance"*, 4.5), will be forgotten in death.

5

The Relationship of Hamlet and the Ghost

"Rest, rest, perturbed spirit!"

Like Ophelia's offering of rosemary (*"for remembrance"*, 4.5), the Ghost represents the preservation of memory. Despite the Ghost's command of *"Pity me not"* (1.5), a dying Prince Hamlet grants to the restless spirit of his *"dear father murdered"* (2.2) something more than the revenge he demanded: atonement for his land-grabbing, *"Extorted treasure in the womb of earth"* (1.1) sins committed *"in his days of nature"* (1.5)—and with it escape from the punishment he suffers in his afterlife *"prison house"* (1.5).

5.1 – Introduction
Hamlet is a play about a young man who has lost a father written by a father who had lost a son. Two of the play's related themes are the duty of remembrance in life and the fear of being forgotten after death.

Sample 1-1
The first sample introduction lists the Ghost's four demands of Prince Hamlet and argues that, by the play's end, the prince has broken every one of them. The son who was instructed to *"Pity me not"* (1.5) ends by atoning for the sins of his suffering-in-purgatory father through his surrender of Denmark to the son of his father's old rival.

'Kill your uncle, ignore your mother, avoid losing your sanity, and don't worry about my suffering in the afterlife' — in simple terms, these are the Ghost's four instructions in 1.5 to the title character of Shakespeare's Hamlet.

The Ghost's demands are unaccompanied by any practical guidance: *"However thou should accomplish this act ..."* But they are tinged with the same emotional blackmail (*"If thou didst ever thy dear father love"*) that King Claudius will later use to manipulate another bereaved young man, Laertes: *"was your father dear to you ... What would you undertake / To show yourself in deed your father's son / More than in words?"* (4.7).

In this essay, I will argue that, by the play's end, Hamlet will have broken every one of the directions issued to him by the *"apparition"* (1.1) who appeared in the *"questionable shape"* (1.4) like *"the King that's dead"* (1.1).

The prince's *"antic disposition"* (1.5) of feigned madness comes dangerously close to real insanity (*"It hath made me mad"*, 3.1; *"My wit's diseased"*, 3.2). As for Queen Gertrude, he does not *"Leave her to heaven"* (1.5) but seeks to uncover her role in his father's death (*"As kill a king ... Ay, lady, 'twas my word"*, 3.4) and save her soul (*"Confess yourself"*, 3.4). As for the killing of the villainous Claudius, it is not the Ghost's sought-for but long-delayed *"Revenge"*

(1.5); it is instead Hamlet's spontaneous response to the king's exposed guilt for the deaths of Gertrude, Laertes and the prince himself: *"In thee there is not half an hour of life"* (5.2).

Although he breaks every element the Ghost's *"dread command"* (3.4), after many *"purposes mistook"* (5.2) and mirroring Laertes' journey from revenge to forgiveness, the prince finds another way to keep the promise he made to his late father's memory: *"Rest, rest, perturbed spirit!"* (1.5).

Sample 1-2

Sample response number two explores two origins of *Hamlet* the play and suggests how Shakespeare altered this raw material to create a story to reminds us of how the dead can persist in our memories through the power of stories.

The storyline of *Hamlet* is in part derived from the Danish legend of Prince Amleth, and it can be assumed that its motifs of death and remembrance are drawn from Shakespeare's personal experience. The reordering of 'Amleth' to 'Hamlet', so that the last letter becomes the first, reflects the two ways in which *Hamlet* the play departs from its two sources of inspiration.

Firstly, the play about a title character who has lost a father is the creation of a playwright who had lost a son. Through drama, Shakespeare transforms his bereavement for a dead son into the Danish prince's grief for a dead father. Shakespeare's son was named Hamnet; his tragedy's protagonist, Hamlet.

Secondly, in place of the sinful pursuit of revenge featured in the Danish legend, Shakespeare substitutes in his play's final 5.2 scene the administration of justice (*"He is justly served"*) and the Christian response of forgiveness (*"Exchange forgiveness with me, noble Hamlet"*).

In *Hamlet*, the title character's memory of his late father is personified in the figure of the Ghost, which, it is believed, was a role played by Shakespeare himself. Significantly, the *"apparition"* (1.1) is seen only by those who remember old King Hamlet and is invisible to others, like his brother King Claudius and first wife Queen Gertrude, who would rather Denmark's former monarch be forgotten.

As he awaits the Players' theatrical performance in 3.2, Prince Hamlet laments that *"a great man's memory may outlive his life"* for only *"half a year"* (3.2). But it is in plays and stories that memories of the dead can be preserved among the living. *Hamlet* begins with Horatio's recounting the tale of Hamlet the father. It ends with him promising to *"truly deliver"* (5.2) the story of Hamlet the son.

Sample 1-3

Two related themes of *Hamlet* are the duty of remembrance in life and the fear of being forgotten after death. Hamlet's dilemma is that he cannot forget his father but, equally, he cannot remember him in the way the Ghost demands.

Like Ophelia's symbolic offering of rosemary (*"that's for remembrance"*, 4.5), the character of the Ghost in Shakespeare's *Hamlet* represents the themes of remembering and forgetting that are continually present throughout the play.

Hamlet's *"fair Ophelia"* (3.1) will fondly recall her Prince of Denmark as he once was: *"O, what a noble mind is here o'erthrown"* (3.1). But she will also wish to erase memories of their relationship by returning his letters and tokens of love: *"My lord, I have remembrances of yours / That I have longed long to redeliver"* (3.1). Rosencrantz and Guildenstern will betray their relationship with the prince (*"young days brought up with him"*) for the promise of financial reward: *"such thanks / As fits a king's remembrance"* (2.1).

Both King Claudius and Queen Gertrude will attempt to replace in the prince's mind the memory of his late father with the substitute figure of his usurping uncle: *"So much for him ... with no less nobility of love / Than that which dearest father bears his son, / Do I impart toward you ... Think of us / As of a father"*, says Claudius (1.2). Speaking of her second husband rather than old King Hamlet, Gertrude will chastise her son: *"thou hast thy father much offended"* (3.4).

Hamlet's dilemma is that he cannot forget his father but, equally, he cannot remember him in the way the Ghost demands: with *"The important acting of your dread command"* (3.4). The prince's challenge is to find another way to keep his promise, expressed after the vengeance-seeking *"apparition"* (1.1) has vanished into Elsinore's dawn air: *"Rest, rest, perturbed spirit!"* (1.5).

5.2 – The Ghost: *"Questionable shape"*

Horatio interpretation of the Ghost as an *"omen... of feared events"* that foretells *"bodes some strange eruption to our state"* (1.1) will prove to be true. Eight deaths will follow its visitation; the Hamlet dynasty will come to a bloody end and Denmark will lose its independence to the rival kingdom of Norway.

Sample 2-1

As the first sample response argues, *Hamlet* begins as a conventional story: we hear about the theft of a throne by a villain and see the assembly of a band of friends, sworn to secrecy and ready to restore order to the *"something rotten"* (1.4) kingdom. But, of course, that is not how the play develops.

As if it could—at least to an extent—foretell how events would unfold, the Ghost appears to Prince Hamlet through two levels of intermediaries. The result of its successive visitations is a shared conspiratorial secret with the potential to spark what is the Ghost's stated aim: the removal of Denmark's newly-crowned King Claudius.

In 1.1, we learn that the spirit first revealed itself to two castle guards on their *"strict and most observant watch."* Its second appearance is both to them and Horatio, Hamlet's friend from Wittenberg University. The guards sent for the *"scholar"* so he may *"avouch"* with his *"own eyes"* that the *"dreaded sight"* witnessed by them is no *"fantasy."* In 1.2, Horatio, in turn, relays to an astonished Hamlet (*"For God's love, let me hear"*) his report of the Ghost (*"My lord, I think I saw him yesternight ... the king your father"*).

As the *"spirit of health or goblin damned"* (1.4) correctly anticipated, neither the guards nor Horatio alert King Claudius of its visitation; it is only the prince in whom they confide, *"As needful in our loves, fitting our duty"* (1.1). Hamlet requests his colleagues continue their *"dreadful secrecy"* (1.4) by swearing on the prince's sword *"Never to speak of this that you have seen."*

But what follows is not a story of a revenge-fueled political rebellion. Instead, the play evolves into an exploration and ultimately a repudiation of the concept of revenge itself; a journey not to vengeance but to justice and forgiveness, culminating in Laertes' words to Hamlet of *"Mine and my father's death come not upon thee"* (5.2).

Sample 2-2

The second sample response contrasts the Catholic and Protestant view of supernatural spirits. Unusually for a soul returned from a Catholic purgatory, the Ghost seeks not prayers to end its suffering in the afterlife but instead demands the murder of a living person. Such a demand for revenge is repugnant to Christians of any denomination.

In addition to his complaint of being *"by a brother's hand / Of life, of crown, of queen at once dispatched"*, the angry Ghost of 1.5 adds a further cause of grievance: he was *"Cut off … With all my imperfections on my head."*

To the Protestant audience of Shakespeare's era, the Ghost presents himself as a soul enduring punishment in the *"fires"* of a Catholic purgatory *"for a certain term"* until his sins are *"purged away"* (1.5). In Catholic doctrine, such souls might be permitted to revisit the living to request prayers to shorten their afterlife suffering. Hence Horatio's first question of the Ghost: *"If there be any good thing to be done / That may to thee do ease … Speak to me* (1.1).

In the Protestant view which Prince Hamlet appears to share, a supernatural apparition may be a truth-revealing figure (*"spirit of health"*) or, more likely, a manipulative demon (*"goblin damned"*, 1.5). The prince first believes the former (*"It is an honest ghost"*, 1.5), but later fears what he has seen *"may be a devil"* who *"Abuses me to damn me"* (2.2).

But the nature of the Ghost's *"dread command"* (3.4) undermines his complaint of 1.5 that the manner of his murder (*"Sleeping within my orchard"*) denied him the opportunity to confess and repent his sins before death (*"No reckoning made"*). For the Ghost's request of Hamlet, which is repugnant to Christians of any denomination, is not a prayer for forgiveness of sins in the next world but a demand for a sinful act of revenge in this one.

Sample 2-3

The third sample response suggests that the Ghost really is a demon. Or, at least, that its command for revenge is demonic. Horatio correctly interprets the Ghost's appearance as foretelling a political upheaval in Denmark similar to the downfall of Julius Caesar in ancient Rome.

Although he does not share his opinion with his friend Prince Hamlet, Horatio's interprets the Ghost as an *"omen ... of feared events"* that foretells a political upheaval in Denmark: *"This bodes some strange eruption to our state"* (1.1). By temperament *"more an antique Roman than a Dane"* (5.2), Horatio is reminded of the supernatural spirits (*"the sheeted dead"*) that appeared before the murder of Caesar (*"ere the mightiest Julius fell"*).

Aside from its unchristian demand for revenge, many clues are provided by Shakespeare to suggest the Ghost is a *"goblin damned"* rather than a *"spirit of health"*, with *"intents"* that are *"wicked"* rather than *"charitable"* (1.5). It disappears at dawn *"like a guilty thing / Upon a fearful summons"* (1.1), and it is from beneath the stage that its voice is afterward heard (*"this fellow in the cellarage"*, 1.5). Significantly, the Ghost's account of poison being poured into the ear of the *"sleeping within my orchard"* (1.5) old King Hamlet is told from the perspective of an observer rather than the victim. How could a sleeping man know how and by whom he has murdered?

More than just Horatio's omen of political disruption, the Ghost brings not *"airs from heaven"* but *"blasts from hell"* (1.5) that lead to eight deaths, the ending of the Hamlet family dynasty, and Denmark's loss of independence to its rival kingdom of Norway. Prince Hamlet, the Ghost's chosen instrument of revenge, is the last to die; and Claudius, the Ghost's intended target of murderous vengeance, is the last to be killed.

5.3 – King Claudius: *"A brother's murder"*

Hamlet is trapped in the middle of a *"cursed spite!"* (1.5) between two brothers. One brother, having stolen the prince's expected inheritance, confines him in the *"prison"* (2.2) of Denmark; the other, returning after midnight from his afterlife *"prison house"* (1.5), wants to steal the prince's soul. *Hamlet* has many echoes of the story of Cain and Abel, two sons of the Bible's first couple, Adam and Eve.

Sample 3-1

The first sample response stresses that Hamlet never actually commits to a vow of revenge. Moreover, the Ghost's command presents the prince with multiple dilemmas: should he murder his uncle on the word of a ghost? And how can he ignore the impact on his mother of making her a widow a second time?

Hamlet responds to his ghost-father in 1.5 as he did earlier to his uncle-father in the court scene of 1.2—with verbal evasion. Then he replied to Claudius' request to *"think of us / As of a father"* with *"I am too much in the sun."* The only allegiance he promised was to his mother: *"I shall do my best to obey you, madam."*

After listening to the Ghost's demand to *"Revenge his foul and most unnatural murder"*, Hamlet records in his scholar's notebook that *"That one may smile, and smile, and be a villain. / At least I'm sure it may be so in Denmark."* Nothing does he *"set ... down"* in his *"tables"* about revenge. And the oath the prince swears is not to avenge the Ghost but only never to forget him: *"Now to my word: / It is 'Adieu, adieu. Remember me.' / I have sworn't."*

We, the audience, hear Claudius' confession (*"a brother's murder"*, 3.3) and are so in no doubt of his guilt. But what if, like Hamlet, we had not? What would we do? Claudius' crime in the palace orchard left behind neither witnesses nor evidence. Such is Hamlet's predicament.

Moreover, the monarch Hamlet is asked to assassinate has been duly elected by the nobles of Denmark. In Claudius' words, *"Your better wisdoms, which have freely gone / With this affair along"* (1.2). An even greater source of conflict for the prince is that Claudius is also the man to whom his mother is very happily—if incestuously—married.

Sample 3-2

As much as Hamlet idolizes his dead father and despises his usurping uncle, in the prince's *"cursed spite"* (1.5) remark there is a recognition that both brothers share blame for the dilemma in which he is placed. Hamlet is trapped between the murderous ambition of a living brother and the vengeful fury of an undead one.

> *"O Hamlet, what a falling off was there!"*—so laments the Ghost in 1.5 as he reflects on the theft of his crown and queen by *"a wretch whose natural gifts were poor / To those of mine."* Hamlet clearly shares this unfavorable comparison. To his mother, the prince describes Claudius as *"A slave that is not twentieth part the tithe / Of your precedent lord"* (3.4). But Hamlet also recognizes both brothers share responsibility for the dilemma in which he finds himself: *"O cursed spite!"* (1.5).
>
> One brother, having stolen the prince's inheritance, confines him in the *"prison"* (2.2) of Denmark; the other, returning after midnight from his afterlife *"prison house"* (1.5), wants to steal Hamlet's soul. Motivated by *"ambition"* (3.3), aided by the *"witchcraft of his wit"* (1.5) and unable to repent (*"Pray can I not"*, 3.3), Claudius is certainly a villainous character. But, in my view, so too is the vengeance-seeking, emotional-blackmailing (*"If thou didst ever thy dear father love"*, 1.5) Ghost of *"the King that's dead"* (1.1).

The fatal flaw or *"vicious mole of nature"* (1.4) of old King Hamlet—at least as he is represented by the figure of the Ghost—is not ambition but an anger so blind, deep and demonic it demands the sacrifice of his son's soul to satisfy it. The Ghost dared not reveal his *"horrible"* afterlife punishment to Hamlet lest *"the lightest word"* of it *"freeze thy young blood"* (1.5). But at least his purgatorial penance is only for a *"certain term"* (1.5). In contrast, the hell which the prince would be damned for yielding to the sin of revenge would last for all eternity.

Sample 3-3

As sample response number three notes, both King Claudius and Prince Hamlet make reference to the Biblical tale of Cain and Abel. The old testament story of brother-murder with its warning against revenge has many echoes in Shakespeare's play.

Hamlet can be viewed as a retelling of the story of Cain and Abel, two sons of the Bible's first couple, Adam and Eve. Motivated by envy, the elder son Cain killed his younger brother, Abel. In the first of the play's two references to the Biblical tale, Claudius in his private chapel acknowledges *"my offence ... hath the primal eldest curse upon't, / A brother's murder"* (3.3). Later, Hamlet imagines a skull tossed about by the gravedigger to be *"Cain's jawbone, that did the first murder!"* (5.1).

On the forehead of the brother-killer Cain, God inscribed a mark as a warning to others against taking revenge upon him, for judgment and justice belonged only to God. As for any human who defied God's injunction, the Bible provides a clear warning of the consequences: *"If anyone kills Cain, vengeance shall be taken on him sevenfold"* (Genesis 4:15). Excluding the guilty Claudius himself, seven is, of course, the number of victims who die in the chain of *"purposes mistook"* (5.2) events that follow Hamlet's conversation with the vengeance-seeking Ghost.

That Claudius identifies with Cain may suggest more than an awareness of his sibling-murdering guilt. If the era of the play, it would have been typical for the firstborn son to succeed to his father's position. Was Claudius, like Cain, the elder of two brothers? If so, why was he passed over for Denmark's kingship in favor of Hamlet's father? Whatever the reason, it is not difficult to imagine Claudius' resentment, accumulating over three decades, tempting him to repeat Cain's sin.

5.4 – Queen Gertrude: *"Leave her to heaven"*

Partly to protect his already-thwarted inheritance from the birth of a rival heir and partly to rescue her soul from damnation, Hamlet attempts to separate his mother from her second husband—contrary to the Ghost's command not to *"let thy soul contrive / Against thy mother aught"* (1.5).

Sample 4-1

The first sample response focuses on how Prince Hamlet uses his play-within-a-play to shame his mother into separating herself from King Claudius. His continued efforts to do in her closet are undermined by the reappearance of the Ghost, which is visible only to him. A terrified Queen Gertrude is left to conclude her son is truly—and dangerously—insane.

If Hamlet struggles with the Ghost's command of 1.5 regarding Claudius (*"Revenge"*), he defies completely his direction about Gertrude (*"Leave her to heaven"*).

During *The Murder of Gonzago* in 3.2, after we hear the grief-stricken Player Queen vow lifelong fidelity to her dying first husband of thirty years (*"Nor earth to me give food, nor heaven light… If, once a widow, ever I be wife!"*), Hamlet pointedly quizzes his mother: *"Madam, how like you this play?"* It seems the prince hopes such a theatrical shaming will *"prick and sting her"* (1.5) to repentance. But the rebuke is lost upon Gertrude. Her later complaint to Hamlet is not that his play has ridiculed her but that Claudius is *"much offended"* (3.4).

The Ghost's first appearance to Hamlet prompted him to pretend to be insane; his second, in Gertrude's closet, convinces Gertrude her son actually is: *"Alas, he's mad"* (3.4). That the Ghost is visible to the prince but unseen by his mother (*"To whom do you speak this?"*, 3.4) reveals the gulf between the haunted-by-the-past Hamlet and the live-in-the-present Gertrude. Also, the Ghost's invisibility to Gertrude undermines her son's credibility and his effort to persuade her to shun Claudius' bed. I believe Gertrude's apparent submission to her son's hectoring (*"Be thou assured"*) is insincere; she is simply terrified of her son (*"Thou wilt not murder me? / Help, help, ho!"*).

When she later informs Claudius that Hamlet is as *"Mad as the sea and wind"* (4.1), I believe Gertrude genuinely believes so; she is not merely acceding to her son's request to conceal from Claudius that he is only *"mad in craft."*

Sample 4-2

The second sample response suggests two reasons why Prince Hamlet ignores the Ghost's direction about Gertrude: he wishes to protect his inheritance and to save her soul from the afterlife torment suffered by old King Hamlet.

Partly to protect his already-thwarted inheritance and partly to rescue her soul from damnation, Hamlet attempts to separate his mother from her second husband—contrary to the Ghost's command not to *"let thy soul contrive / Against thy mother aught"* (1.5).

In their encounter of 3.4 in her closet, the prince voices his suspicion that his mother was an accessory to murder: *"As kill a king ... Ay, lady, 'twas my word."* But satisfied by Gertrude's denial of complicity, Hamlet directs her to shun sexual relations with Claudius: *"go not to mine uncle's bed."*

Having had his expected inheritance stolen once by Claudius (*"He that hath ... Popped in between th'election and my hopes"*, 5.2), Hamlet does not want it jeopardized a second time by the birth of a rival heir to his *"uncle-father and aunt-mother"* (2.2).

As Hamlet subjects Gertrude to a barrage of verbal violence (*"I will speak daggers to her"*, 3.2), the Ghost appears and begs the prince to cease: *"O, step between her and her fighting soul."* Indeed, such That the Ghost is invisible to his former wife of thirty years (*"This the very coinage of your brain"*) reveals how his memory is as dead to her as it is alive to the prince. is Gertrude's self-absorption that her son's imminent departure to England has slipped her mind: *"Alack, I had forgot."*

After the Ghost *"steals away,"* Hamlet's behavior and tone towards his mother change: from hectoring *"scourge"* to righteous *"minister."* I believe Hamlet genuinely does want Gertrude to *"Confess yourself to heaven"* and so avoid afterlife punishment for what Shakespeare's audience would have regarded as a sinfully incestuous marriage.

Sample 4-3

Sample response number three argues that Hamlet wishes to separate his mother from King Claudius to minimize the devastation she will experience at her second husband's death. A further suggested motivation is the prince's wish to reunite his parents in the afterlife.

The ghost, which in 1.5 pleaded *"Remember me"*, returns in 3.4 with this reminder to the prince: *"Do not forget."* In act one, three witnesses see the apparition with whom only Hamlet speaks. In his mother's closet, only Hamlet sees and converses with the spirit (*"My father, in his habit as he lived"*). Gertrude, who sees and hears nothing, asks her son: *"how is't with you, / That you ... with th'incorporal air do hold discourse?"* But by representing the Ghost onstage by an actor, I believe Shakespeare intends us to regard the Ghost as real and not a hallucination of the prince. Old King Hamlet's Ghost is invisible to Gertrude because his memory is dead to her.

In the closet scene and the chapel scene which precedes it, we see that Hamlet's purpose has evolved from mere revenge to another, more poignant one: to reunite in the afterlife his fractured-by-Claudius family of mother and father. Hence the prince's desire both to rescue his mother's soul (*"Confess yourself to heaven. / Repent what's past. Avoid what is to come"*, 3.4) and condemn his uncle's (*"as damned and black / As hell, whereto it goes"*, 3.3).

I believe Hamlet's motivations for seeking to separate Gertrude from Claudius are two-fold: to minimize the Hecuba-like devastation she will feel at her second husband's death, and to save her soul from hell. The prince's words over Polonius' lifeless body make it clear who he intends his next victim to be: *"Thus bad begins and worse remains behind."* Echoing Gertrude's earlier request of him (*"Let not thy mother lose her prayers, Hamlet"*, 1.2), he departs her closet hoping she will reform so that as a son he can ask his mother's blessing: *"And when you are desirous to be blessed, / I'll blessing beg of you."*

5.5 – Madness: *"Taint not thy mind"*

The *"noble youth"* who was warned by the Ghost in act one to *"Taint not thy mind"* (1.5) has by act five come to be regarded as a dangerous lunatic: as *"he that is mad and sent into England"* in the hope *"he shall recover his wits there"* (5.1).

Sample 5-1

Hamlet never explains why he puts on his act of insanity. This first sample response offers one theory: the prince devises his antic ploy to disguise his real—and kingship-disqualifying—mental fragility.

"Taint not thy mind", the Ghost directs Hamlet in 1.5. But it is difficult to imagine how the prince could react with anything other than shock and psychological distress to what he sees and hears.

From the *"dead corse"* of his late father, which has seemingly returned from the grave *"Wherein we saw thee quietly interred,"* Hamlet is offered a terrifying glimpse of the afterlife torment that awaits sinners: *"O, horrible! O, horrible! Most horrible!"* Yet he is also directed to assassinate his country's monarch in a sinful act of private vengeance. And the same Ghost who instructs Hamlet to remove his mother from his thoughts also burdens the prince with the mental image of her and his uncle Claudius sharing *"the royal couch of Denmark."*

When Horatio sought to restrain Hamlet from conversing with the Ghost, his concern was not for his friend's body or soul, but his sanity: *"What if it … deprive your sovereignty of reason / And draw you into madness?"* On hearing the prince afterward speak in *"wild and whirling words"*, Horatio must fear his concern was well-founded.

But Hamlet appears instead to be preparing for the new role he has decided—without explanation—to adopt: the pretend madman. Aware that any public signs of mental weakness might disqualify him from replacing Claudius on the throne, I believe the prince's intention is this: to mask his real distress (*"my weakness and my melancholy"*, 2,2) with episodes of feigned madness. Should he later need proof of his claim that he was never really insane, Hamlet can release from their oath of secrecy two credible witnesses: one of Elsinore's loyal soldiers, Marcellus, and Horatio, a man trusted by them (*"thou art a scholar"*, 1.1).

Sample 5-2

A second theory is that Hamlet's 'antic disposition' charade is a cunning plan to prepare an insanity defense should he actually murder King Claudius. This theory also offers one interpretation of the prince's behavior towards Polonius' daughter, Ophelia.

After his conversation with the Ghost, in which he is warned *"Taint not thy mind"* (1.5), Hamlet immediately and without explanation declares he will *"put an antic disposition on"* (1.5). Why?

In my view, the intention of the *"Looking before and after"* (4.4) prince is to set in place a defense of temporary insanity should he kill Claudius and face a trial for the crime of regicide. He shares his ploy with Horatio and the guard Marcellus for one purpose: to assure them of his fitness to rule as a future king capable of protecting the *"safety and health of this whole state"* (1.3). So, in the interim, they should not lose confidence in him, however *"strange or odd soe'er I bear myself"* (1.5). It is this same excuse of temporary insanity that Hamlet will later use with Laertes in explanation for his murder of Polonius: *"Was't Hamlet wronged Laertes? Never Hamlet ... His madness is poor Hamlet's enemy"* (5.2).

After Polonius's ending of his daughter's relationship with Hamlet, the prince adds a further element to his feigned insanity. He presents himself as a man driven temporarily mad by rejected love rather than on the more suspect grounds of thwarted political ambition. Hence, Hamlet's disheveled *"doublet all unbraced"* (2.1) visit to Ophelia's closet, his teasing of Polonius (*"Have you a daughter?"*, 2.2) and his uncouth *"I must be idle"* (3.2) conduct during *The Murder of Gonzago*.

Unfortunately, Ophelia belief that her rejection of the prince's advances has caused his insanity—and with it, his murder of Polonius—sends her into real and suicidal madness.

Sample 5-3
As he realizes at the play's end, Hamlet's cultivated reputation of a madman has become the one for which he becomes known throughout the kingdom. Hence the prince's dying wish to Horatio that his friend repair Hamlet's *"wounded name"* (5.2).

When a dying Hamlet pleads with Horatio in 5.2 to *"set my cause aright"*, it is to correct the *"wounded name"* he leaves behind. At the play's beginning, the prince shared with Horatio his concern at Denmark's national reputation for excessive drinking: *"traduced and taxed of other nations: / They clepe us drunkards"* (1.4). At the end, it is the damage to his own personal reputation that worries Hamlet.

The *"noble youth"* who was warned by the Ghost in act one to *"Taint not thy mind"* (1.5), has by act five come to be regarded as a dangerous lunatic. We can assume that the grave-digger's words about the prince reflect the opinion of Danish court and public generally: *"he that is mad and sent into England"* in the hope *"he shall recover his wits there"* (5.1).

Shakespeare leaves us guessing why Hamlet decides to *"put an antic disposition on"* (1.5). What is certain is that Hamlet's feigned madness adds another element of deception to a play in which almost every character at some point hides their true motives and self behind a mask of falsity. King Claudius' exterior pose of a grieving brother and benevolent monarch conceals the true *"inward man"* (2.2); a murderous usurper who deceives others but who with himself is brutally honest: he knows his kingship is a charade—a *"painted word"* (3.1).

While Hamlet's pretense mirrors Claudius falsity, the key difference is that the king impersonates someone he is not; the prince, in his clear mental distress (*"my weakness and my melancholy"*, 2.2), impersonates himself. For his outward feigned insanity both conceals and yet reveals his very real inner anguish.

5.6 – Conclusion: *"Rest, rest, perturbed spirit!"*

What if the Ghost had not returned from the grave? Or instead of demanding revenge had asked instead for prayers to end the suffering of two souls: his in the *"sulfurous and tormenting flames"*, (1.5) of purgatory; and his brother's in Elsinore's chapel, *"limed"*, and *"struggling to be free"* (3.3)?

Sample 6-1

With Polonius and Ophelia already dead, the final scene adds six more victims—Gertrude, Hamlet, Laertes, Claudius, Rosencrantz and Guildenstern-to the play's list of lives lost. The first sample conclusion asks the question: which of the play's characters is principally responsible for all this carnage?

> A conscience-stricken Laertes brings the play to its conclusion with his truth-revealing declaration: *"The King, the King's to blame"* (5.2). But which king?
>
> Claudius is the obvious candidate, for he is exposed to the Danish court as responsible, if indirectly, for Gertrude's and Laertes' deaths, and vicariously for Prince Hamlet's. Moreover, Horatio can provide documentary evidence (*"Here's the commission: read it at more leisure"*, 5.2.) of Claudius' attempt to execute his nominated successor, the prince. His guilt for the murder of old King Hamlet, however, goes unmentioned.
>
> But what of old King Hamlet, *"the King that's dead"* (1.2)? Perhaps the blame lies ultimately with him? What if the Ghost had not returned from the grave? Or had asked instead for prayers to end the suffering of two souls: his in the *"sulfurous and tormenting flames"* (1.5) of purgatory; and his brother's in Elsinore's chapel, *"limed"* and *"struggling to be free"* (3.3)?
>
> The third candidate for blame is the play's title character, who on his return to Elsinore introduced himself with the kingly title of *"Hamlet the Dane"* (5.1). Had he heeded Horatio's advice against conversing with the Ghost, lest it *"deprive your sovereignty of reason / And draw you into*

madness" (1.4), perhaps Polonius would yet be alive, Laertes still in France (*"drinking, fencing, swearing"*, 2.2), and his *"fair Ophelia"* (3.1), to whom the prince made *"made many tenders / Of his affection"* (1.3), would not have become *"Divided from herself"* (4.5) and surrendered in despair to death in the *"weeping brook"* (4.7)?

Sample 6-2

Sample conclusion number two contrasts the conflict of *"emulate pride"* (1.1) between old King Hamlet and old King Fortinbras with the *"cursed spite"* (1.5) conflict between the two brothers of the Hamlet family, one living and one undead. Horatio began the play by recounting the first story. He ends it with a promise to *"truly deliver"* (5.2) the second.

"Good now, sit down and tell me, / he that knows ..." In 1.1, Horatio responds to the guards' request for an explanation of Denmark's frenzied military preparations (*"That can I"*). Again, in the final 5.2 scene, he takes on the role of storyteller with his vow to the dying *"sweet Prince"*: to recount of *"how all this came about"* to the *"unknowing world."*

Horatio's opening tale (*"At least the whisper goes so"*, 1.1) was of a duel between two kings from two countries, Denmark and Norway. His second, will be of a conflict between two kings from the same country; two brothers, one living and one undead. The first contest was prompted by *"emulate pride"* (1.1); the second, by a *"cursed spite"* (1.5).

The first was fought directly between the two combatants; the second, through two surrogates whose lives it both destroyed. Claudius successfully exploited Laertes to do his killing; the Ghost sought but ultimately failed to make to Prince Hamlet his instrument. Laertes, the avenger Hamlet's obsession with revenge created, is also the man who pardons the prince: *"Mine and my father's death come not upon thee, / Nor thine on me."*

Claudius dies as he lived—an unrepentant villain. As for the suffering-in-purgatory old King Hamlet, his son reverses the outcome of the duel fought thirty years before. By restoring Young Fortinbras' inheritance and adding to it the entire kingdom of Denmark, he atones for his father's sins and so shortens his afterlife torment *"in fires"* (1.5). Whereas the Ghost ignored Horatio's question *"If there be any good thing to be done / That may to thee do ease and grace to me"* (1.1), the prince answers it in his one action as Denmark's king: *"Fortinbras ... has my dying voice"* (5.2).

Sample 6-3

The third sample conclusion links Prince Hamlet's fate with that of old King Hamlet. There is indeed revenge at the end of the play, but it is, in effect, revenge *on* old King Hamlet rather than by him. In his one and final act as Denmark's monarch, Prince Hamlet surrenders his throne to Young Fortinbras. It is the price that must be paid for ending his father's suffering in purgatory.

The play ends with the Prince Hamlet's fate echoing that of old King Hamlet. His father's death was a secret murder disguised as an accidental snake-bite, a *"forged process"* with which *"the whole ear of Denmark"* was *"rankly abused"* (1.5). Similarly, as Claudius assures the blinded-by-vengeance Laertes, Prince Hamlet's demise in front of the assembled court will appear so unsuspicious that *"no wind of blame shall breathe"* and *"even his mother shall ... call it accident"* (4.7).

But unlike the original crime in the palace orchard, the rigged fencing duel is exposed publicly to the court. And the last members of the Hamlet and Polonius families perish in the *"feast"* of *"death"* (5.2) that greets Norway's Young Fortinbras, who arrives fortuitously to occupy Denmark's empty throne.

As for old King Hamlet (*"Alas, poor Ghost"*, 1.5), by surrendering Denmark to his rival's son perhaps the prince granted his *"dear father murdered"* (2.2) something more than the revenge he demanded: forgiveness for his land-grabbing, *"Extorted treasure in the womb of earth"* (1.1) sins committed *"in his days of nature"* (1.5)—and with it escape from his suffering in the *"sulfurous and tormenting flames"* (1.5) of purgatory.

The passage of Denmark's crown to the son of Norway's King Fortinbras is the play's final irony and instance of *"purposes mistook / Fallen on th'inventors' heads"* (5.2). For the revenge sought by the Ghost of old King Hamlet on his brother in act one becomes in act five the revenge of old King Fortinbras on old King Hamlet.

6

The Relationship of Hamlet and Claudius

"Think of us as of a father"

Prince Hamlet and King Claudius are two men at war with each other—and themselves. Claudius is haunted by the murder he has committed (*"O heavy burden!"*, 3.1). Hamlet by the one he hasn't yet (*"Am I a coward?"*, 2.2). They both *"stand in pause"* (3.3). The prince enjoys play-acting in theater. His uncle excels at play-acting in politics.

6.1 – Introduction

King Claudius begins the play at his highest point, Prince Hamlet at his lowest. One is a scheming manipulator, but with a conscience (*"O, what form of prayer, / Can serve my turn?"*, 3.3); the other a truth-seeking scholar, but with a violent streak (*"Yet have I something in me dangerous, / Which let thy wisdom fear"*, 5.1). In the middle of this conflict between two men who hate each other is a woman who loves and is loved by both, Queen Gertrude.

Sample 1-1
The first sample introduction contrasts the two personalities of King Claudius and his nephew, Prince Hamlet—the conscience-troubled cynic and the impulsively-violent idealist. Over the course of the play, their conflict escalates until it concludes with their mutual destruction and the end of the Hamlet family dynasty.

> The characters of Prince Hamlet and his uncle King Claudius in Shakespeare's *Hamlet* provide examples of both external and internal conflict: they are two individuals at war with each other—and themselves. Also divided is a third character, Queen Gertrude. As she admits, the hostility between her second husband, Claudius, and her son, the prince, *"has cleft my heart in twain"* (3.4).
>
> Although Prince Hamlet is the protagonist and Claudius his antagonist, nephew and uncle share in common a capacity for and love of play-acting: one in theater; the other in politics. Hamlet's happiest moment is his welcoming of the visiting Players (*"there did seem in him a kind of joy"*, 3.1). In 4.7, Claudius delights in conspiring *"a little shuffling"* with Laertes: a sharpened, tainted sword and—in the event of a *"bad performance"*—a goblet of poisoned wine.
>
> Fundamentally, the difference between Hamlet and Claudius is between the idealist and cynic. Hamlet decries the character flaws of others. To Rosencrantz, he says: *"There is a kind of confession in your looks which your*

> modesties have not craft enough to colour" (2.2). In contrast, Claudius recognizes human imperfections as a reality ("'Tis a fault to heaven", 1.2) and exploits them for his own purposes: Gertrude's desire to retain her queenly role; Polonius' craving for flattery; Rosencrantz and Guildenstern's greed for financial reward; and Laertes' impulsive and vengeful grief.
>
> In this essay, I will describe the conflicting relationship between Claudius and Hamlet, and how it ends not with a victory for either but with the destruction of the entire Hamlet family and the defeat of Denmark itself.

Sample 1-2

Sample response number two stresses the difference in circumstances between Prince Hamlet and King Claudius at the beginning of the play. No longer is Claudius living in the shadow of his brother; he now possesses both the throne and queen of Denmark. In contrast, his nephew has lost everything. Even his wish to return to the life he loved at Wittenberg University is denied to him.

> Shakespeare's *Hamlet* is chiefly celebrated for its portrayal of the title character's internal conflict—expressed most eloquently in his *"To be or not to be"* speech (3.1). However, the external conflict that drives the play's storyline to its tragic conclusion is between Prince Hamlet and his uncle, King Claudius.
>
> In the play's opening scenes, the two could not be further apart in circumstances. King Claudius strikes an impressive figure as he addresses his royal court; obediently and happily at his side sits Queen Gertrude—Hamlet's mother, his late brother's widow and now his wife. No wonder Denmark's new king celebrates late into the night, with the canons at Elsinore castle firing off celebratory rounds each time the king drinks down another cup of German wine.

While Claudius has won the crown and queen we can imagine he long coveted, Prince Hamlet is at his lowest imaginable level. In the space of two short months he has been afflicted by *"a sea of troubles"* (3.1): the father he idolized, dead (*"I shall not look upon his like again"*, 1.2); respect for his hastily remarried mother gone too (*"A beast would have mourned longer"*, 1.2); and his succession hopes crushed (*"I lack advancement"*, 3.2). The country his father old King Hamlet ruled is now a *"prison"* (2.2) from where his *"uncle-king and aunt-mother"* (2.2) allow him no escape: *"Go not to Wittenberg ... remain / Here in the cheer and comfort of our eye"* (1.2).

In the middle of this conflict between two men who hate each other is a woman who loves and is loved by both, Queen Gertrude. The play ends with the deaths of all three characters and their country's loss of independence to Norway.

Sample 1-3

This third sample introduction focuses on the mutual antagonism of Prince Hamlet and King Claudius. But, because of their shared relationship with Queen Gertrude, each is restrained from striking openly against one another.

It has been said of Prince Hamlet that had he obeyed the Ghost's command by killing Claudius immediately, seven of the play's eight violent deaths would have been prevented. But the same could be said of King Claudius: had he murdered Hamlet junior as well as senior, then he, his wife, the three members of Polonius' family and the prince's two old school friends would have escaped their untimely deaths.

The play's protagonist and antagonist share a mutual contempt that is revealed by their speaking of one another in the language of sickness, disease, and death. To the prince, his uncle is a *"canker of our nature"* (5.2). Claudius calls Hamlet an *"ulcer"* (4.7) and *"the hectic in my blood"* (4.3).

Over the course of the play, the relationship uncle and nephew share with Queen Gertrude inhibits them from striking openly against one another. As Claudius says to Laertes of Hamlet: *"The queen his mother / Lives almost by his looks"* (4.7). From Hamlet's perspective, he can see in the First Player's enactment of Hecuba's grief in 2.2 the heartbreak his mother would experience should he kill Claudius and make her a widow a second time in four months. There are also political considerations. Claudius must take account of the prince's popularity, for he is admired by "*the distracted multitude*" (4.3) and enjoys the "*great love the general gender*" (4.7).

In this essay, I will describe the conflict between Hamlet and Claudius which begins with a psychological battle of wits and culminates in a bloodbath that leads Young Fortinbras of Norway to Denmark's vacant throne.

6.2 – The imposter king and the player prince: *"Who's there?"*

This second section of the sample essay describes the mutually suspicious relationship of Hamlet and Claudius from the play's beginning up until when the prince devises his plan for testing the Ghost's truthfulness (*"The spirit that I have seen / May be the devil"*, 2.2) by using the Players to stage the 'play-within-a-play.'

Sample 2-1
As this first sample response notes, uncle and nephew each suspect the other is hiding a secret behind a false exterior. Prince Hamlet's secret is that he knows of Claudius' secret murder of his father.

"Who's there?"—the guard Barnardo's question from the play's first line is asked by Prince Hamlet and King Claudius of each other over the first three acts. Each one suspects—correctly—that other is hiding a secret. Prince Hamlet's secret is that he knows Claudius' secret: that the new king murdered his father. Or at least, so the prince has been informed by an *"apparition"* (1.1) in the *"questionable shape"* (1.4) of a *"figure like the King that's dead"* (1.1). With neither uncle nor nephew having sufficient grounds to strike openly against the other, both are locked in a mutually hostile stalemate.

In the court scene of 1.2, Prince Hamlet is compelled against his wishes to remain at Elsinore in *"the cheer and comfort of our eye"* as the king phrases it. But Claudius dares not challenge the prince's public refusal to swear loyalty to his new kingship and his offer of allegiance only to Queen Gertrude: *"I shall do my best to obey you, madam."*

Hamlet's feigned madness that follows the Ghost's revelations about *"The serpent that did sting thy father's life"* (1.5) is met with successive *as "'twere by accident"* (3.1) ploys by Claudius and Polonius to uncover the true state of mind of Gertrude's *"too much changed son"* (2.2).

When in 3.1 the prince rants at Ophelia about how *"Those that are married already, all but one, shall live,"* Claudius reverses his earlier decision to confine Hamlet at Elsinore: *"he shall with speed to England."* But Polonius persuades him to arrange one further eavesdropping scheme: a staged conversation between the prince and his mother in her closet to uncover that *"something-settled matter in (Hamlet's) heart."*

Sample 2-2

A scheming Claudius must have wondered how Prince Hamlet would respond to his father's suspicious death and his mother's quick remarriage. Would the scholarly prince strike back—and how?

A secret murder in the palace orchard, a quick marriage to the widowed queen, and a successful election by the country's nobles—as Claudius plotted his three-step path to Denmark's throne, we can imagine his scheming mind pondering one question: how would his nephew and victim's son react? Ophelia's description of Hamlet as *"The expectancy and rose of the fair state"* (3.1) suggests the prince was regarded as the likely heir in an era when it was more usual for a son rather than a brother to succeed a dead king.

Would a suspicious and hostile Hamlet strike back with some devious act of private vengeance? Or perhaps the disinherited prince, who Claudius recognizes as *"loved of the distracted multitude'* (4.3), might lead a public revolt against Claudius' kingship, much as we see Laertes doing later?

In fact, Hamlet's responds with an act of feigned madness that draws the king into a psychological battle of wits. Hamlet's put-on *"antic disposition"* (1.5) clearly unnerves Claudius. An anxious king recruits Rosencrantz, Guildenstern and Ophelia to uncover the *"some danger"* in the prince's soul *"o'er which his melancholy sits on brood"* (3.1).

When in 2.2 Polonius reports that the ambassadors to Norway have *"joyfully returned",* and, as *"the fruit to that great feast,"* he has also uncovered *"the very cause of Hamlet's lunacy,"* the king is chiefly interested in the mental state of Hamlet: *"O, speak of that! That do I long to hear."* Claudius' reaction reveals his concern for his country's safety ranks second to his obsession with the potential threat posed by his nephew.

Sample 2-3
As this third sample response illustrates, his gaining of Denmark's throne and queen has not brought Claudius peace of mind. The king's troubled conscience mirrors his nephew's inner struggle with the moral dilemma of revenge.

Claudius' remark about Prince Hamlet that neither *"th'exterior nor the inward man / Resembles that it was"* (2.2) applies as much to the king himself as it does to his antic nephew. Outwardly, Claudius has achieved *"My crown, mine own ambition, and my queen"* (3.4). But privately he compares his masquerade as a legitimate monarch with a *"harlot's cheek ... beautied with plastering art ... my conscience ... O heavy burden!"* (3.1).

If Claudius is haunted by the *"brother's murder"* (3.3) he has secretly committed, Hamlet is burdened by the retributive killing demanded of him by vengeful Ghost: *"Revenge this foul and most unnatural murder"* (1.5). The prince is torn between facing hell in *"that sleep of death"* (3.1) for the sin of revenge or suffering feelings of inadequacy in this world: *"Am I a coward?"* (2.2). Hamlet's put-on act of insanity reflects Claudius' charade of rightful kingship.

Clearly, Hamlet does not trust the Ghost—a possible *"goblin damned"* (1.4)—any more than he does most of the living characters at Elsinore: *"To be honest, as this world goes, is to be one man picked out of ten thousand"* (2.2). He swears only never to forget his dead father rather than avenge him: *"Now to my word. / It is 'Adieu, adieu. Remember me.' / I have sworn't"* (1.5).

After attempts by Rosencrantz, Guildenstern, Polonius, and Ophelia to discover the cause of Hamlet's *"antic disposition"* (1.5) are quickly exposed and scornfully repelled by the prince, a suspicious Claudius grows increasingly fearful about what lies beneath his nephew's *"turbulent and dangerous lunacy"* (3.1).

6.3 – The reverse revelation: *"The play's the thing"*

Section three of the sample essay addresses the performance of the 'play-within-a-play.' Hamlet's behavior during *The Murder of Gonzago* reveals the prince's secret knowledge to Claudius rather than exposing the king's guilt to the court.

Sample 3-1

Hamlet sabotages his stated purpose for staging *The Murder of Gonzago*. This first sample response asks: 'why?'

Why does Hamlet's behavior during *The Murder of Gonzago* depart from his stated motive for requesting the visiting Players to stage the play-within-a-play: *"to catch the conscience of the King"* (2.2)? As the prince confides in Horatio, the play will include a scene that *"comes near the circumstance / Which I have told thee of my father's death"* (3.2). Everything is set for the two friends to observe quietly the reaction of Claudius for evidence of his *"occulted guilt"* (3.2).

One explanation for Hamlet's provocative commentary on the Players' performance is that the reenactment of his father's murder and mother's seduction is too much for the prince to endure. His repeated, single-word aside of *"Wordwood, wormwood"* (3.2)—a plant signifying bitterness—in response to the Player Queen's vow of lifelong fidelity to her deceased first husband supports this interpretation.

Another view is that, for a man who two months previously was forced to bow before a throne he expected to occupy, the play provides an opportunity too tempting for Hamlet (*"I ... the son of a king"*, 4.2) to resist: to goad the uncle he despises to the point where, in front of the nobles who elected him, Claudius is intimidated into fleeing in panic from the great hall of Elsinore castle.

Whatever the reason, the original plan of testing the Ghost's truthfulness is forgotten. Swept up with *"the motive and cue for passion"* (2.2) that the Players' performance has provided, Hamlet is ready to take on the role of the theatrical uncle-killer Lucianus: to *"do such bitter business as the bitter day / Would quake to look on"* (3.2). The two-month long psychological battle of wits between uncle and nephew is now set to turn violent.

Sample 3-2

Sample response number two argues that Claudius' hasty exit is a more likely prompted by Hamlet's threat to his life than the theatrical reenactment of his past crime against his brother.

From Rosencrantz and Guildenstern, King Claudius learns of Hamlet's excitement at the arrival of a troupe of Players: *"there did seem in him a kind of joy"* (3.1). The king instructs the pair to encourage his nephew's interest: *"drive his purpose on to these delights"* (3.1). But just as Claudius knows nothing about the Ghost's revelations, he is also unaware of the prince's plan to use the Players' performance to test his guilt: *"If he do blench ... I know my course"* (2.2).

As they view *The Murder of Gonzago*, which Hamlet has adapted so that it *"comes near the circumstance"* (3.2) of his father's murder, the prince does not lean over to his uncle and whisper: 'I know you poisoned my sleeping father.' But that is what his every action amounts to. Earlier, he and Horatio agreed to scrutinize closely the king's countenance during the performance: *"Observe mine uncle"* (3.2). But as the play-within-play unfolds, Hamlet abandons his plan in favor of a provocative verbal assault on the king.

Claudius' questioning about the play is met with the prince's response that it is *"the image of a murder done."* After which he adds sarcastically: *"but what of that? ... we that have free souls, it touches us not."* (3.2). It is when Hamlet identifies the stage murderer Lucianus as the *"nephew to the king"* (3.2) that Claudius makes his hurried and undignified exit.

The play Hamlet devised to determine Claudius' guilt instead reveals to the king his nephew's knowledge of his secret crime—and the prince's murderous intent towards him.

Sample 3-3

Hamlet is clearly elated with the result of the Players' performance. But the ever-skeptical Horatio does not appear to share his friend's certainty that Claudius' flight from the hall is proof of the king's guilt.

After Claudius has fled the palace hall following the abandoned staging of *The Murder of Gonzago*, Guildenstern reports to Hamlet that the king is *"marvelous distempered"* (3.2). An almost manically delighted prince confides in Horatio that *"I'll take the ghost's word for a thousand pound"* (3.2). But his trusted and level-headed confidant appears unconvinced that the king's panicked reaction (*"I did very well note him"*, 3.2) is proof of his guilt, and with good reason.

Hamlet's ploy with Horatio of using professional actors to investigate Claudius' possible *"occulted guilt"* (3.2) mirrors the king's and Polonius' earlier casting of Rosencrantz, Guildenstern and Ophelia as amateur players in contrived performances to uncover what lies beneath Hamlet's *"turbulent and dangerous lunacy"* (3.1).

But Hamlet is disappointed in his hope for a public confession from Claudius, for the king displays the same self-composure as he does later when faced with Laertes' mob-leading castle invasion. Claudius sits unperturbed as the Players twice reenact the Ghost's account of old King Hamlet's murder, first in the dumb show and again in the spoken version. In my view, Claudius' abrupt exit is prompted not by the theatrical reenactment of his past crime but the threat of a future one—via the uncle-killer Lucianus—with him as the intended victim.

The assembled court remains unaware of Claudius' still hidden crime. And Hamlet's obnoxious behavior at the play—his uncouth taunting of Ophelia and his humiliation of the royal couple—only further damages the prince's reputation. As the words of the grave-digging sexton later reveal, Hamlet comes to be regarded among the *"general ear"* (2.2) as *"he that is mad, and sent into England"* to *"recover his wits there"* (5.1).

6.4 – The two delayers: *"I stand in pause"*

Section four of the sample essay deals with the 3.3 chapel scene. Note that the Ghost who minutes later appears to Hamlet in Gertrude's closet does not show himself in the chapel. This suggests that, while the Ghost may not be necessarily a *"goblin damned"* (1.5), the revenge it calls for represents *"blasts from hell"* rather than *"airs from heaven"* (1.5).

Sample 4-1

The Ghost instructed Hamlet to take no action against his mother, but to *"Leave her to heaven / And to those thorns that in her bosom lodge / To prick and sting her"* (1.5). As the chapel scene demonstrates, however, it is not Gertrude but Claudius who is tormented by pangs of conscience.

In the nunnery scene of 3.1, Ophelia only pretended to be deep in prayer—complete with a devotional book helpfully supplied as a prop by her father. The Claudius who Hamlet accidentally encounters in 3.3 actually is (*"Help, angels ... Bow, stubborn knees"*), if ultimately without success (*"My words fly up, my thoughts remain below"*).

On his knees in his private chapel, the usurping king is an easy target for the prince's sword: *"Now I might do it pat, now he is praying"* (3.3). But having convinced himself of his uncle's guilt, Hamlet now finds something else to be uncertain about: would the king's soul ascend to heaven rather than fall to hell if Hamlet murdered him while he is at prayer: *"A villain kills my father, and, for that, / I, his sole son, do this same villain send / To heaven"*?

But does Hamlet really believe that Claudius has chosen the path of repentance? For like the king the prince knows that earning divine forgiveness would require Claudius surrender *"those effects for which I did the murder"* (3.3). Yet the king does not rise from his knees, depart his private chapel, make a public confession to the court, and vow to spend the remainder of his days in penance.

Hamlet shows himself capable of committing murder when motivated by manic rage (Polonius) or a callous sense of poetic justice (Rosencrantz and Guildenstern). But perhaps the act of killing another human being in cold blood is too much for him to face, and he uses his speculation about Claudius' soul to rationalize his decision to defer striking Claudius until another, more opportune time (*"When he is fit and seasoned for his passage?"*).

Sample 4-2
The second sample analysis of the chapel scene suggests that Hamlet sees in the forgiveness-seeking Claudius an image of his future self should he murder his uncle in such cowardly circumstances.

Hamlet's staging of *The Murder of Gonzago* does indeed cause Claudius to be *"struck so to the soul"* and sends him to his knees to *"proclaim"* his *"malefactions"* (2.2). Unfortunately for the prince, his uncle confesses his crime (*"Oh, my offence is rank ... A brother's murder"*, 3.3) in his private chapel rather than publicly in front of the court. Such an admission to the *"general ear"* (2.2) would have relieved Hamlet of the burden of revenge and virtually assured the prince of his succession to the throne.

En route to his mother's closet, Hamlet passes the king's private chapel where he encounters but defers striking the kneeling-in-prayer Claudius. His stated reason is that he will wait until he catches the king in a state of sin (*"some act / That has no relish of salvation in't"*, 3.3). For to kill Claudius while at prayer might this *"villain send / To heaven."* To Hamlet, this seems unfair given that the prince's *"dear father murdered"* (2.2) had no opportunity to repent his sins, but was taken *"full of bread ... With all his crimes"* on his head (3.3).

But perhaps the prince also recognizes that were he to depose Claudius through such a cowardly action he would acquire more than Denmark's crown. Along with it would come Claudius' *"limed soul"* (3.3). For how does taking a man's life as he prayed in his chapel differ from doing the same to another while he slept in his garden? Afterward, would Hamlet not too struggle with a tormented conscience (*"May one be pardoned and retain th'offence?"*, 3.3) as he knelt in Elsinore's chapel? And like Claudius, could Hamlet find forgiveness only by giving up *"those effects for which (he) did the murder"* (3.3)?

Sample 4-3
The third sample response stresses the double irony of the chapel scene: Hamlet's desire to send Claudius to hell not only extends the king's earthly life but also spares his still unrepentant soul.

The Claudius we see in the chapel scene of 3.3 is no smiling villain (1.5), but an imperfect man tortured by a troubled conscience. Torn between repenting his sins or retaining *"My crown, mine own ambition, and my queen"*, Claudius feels *"like a man to double business bound."*

The man he is like is, of course, Hamlet. The prince's twin purpose is part poignant, part demonic (*"Up, sword ... My mother stays"*): it is both to rescue his mother's soul and condemn his uncle's (*"as damned and black / As hell, whereto it goes"*).

In his wish to murder both Claudius' soul and body, the prince resembles the politician he later condemns in the graveyard scene because he *"would circumvent God"* (5.1). As for his quest to reunite in the afterlife his fractured-by-Claudius family, it shows a son's longing to turn back time to when his mother *"would hang on"* his father *"As if increase of appetite had grown / By what it fed on"* (1.2). And so, like *"hellish Pyrrhus"* in the Player's speech of 2.2, Hamlet's sword must *"i'th'air to stick"*, awaiting the right moment to strike.

The double irony of the chapel scene is that Hamlet's desire to send Claudius to hell not only extends both the king's earthly life but also spares his still unrepentant soul. For the king's attempts at prayer are unsuccessful: *"My words fly up, my thoughts remain below."*

But Hamlet's delay also helps protect the *"safety and health of this whole state"* (1.3). For a Denmark in political disarray following the king's assassination could well have prompted an opportunistic attack from Fortinbras' army, which at that very moment is assembled in force outside Elsinore castle.

6.5 – The queen in the middle: *"My heart is cleft in twain"*

This fifth section of the sample essay describes the role of Queen Gertrude, the woman who is at the center of the antagonism between Hamlet and Claudius. What she admits is her *"o'erhasty marriage"* (2.2) to her brother-in-law Claudius overshadows her relationship with her son.

Sample 5-1

The first sample response argues that the term 'wretch' that Gertrude and Hamlet apply to one another reveals the huge gulf in personality and outlook between mother and son. She seeks to smooth over everything without thinking too deeply; he cannot but think deeply about everything.

At the center of this conflict between uncle and nephew is Queen Gertrude. Her relationship with her second husband Claudius is tainted with mutual ambition. And her relationship with her son is overshadowed by Hamlet's disgust at her remarriage and Gertrude's incomprehension at his unhappiness.

Only twice do we see Gertrude shedding the submissive role she plays in her union with Claudius. The first is when she leaps from the throne to confront Polonius' sword-wielding, rebellion-leading son whose followers cry out *"Laertes shall be king, Laertes king!"* (4.5). It illustrates how fearlessly she will defend her role as Denmark's queen. The second occasion is in the final scene when she defies her husband's plea not to drink from the poisoned wine goblet he intended for her son. It is then that Gertrude pays the ultimate price for what she earlier admitted to Hamlet were the *"black and grained spots"* (3.4) in her soul.

At two different points the play, Gertrude and Hamlet use the same word to describe each other: 'wretch', a term of pity rather than respect. She fails to understand why Hamlet will not *"look like a friend on Denmark"* (1.2) but instead loiters sadly about Elsinore like a *"poor wretch"* (2.2). Hamlet's final words to his mother as she expires from the same poison that killed his father are *"Wretched Queen, adieu!"* (5.2). For his mother traded Prince Hamlet's *"proper life"* (5.2) and even his sanity so she could retain by means of a second marriage to Claudius the queenly position she enjoyed for thirty years through her first marriage to old King Hamlet.

Sample 5-2

Despite Hamlet's accusation of *"Frailty"* (1.2) towards his mother, Gertrude remains steadfastly at her second husband's side. Gertrude's tragic flaw is what she does not know—or perhaps by what she suspects but refuses *"hoodman-blind"* (3.4) to see—until it is too late.

Despite Hamlet's complaint that *"Frailty thy name is woman"* (1.2), his mother Queen Gertrude never wavers in her relationship with the man she married so quickly— *"A little month, or ere those shoes were old"* (1.2)—after her first husband's death. She provides a listening ear to his cares (*"O Gertrude, Gertrude, / When sorrows come, they come not single spies / But in battalions"*, 4.5) and defends him when Laertes leads an angry mob to threaten their shared throne.

According to Hamlet, *"Father and mother is man and wife, man and wife is one flesh"* (4.3). As long as she is joined in marriage to Claudius, she is one person with him, and in Hamlet's mind, they cannot be fully son and mother.

In closet scene, he berates her remorselessly: *"You are the queen, your husband's brother's wife and—would it were not so—you are my mother"* (3.4). That she afterward protects one of Hamlet's secrets (that he is only feigning madness) but discloses another (that he did kill Polonius) reveals how her loyalties are divided between her husband and her son. As she admits to him: *"O Hamlet, thou hast cleft my heart in twain."* (3.4).

In the final scene, Gertrude dies by the same means used to murder both her first husband and her only son: Claudius' *"leprous distilment"* (1.5). In a play where so many characters set out to deceive one another, Gertrude fooled only herself: her wished-for 'happily ever after' descended into a nightmare and ended ultimately in the death of her entire family.

Sample 5-3

Whatever the extent of Gertrude's guilt, Hamlet's parting words in 5.2 to her (*"Wretched Queen, adieu"*) reveal that the prince is unwilling to grant to his mother the forgiveness a repentant Laertes extended to him: *"Mine and my father's death come not upon thee."*

When in 4.7 Claudius is asked by an angry Laertes (*"I a noble father lost; / A sister driven into desperate terms"*) why he cannot strike openly against Hamlet, the king replies that doing so would jeopardize his relationship with Gertrude, for *"The queen his mother / Lives almost by his looks."*

Although the relationship between mother and son is undermined by her marriage to Claudius—*"thou hast my father much offended"* (3.4)—there is always a spontaneous tenderness in her love for him: *"Come hither, my dear Hamlet, sit by me"* (3.2) she says before the performance of *The Murder of Gonzago*. Later in 5.1, Gertrude is so thrilled at her exiled son's reappearance that she calls out his name twice—*"Hamlet, Hamlet!"* As the prince jostles with Laertes in Ophelia's grave, she orders Polonius' son to unhand him (*"For love of God, forbear him"*), saying that her son's *"mere madness"* will pass.

If Hamlet struggles with the Ghost's command of 1.5 regarding Claudius (*"Revenge"*), he defies completely his direction about Gertrude (*"Leave her to heaven"*). In their confrontation in the closet scene of 3.4, he instead tries to separate her from the king—*"Assume a virtue, if you have it not"* (3.4)—so that she might avoid the *"sulfurous and *tormenting flames"* (1.5) suffered by the Ghost. After Gertrude's death from Claudius' poisoned wine goblet, however, the prince's final words to the villainous Claudius—*"Follow my mother"* (5.2)—suggests the prince does not believe he has succeeded.

6.6 – Conclusion: *"As kill a king"*

Claudius stole two roles previously played by his brother: husband and king. For her part in the first, Gertrude forfeits her life when she drinks from the wine goblet that contains *"juice of cursed hebenon"* (1.5). For colluding in the second, the country's nobles lose their political power to Norway. His third role-grabbing attempt was directed at his nephew: *"think of us / As of a father"* (1.2). But Hamlet could and did not.

Sample 6-1

In the final 5.2 scene, the *"incestuous, murderous, damned Dane"* is *"justly served"* by *"a poison tempered by himself."* If at the cost of his life, but without the taint of private vengeance, Hamlet removes from Denmark's throne the usurper who twice plotted his murder and whose villainy led to the deaths of his two parents.

Claudius' exile of one revenge-seeking son from Denmark is followed only by the return of another—an angry, bereaved Laertes who leads a castle-storming revolt against him. And then much as old King Hamlet reappeared from the dead, Prince Hamlet returns from his death sentence in England. The Claudius who turned his soul *"black as death"* (3.3) to gain his brother's throne and wife now finds even a king cannot entirely control events. As he complains to Gertrude: *"When sorrows come, they come not single spies / But in battalions"* (4.5).

With one final example of the *"witchcraft of his wit"* (1.5), Claudius sets the two fatherless sons against each other in a *"forgery of shapes and tricks"* (4.7): a plot to murder Hamlet disguised as a fencing duel of honor.

But the king's words about Hamlet—*"He shall not choose but fall"* (4.7)—now rebound on him in the final 5.2 scene when Gertrude (*"I could not but by her"*, 4.7) reaches for the goblet of poisoned wine he prepared for her son. Torn between revealing his murderous plot or saving her life, all Claudius can do is utter: *"Gertrude, do not drink."* The queen's dying words of *"I am poisoned"* prompt Laertes' conscience-stricken confession of *"The King's to blame."*

Without mentioning Claudius' murder of his father, but with deadly symbolism, Hamlet by two methods kills the *"arrant knave"* (1.5) who had twice schemed to murder him and whose poison claimed the lives of both his parents.

Sample 6-2

Sample conclusion number two focuses on the enormity of Claudius' crimes and the scale of the catastrophe that follows them.

Laertes from France (*"O'erbears your officers. The rabble call him 'lord'"*, 4.5), Prince Hamlet from his English voyage (*"I am set naked on your kingdom"*, 4.7) and Young Fortinbras from Poland (*"What warlike noise is this?"*, 5.2)—all three fatherless sons arrive at Elsinore in the last movement of a storyline that began with disorder (*"something rotten in the state of Denmark"*, 1.4), descended into the chaos (*"purposes mistook"*, 5.2) and with tragic inevitability concludes in a final catastrophe (*"The sight is dismal"*, 5.2).

So *"unnatural"* (1.5) were Claudius' brother-murdering, *"sometime sister"*-marrying (1.2) and kingdom-stealing crimes that Shakespeare's audiences would have regarded them as an affront to what was then called the Great Chain of Being. Young Fortinbras' military threat led to feverish preparations that did *"not divide the Sunday from the week"*

(1.2). Claudius' villainy was followed by a breach in the natural boundary between this world and the next. A *"dreaded sight"* (1.1) was released from beyond the grave with the command *"Bear it not"* (1.5). The rightful heir to Denmark's stolen throne was fated to play the role of *"scourge and minister"* for *"heaven hath pleased it so"* (3.4).

Although Laertes describes both Claudius and himself as *"justly served"* (5.2), the sheer scale of the *"casual slaughters"* (5.2) that followed the original crime in the Elsinore palace orchard extended far beyond the punishment of the guilty. It reminds us of what tragically catastrophic consequences ensue when *"he that plays the king"* (2.2) is an amoral villain. Denmark lost its political independence, and even the *"green girl"* (1.3) Ophelia did *"not escape calumny"* (3.1)

Sample 6-3

The *"providence"* (5.2) to which Hamlet has surrendered his fate he now believes will provide the circumstances for him to complete the task for which *"my fate cries out"* (1.4). All the prince need do is be prepared to act his assigned part when the moment comes, for *"the readiness is all"* (5.2). Claudius, in contrast, remains unrepentant to the very end.

Ophelia's surrender to the water and death, as described by Queen Gertrude in 4.3, foreshadows the suicidal return of her *"bonny sweet Robin"* (4.5) to Elsinore. As the prince must surely expect, the villainous Claudius has some fatal *"exploit"* (4.7) prepared for him.

Gertrude's *"my too much changed son"* (2.2) has undergone a second transformation. Gone is his *"antic disposition"* (1.5), his Polonius-like struggle to *"find / Where truth is hid"* (2.2) and his Claudius-style stratagems of deception and *"a little shuffling"* (4.7). He returns without a plan of action; as he writes to Claudius: *"I am set naked on your kingdom"* (4.7). In his graveyard conversation with

Horatio, Hamlet states his belief that the *"providence"* (5.2) to which he attributes his escape from execution will provide the circumstances *"To quit (Claudius) with this arm"* (5.2).

Claudius dies as he lived—an unrepentant villain who is duplicitous to the very last. His final deceit is an attempt to portray Gertrude's fainting as a reaction to the fencing duel of Hamlet and Laertes: *"She swoons to see them bleed"* (5.2). But Gertrude's dying cry of *"I am poisoned"* is a damning contradiction of her husband and echoes the Ghost's contradiction of the *"forged process"* (1.5) that concealed the true cause of his death. But the man who lived a lie all throughout the play—a false king, false husband and false uncle—meets his comeuppance. Hamlet finally kills Claudius when he is *"fit and seasoned for his passage"* (3.3) and bids him farewell with the words *"thou incestuous, murderous, damned Dane"* (5.2).

7

The Relationship of Hamlet and Gertrude

"Would it were not so—you are my mother"

A haunted-by-the-past (*"Must I remember?"*, 1.2) son seeks the truth about his father's death. A live-in-the-present (*"all that is I see"*, 3.4) mother seeks to protect her second husband and throne. To secure his inheritance from the birth of a rival heir, and to lessen the Hecuba-like grief she will feel at his killing of Claudius, Hamlet attempts to separate his mother from his usurping uncle.

7.1 – Introduction

Gertrude's *"o'erhasty marriage"* (2.2) marriage to Claudius and her collusion with the prince's confinement at Elsinore creates a barrier between mother and son who are as different from one another as is humanly possible. Hamlet's last words to Claudius in 5.2 (*"Follow my mother"*) suggest the prince believes it will be in the company of his villainous uncle rather than his *"dear father murdered"* (2.2) that the *"Wretched Queen"* (5.2) will be eternally united.

Sample 1.1

The first sample introduction contrasts the two figures of Prince Hamlet and Queen Gertrude. Although mother and son, they are as different as two people can be. He is a scholarly truth-seeker who torments himself that his thinking is but an excuse for cowardice. She is a contented, status-loving materialist who lives only in the present and is puzzled why her son struggles to do the same.

> No two characters in Shakespeare's *Hamlet* are further apart in personality and outlook than Denmark's prince and his mother, Queen Gertrude. Hamlet shares Claudius' capacity for deception (*"put an antic disposition on"*, 1.5) and Polonius' curiosity (*"How long will a man lie i'th'earth ere he rot?"*, 5.1). In happier times, we can imagine he was the closest of friends with Rosencrantz and Guildenstern (*"Good gentlemen, he hath much talked of you"*, 2.2).
>
> Between mother and son, however, there exists a huge gulf. He is a seeker of truth and meaning; she, a superficial, status-loving materialist. Hamlet is continually *"Looking before and after"* for he cannot accept that our *"godlike reason"* should waste in us *"unused."* Yet he torments himself that his *"thinking too precisely on th'event"* is but an excuse for inaction: *"A thought which, quartered, hath but one part wisdom / And ever three parts coward"* (4.4).

In contrast, Gertrude lives only in the present and is puzzled why her son struggles to do the same. In 1.2, we see her as a woman quick to move on from the past: *"All that lives must die, / Passing through nature to eternity."* But later in 5.1, with *"my Hamlet"* exiled in England, a grieving Gertrude recognizes her family's future is slipping away from her as she scatters flowers over Ophelia's grave. There will be no grandchildren at Elsinore to carry the dynasty of Hamlet: *"I thought thy bride-bed to have decked, sweet maid, / And not have strewn thy grave."* In this essay, I will give my opinion on the relationship between the tragic prince and his mother, *"the beauteous Majesty of Denmark"* (4.5).

Sample 1.2

Sample introduction number two argues that the theft of Hamlet's expected inheritance—and all the tragic events that followed from it—was as much the result of his mother's desire to retain Denmark's throne as his uncle's ambition to acquire it.

In 4.5 of *Hamlet*, Polonius' bereaved and angry son storms into Elsinore castle at the *"riotous head"* of a rebellious mob who cry out *"Choose we! Laertes shall be king!"* It is a scene that leaves us wondering: why Prince Hamlet—who by then has been sent by King Claudius to execution in England—did not do the same? After all, as Claudius acknowledges, the prince is admired by *"the distracted multitude"* (4.3) and enjoys the *"great love the general gender"* (4.7).

In part, I believe, it is because Hamlet, being of royal blood and *"to the manor born"* (1.4), knows that those who are swept to power by a popular uprising—with *"Antiquity forgot, custom not known"* (4.5)—can just as easily be brought down by one. More fundamentally, in my view, it is because of the figure who leaps fearlessly from the throne to confront the sword-wielding Laertes.

That defiant, throne-protecting figure is not the play's villain and Hamlet's antagonist, King Claudius. It is old King Hamlet's widow, Claudius' new wife and Prince Hamlet's mother, Queen Gertrude, *"the beauteous Majesty of Denmark"* (4.5).

In this essay, I will argue that the theft of Hamlet's expected inheritance—and all the tragic events that followed from it—is as much the result of his mother's desire to retain Denmark's throne as his uncle's ambition to acquire it. What Gertrude admits is her *"o'erhasty marriage"* (2.2) to her brother-in-law overshadows the relationship between mother and son, ultimately costs them both their lives and ends the royal dynasty of the Hamlet family.

Sample 1.3

This third sample introduction suggests that Hamlet's request to the arriving Players (*"One speech in it I chiefly loved. 'Twas Aeneas' tale to Dido …"*, 2.2) reveals how Gertrude's love for her second husband complicates his mission to revenge his late father.

"This is too long"—Polonius' comment in 2.2 on a speech delivered by one of Elsinore's visiting Players is more than an ironic statement on the over four-hour play that contains it. The speech that continues at Hamlet's insistence reveals the dilemma in which the prince finds himself.

In a *"broken voice"* and with *"Tears in his eyes"*, the Player describes the harrowing grief of Hecuba, the wife who witnessed *"hellish Pyrrhus"* savagely murder her husband Priam in revenge, *"mincing with his sword her husband's limbs."* In Hamlet's *"mind's eye"* (1.2), we sense that Hecuba stands for Queen Gertrude. In the Player's presentation of her grief, he sees the heartbreak his mother would experience should he kill Claudius and make her a widow a second time in four months.

In my view, Hamlet's hesitancy in pursuing the Ghost's first demand of 1.5 (*"Revenge his foul and most unnatural murder"*) stems from his inability to follow the second (*"let thy soul contrive / Against thy mother aught. Leave her to heaven"*). Hamlet's goal evolves beyond bloody revenge (*"hire and salary"*, 3.3) to another, more poignant purpose: to reunite in the afterlife his fractured family of mother and father. Hence the prince's desire both to condemn Claudius' soul (*"as damned and black / As hell, whereto it goes"*, 3.3) and rescue his mother's (*"Confess yourself to heaven. / Repent what's past. Avoid what is to come"*, 3.4).

However, Hamlet's last words to Claudius in 5.2 (*"Follow my mother"*) suggest he believes it will be in the company of the prince's villainous uncle rather than his *"dear father murdered"* (2.2) that the *"Wretched Queen"* will be eternally united.

7.2 – The prisoner of Elsinore: *"Stay with us. Go not to Wittenberg"*

It has been said of Prince Hamlet that had he obeyed the Ghost's command by killing Claudius immediately there would have been no tragic play named *Hamlet*. But the same is true had Gertrude insisted her son be granted his wish to return to Wittenberg University.

Sample 2.1

The first sample response contrasts Gertrude's desire for Hamlet to remain at Elsinore with her behavior throughout the remainder of the play. She seems in no need of her son's company, and her interest in his well-being does not extend beyond colluding with the spying operations of Claudius and Polonius.

In the 1.2 ceremonial scene, we see Claudius and Gertrude united in their court-approved marriage, their shared possession of Denmark's throne, and their decision regarding the future of Prince Hamlet. Unlike Laertes, who is permitted to resume his pleasure-seeking ways in Paris, Prince Hamlet is denied his request to return to his former life at university. We can assume Claudius wishes to keep his potentially troublesome nephew under close surveillance, *"in the cheer and comfort of our eye."* Gertrude's echoing of her new husband's command is less easy to understand: *"Let not thy mother lose her prayers, Hamlet ... stay with us. / Go not to Wittenberg."*

After *"a little month"* (1.2) following old King Hamlet's death, Gertrude accepted a proposal of marriage from Claudius: *"O God, a beast that wants discourse of reason / Would have mourned longer!"* (1.2). Accordingly, she is in no need of the emotional support a recently widowed mother might seek from her only child.

Conversely, we never see Gertrude express a motherly desire to spend time in the company of her very obviously downcast son. In fact, his continuing grief leaves her puzzled: *"All that lives must die ... Why seems it so particular with thee?"* (1.2). Although aware of his *"poor wretch"* (2.2) state, never once does she seek him out. Their encounter in her closet is just another of Polonius' spying operations, during which she admits that her son's imminent departure to England had slipped her mind: *"Alack, / I had forgot"* (3.4). His father's castle has indeed become Hamlet's *"prison"* (2.2). And his jailers are the royal couple of his *"uncle-father and aunt-mother"* (2.2).

Sample 2.2

Old King Hamlet permitted his scholarly and the theater-loving son to pursue his interests as the prince awaited his expected inheritance of Denmark's throne. His mother's relationship with Hamlet seems devoid any such empathy. Moreover, the prince's only happy childhood memories are of his boyhood companion Yorick.

> *"Have you your father's leave?"* (1.2)—Claudius' response to Laertes' request to return to France reveals that, among Denmark's aristocratic families at least, a son required such permission before departing to another country.
>
> Prince Hamlet may have had little in common with his triumphantly warlike father, who *"smote the sledded Polacks on the ice"* (1.1). But old King Hamlet at least allowed his son to follow his chosen path in life as he awaited his expected inheritance of Denmark's throne. In Ophelia's estimation, Hamlet's time at Wittenberg University did indeed produce an ideal Renaissance prince: *"The courtier's, soldier's, scholar's, eye, tongue, sword, / Th'expectancy and rose of the fair state"* (3.1).
>
> That Hamlet's mother should collude with Claudius in denying him that freedom appears at best unthinking. At worst, it suggests that Gertrude valued her son's happiness second to a desire to appease the second husband through whom she has extended into the future the queenly role she had for three decades enjoyed. In her second marriage, Gertrude no more of a nurturing mother to her son than she was in her first.
>
> In Hamlet's recollections of Yorick in the 5.1 graveyard scene, there is a deep sense of human connection that is strikingly absent from his family relationships. The jester seemed not only a substitute for an often absent-at-war father (*"he hath borne me on his back a thousand times"*). But a surrogate mother too for an emotionally distant, self-absorbed Gertrude (*"those lips that I have kissed I know not how oft"*).

Sample 2.3
Old King Hamlet's death left his widow Gertrude as Denmark's reigning monarch. That she did not use her power to grant her son his wish to resume the life he loved at Wittenberg University hardly seems like the act of a loving and nurturing mother.

In an era when kings and queens were regarded as God's representatives on earth, old King Hamlet's death in the palace orchard left his widow Gertrude as her country's reigning monarch. As such, she would have been in a strong bargaining position in response to the proposal of marriage from her brother-in-law, which, as Horatio notes, *"followed hard upon"* (1.2) her first husband's passing.

One of her terms of agreement might have been that both partners renounce any claim to the throne and vacate Elsinore castle to pursue their relationship as a middle-aged couple in some quiet corner of Denmark. Doing so would have cleared the path for the thirty-year-old prince to claim his expected inheritance, perhaps with *"fair Ophelia"* (3.1) reigning as queen by his side.

At a minimum, Gertrude could have insisted that her second husband extend to her son the same freedom as did her first: that the prince be permitted to spend his time as *"most immediate to our throne"* (1.2) in an environment he so obviously loved—far from Elsinore in the intellectual and artistic world of Wittenberg University.

But Gertrude imposed neither of these two conditions before saying 'I do' to her former brother-in-law. When Hamlet talks to Rosencrantz and Guildenstern about his *"bad dreams"* (2.2), I can imagine that among his nightmares is the prospect of many years of bored captivity. Hamlet's delight at the Players' arrival (*"Buzz, buzz"*, 2.2) is his happiest moment in the play. It is then we can see the joy he had in his life before his mother colluded in her son's captivity at Elsinore in the *"cheer and comfort"* (1.2) of Claudius' watchful eye.

7.3 – The Player Queen: *"The lady doth protest too much, methinks"*

"Madam, how like you this play?" Hamlet's pointed question of his mother during *The Murder of Gonzago* suggests that the conscience-catching target of the Players' performance is as much Hamlet's *"seeming virtuous"* (1.5) mother as his despised uncle. But the *"hoodman-blind"* (3.4) Gertrude lacks the empathy to recognize herself in the theatrical figure of the Player Queen.

Sample 3.1
By reenacting Claudius' crime (*"A poisons him i'th'garden for his estate"*) and Gertrude's willing seduction (*"you shall see anon how the murderer gets the love of Gonzago's wife"*) Hamlet's *The Murder of Gonzago* seeks to shame both his uncle and mother on stage in front of the assembled court.

In 3.2, why does Hamlet give the title of 'The Mousetrap' to his adapted version of *The Murder of Gonzago*? Perhaps a clue lies in Claudius' term of affection for Gertrude (*"calls you his mouse"*, 3.4). For as the performance unfolds, it becomes clear that the conscience-catching target of the Players' show is as much Hamlet's *"seeming virtuous"* (1.5) mother as his uncle.

The spoken play features a dying king saying goodbye to his loving wife of thirty years (*"Full thirty times hath Phoebus' cart gone round"*) with the hope that she will find love again. Her response is a vow never to remarry: *"Both here and hence pursue me lasting strife / If, once a widow, ever I be wife!"* It is then that Hamlet pointedly questions his mother: *"Madam, how like you this play?"*

But the prince's attempt to shame the royal couple into a public confession (*"proclaimed their malefactions"*, 2.2) is unsuccessful. Claudius is far too composed a character to betray himself publicly. It is only after Hamlet's threat on his life (*"nephew to the king"*) that he flees the performance.

With Gertrude, it is her complete lack of empathy that ensures her *"withers are unwrung."* In the closet scene which follows shortly afterward, her complaint to Hamlet is not that his play has ridiculed her but that Claudius is *"much offended"* (3.4). But what is surely clear to the king and Denmark's court is that Hamlet's 'The Mousetrap' is a public humiliation his mother as a faithless destroyer of old King Hamlet's memory.

Sample 3.2

Sample response number two focuses on one of the play's most memorable lines: Queen Gertrude's remark that *"The lady protests too much, methinks"* (3.2) Gertrude is unable to understand why a widow would not want to remarry in any circumstances. Ironically, her observation is echoed in the words of the Player King.

Hamlet shares with Horatio in 3.2 his motive for requesting the visiting Players to stage *The Murder of Gonzago* with additional lines that *"comes near the circumstance ... of my father's death."* It is to *"catch the conscience of the King"* (2.2). What the prince never tells us is why he calls his play-within-a-play 'The Mousetrap.' One explanation is that the prince is inspired by his uncle's pet name for his mother (*"call you his mouse"*, 3.4). Certainly, Gertrude individually and the couple's royal marriage seems as much a target of the Players' performance as Claudius himself.

Along with his cruel taunting of Ophelia, Hamlet directs his attention on Gertrude with the same focus with which he asked Horatio to scrutinize Claudius' reaction: *"Observe mine uncle."* After we hear the grief-stricken Player Queen vow lifelong fidelity to her dying first husband of thirty years—*"Nor earth to me give food, nor heaven light ... If, once a widow, ever I be wife!"*—Hamlet quizzes his mother: *"Madam, how like you this play?"*

Her response is one of the play's most well-known lines: *"The lady protests too much, methinks."* It reveals she is unable to understand why a widow would not want to remarry in any circumstances. In contrast, Hamlet seems to regard Gertrude's remarriage as comparable with Claudius' actual murder of old King Hamlet. Yet, ironically, his mother's pragmatic attitude is echoed in the Player King's own words: *"So think thou wilt no second husband wed, / But die thy thoughts when thy first lord is dead."*

Sample 3.3

The third sample response notes the irony of Hamlet's purpose in staging the play-within-a-play: to rebuke Gertrude for her disloyalty to his father's memory. For the same performance also highlights his own lack of faithfulness to the Ghost's command for revenge.

Before a later scene when a traumatized Ophelia will hand out symbol-laden flowers, Prince Hamlet at *The Murder of Gonzago* in 3.2 uses a botanical metaphor of his own. What Ophelia will present the queen with is a gift of rue, a plant symbolizing regret. Hamlet's figurative expression is the repeated word *"Wordwood, wormword"* (3.3), a reference to a bitter-tasting plant. That the prince utters this remark to himself in an aside at a time when he is interacting animatedly with other audience members suggests this exclamation is not part of his *"I must be idle"* act but is entirely genuine and deeply-felt.

What prompts Hamlet's remark are the protestations of the soon-to-be-widowed Player Queen that she will never remarry after the Player King's death: *"Such love must needs be treason in my breast ...In second husband let me be accursed! / None wed the second but who killed the first"* (3.3). Immediately afterward, in an echo of Hamlet's earlier *"Thrift, thrift, Horatio!"* (1.2) remark, she continues: *"The instances that second marriage move / Are base respects of thrift, but none of love."*

If the purpose of Hamlet's play was in part to rebuke Gertrude for her disloyalty to his father's memory, the prince also finds the performance pointing accusingly back at him. For his infidelity to the Ghost's command for *"Revenge"* (1.5) is mirrored in the observation of the Player King: *"What to ourselves in passion we propose, / The passion ending, doth the purpose lose."*

7.4 – The closet scene: *"Cruel only to be kind"*

For three reasons, Hamlet in the 3.4 closet scene seeks to separate his mother from Claudius: to protect his already-thwarted inheritance from the birth of a rival heir (*"Good night: but go not to mine uncle's bed"*); to minimize the loss she will feel at her second husband's death (*"Is it the King? ... This bad begins, and worse remains behind"*); and, most poignantly, to save her soul from the sin of incest (*"Confess yourself to heaven"*) so that his two, separated-by-Claudius parents may be reunited in the afterlife as he remembers them in a loving union on earth (*"Why, she would hang on him"*, 1.2).

Sample 4.1

At Polonius's direction, Gertrude attempts to scold her son for his *"pranks"* (3.4). But it is Hamlet who takes on the role of chastising parent who scolds his mother for what he sees as her infidelity to his father's memory.

> *"Pray you, be round with him"*—Polonius' guidance in 3.4 to Gertrude as he conceals himself behind the arras in the queen's closet recalls his earlier directions to his daughter (*"Ophelia, walk you here"*, 3.1) in the nunnery scene. On that occasion, Hamlet only voiced his suspicion that the king's meddlesome advisor was eavesdropping nearby (*"Where is your father?"*, 3.1). Now, in what the queen calls *"a rash and bloody deed"*, Hamlet runs his sword through the arras to kill the concealed figure after he cries out (*"What, ho! Help!"*) in

response to Gertrude's panic at her son's rage: *"Thou wilt not murder me? / Help, help, ho!"*

Given that the prince was familiar with Polonius' voice, and that only moments before he had left Claudius in his chapel, I do not believe Hamlet's question of *"Is it the King?"* is genuine. Instead, I see it as part of his overall *"cruel only to be kind"* (3.4) strategy displayed throughout the closet scene. Hamlet is putting the queen on notice that she should distance herself from the second husband towards whom he intends to *"do such bitter business"* (3.2). For the prince's words over Polonius' lifeless body are clear who he intends his next victim to be: *"Thus bad begins and worse remains behind."*

The first appearance of the Ghost prompted Hamlet to pretend to be insane; his second appearance in her closet convinces Gertrude that he actually is (*"Alas, he's mad"*). That Gertrude does not see the Ghost reveals how she has moved on from one brother to the other. When she later informs the king that Hamlet is as *"Mad as the sea and wind"* (4.1), I believe Gertrude genuinely believes so; she is not merely acceding to her son's request to conceal from Claudius that he is only *"mad in craft."*

Sample 4.2

The second sample response presents son and mother as examples of the truth of the Player King's observation: *"Purpose is but the slave to memory"* (3.2). He wishes to extend forever in heaven the marriage that died with his father. She by means of a second marriage wishes to prolong her thirty-year reign as queen.

In the chapel scene of 3.3, the conscience-stricken Claudius is torn between repenting his sins or retaining *"My crown, mine own ambition, and my queen."* The king declares himself *"like a man to double business bound."* The man he is like is, of course, Hamlet, who stands behind him with his sword drawn and ready to strike.

The prince's *"double business"* is to damn his uncle's soul to hell and rescue his mother's for heaven, so that his two parents may be reunited in the afterlife as he remembers them in a loving union on earth (*"Why, she would hang on him"*, 1.2). In different ways, both Gertrude and Hamlet reveal the truth of the Player King's observation that *"Purpose is but the slave to memory"* (3.2). She wishes to prolong her time as *"the beauteous majesty of Denmark"* (4.5), a queenly role she should have yielded when old King Hamlet passed. Her son wishes to extend forever in heaven the marriage that died with his father.

In 3.4, Gertrude submits to her son's shaming (*"No more, sweet Hamlet!"*), seeks his advice (*"What shall I do?"*), and agrees to his request to no longer share her bed with Claudius (*"Be thou assured"*). In my opinion, Gertrude is not sincere in her promise; she is simply terrified of her son (*"Alas, he's mad!"*) who has just murdered Polonius and spoken with an invisible—to her—ghost. Hamlet's blind, through-a-curtain stabbing of Polonius sends the play's storyline on its tragic, downward course. It drives Ophelia into madness and apparent suicide, and in Laertes creates a second fatherless son whose obsession with revenge will end both his and Hamlet's lives.

Sample 4.3

Sample response number three addresses Sigmund Freud's diagnosis of the prince as suffering from a so-called Oedipal complex. This theory has prompted many modern versions of the play to transform 3.4 from a closet scene into a bedroom scene. But we have the lines of three characters—Rosencrantz, Polonius, and Claudius—to support the fact that mother and son meet in her closet, not her bedroom.

Hamlet productions that include a bed in 3.4 and show son and mother kiss full on the lips take their inspiration from Sigmund Freud's theory that the prince subconsciously desires to possess his mother sexually. But Shakespeare's text describes 3.4 not as a bedroom scene but a closet scene. It seems unlikely that Gertrude would have a second *"royal bed of Denmark"* (1.5) in her closet in addition to the one in her bedroom. Moreover, Hamlet's directions to his mother in the scene—*"Sit you down"* and *"You shall not budge"*—hardly suggest sexual interaction between the two.

Hamlet resorts to using sexually charged language against his mother only after the following have left her unmoved: his stabbing of Polonius (*"a foolish prating knave"*); an accusation of murder (*"As kill a king"*); the dismissal of her remarriage as a loveless fraud (*"As false as dicers' oaths"*); and moral exhortation (*"Heaven's face doth glow"*). All of which leaves Gertrude in fear of her son's rage but still puzzled as to its cause: *"Ay me, what act?"*

It is then that Hamlet asks her to compare visually her two husbands as if her remarriage represented a lapse in taste rather than morals (*"Ha, have you eyes?"*). It is by assaulting her senses (*"Ears without hands or eyes, smelling sans all"*) that Hamlet reaches her conscience (*"Thou turn'st mine eyes into my very soul"*). Such is the prince's *"speak daggers"* verbal violence that the Ghost appears and begs him to cease: *"O, step between her and her fighting soul."* Hamlet departs with the hope that she will reform so that as a son he can ask his mother's blessing: *"And when you are desirous to be blessed, / I'll blessing beg of you."*

7.5 – Departure and return: *"Hamlet, Hamlet!*

With Hamlet dispatched to England, Gertrude shows no sign of wavering in her relationship with Claudius. But the throne she shares with the king provides no defense against the *"guilt"* she now feels in her *"sick soul"* (4.5). After his escape from Claudius' execution plan and return to Denmark, Gertrude's *"my too much changed son"* (2.2) has undergone a second transformation.

Sample 5.1

The first sample response focuses on Gertrude's sincere joy at her son's return to Denmark. The Hamlet who escaped Claudius' execution plot in 5.1 is a changed man, both on the outside and inside. Gone are both his *"inky cloak"* (1.2) and *"antic disposition"* (1.5). The prince now entrusts his fate to the *"providence"* (5.2) which he claims guided his escape.

In 4.1, the king's first response to news of Polonius' murder is not concern for his wife's distress but fear for his own safety: *"It had been so with us, had we been there."* Claudius declares Hamlet must be exiled, for *"His liberty is full of threats to all."* What Gertrude does not know is that Hamlet's voyage to England will see him executed there on her husband's secret order.

We can only speculate whether Gertrude followed her son's request to shun her husband's bed. And we are never told of the contents of Hamlet's letter to her which arrives along with his defiant *"High and mighty"* missive to Claudius: *"Letters, my lord, from Hamlet / This to your majesty, this to the queen"* (4.7). However, there is no doubting Gertrude's joy on seeing her son again. In 5.1, she shouts out his name twice (*"Hamlet, Hamlet!"*), orders Laertes to unhand him in Ophelia's grave (*"For love of God, forbear him"*) and excuses his outburst as a *"fit"* that will last only *"awhile."*

We see that Gertrude's *"my too much changed son"* (2.2) has undergone a second transformation. Gone are both his *"antic disposition"* (1.5) and Claudius-like stratagems of *"a little shuffling"* (4.7). The prince now entrusts his fate to the *"providence"* (5.2) which he claims guided his escape from execution. And in his graveyard reflections, he has recognized the truth of his mother's observation that *"All that lives must die, / Passing through nature to eternity"* (1.2). As he tells Horatio, *"If it be not to come, it will be now. If it be not now, yet it will come—the readiness is all"* (5.2).

Sample 5.2

Sample response number two asserts that, up until the very last scene, Queen Gertrude remains steadfastly at the side of the man she married so quickly after old King Hamlet's death. But the throne she shares with the king provides no defense against the *"guilt"* she now feels in her *"sick soul"* (4.5).

With Hamlet sent to England, Gertrude shows no sign of wavering in her relationship with Claudius and remains steadfastly at his side up until the very last scene. In 4.5, when the king casts himself as the play's victim and his nephew as the *"most violent author"* of his own misfortunes, she provides a listening ear to his cares: *"O Gertrude, Gertrude, / When sorrows come, they come not single spies / But in battalions."* Against the enraged, sword-wielding Laertes, she defends her husband from any role in Polonius' death: *"But not by him."*

But, however fearlessly she clings to her role of the *"beauteous majesty of Denmark"* (4.5), her crown provides no defense against the *"guilt"* she feels in her *"sick soul"* (4.5). I suspect that when a traumatized Ophelia sings of lost love and offers her a rue plant, Gertrude was already reflecting ruefully on how much unhappiness had followed her *"o'erhasty marriage"* (2.2).

Gertrude's delight at her son's return (*"Hamlet, Hamlet!"*, 5.1) is matched by Claudius shock and Laertes' blood-thirsty exclamation: *"But let him come. / It warms the very sickness in my heart"* (4.7). Blinded by anger and consumed with a desire for revenge, Polonius' son is easy prey for Claudius' manipulative skills. The king exploits Laertes' vanity as a swordsman—*"a quality / Wherein, they say, you shine"*—to draw him into his scheme of the rigged fencing duel to dispose of Hamlet. And as he assures Laertes, *"even his mother shall uncharge the practice / And call it accident."*

Sample 5.3
The third sample response notes the change in Gertrude's outlook. As act four unfolds, the queen finds she can no longer reconcile her optimistic view of life and her hopes for her family's future with all the calamities that have followed her remarriage.

The queen who in 3.1 told Ophelia of her hopes *"That your good beauties be the happy cause / Of Hamlet's wildness"* was still possessed of her romantic even simple-minded view of life. Now, with Hamlet in exile, Polonius dead and his daughter in the grip of madness, there are signs of character change in Queen Gertrude.

I see Gertrude's reluctance to meet with a distressed Ophelia in 4.5 as typical of her instinct to turn away from uncomfortable realities; in this case, from the sight of a woman driven insane and her heart torn by divided love and loyalties. In my opinion, it is evidence that something inside her has changed. It is also at this very moment she talks in an aside about the *"guilt"* she feels in her *"sick soul."*

Her words at Ophelia's funeral—*"I hoped thou shouldst have been my Hamlet's wife ... sweet maid* (5.1)—tell me Gertrude has recognized she can no longer reconcile her optimistic view of life and her hopes for her family's future with all the calamities that have followed her remarriage when *"the funeral baked-meats / Did coldly furnish forth the marriage tables"* (2.1).

In 5.1, Gertrude is obviously thrilled at her exiled son's reappearance: *"Hamlet, Hamlet!"* In this double-greeting, I hear both joy from a mother's heart and relief from a guilty soul. I suspect she feared their fraught exchange in her closet was the last time they would ever see each other, and that her marriage to Claudius came at the cost of losing her son forever to exile from Denmark and him losing his mind to unhappiness and insanity.

7.6 – Conclusion: *"Wretched Queen, adieu"*
In 5.2, Gertrude's defiant drinking from the poisoned wine goblet (*"I will, my lord. I pray you, pardon me"*) and her damning contradiction of Claudius' excuse for her fainting (*"She swoons to see them bleed"*) prompts Laertes' confession (*"the King's to blame"*) and Hamlet's killing of the man who killed his father.

Sample 6.1
The first sample response summarizes the trajectory of Hamlet's relationship with his mother: from disappointment at her remarriage in the beginning to callous dismissal of her soul at the end. And it explores the triple pun in the prince's final words to Claudius.

> Hamlet began the play in despair at his mother's within *"A little month"* (1.2) marriage to Claudius: *"It is not nor it cannot come to good, / But break, my heart, for I must hold my tongue"* (1.2). But the prince ends it, in his own mind at least, by extending forever into an eternity of *"sulfurous and tormenting flames"* (1.5) the incestuous union of his *"uncle-father and aunt-mother"* (2.2).
>
> Distressed and confused in 1.5 by his encounter with his ghost-father, Hamlet used the triple pun of *"this distracted globe"*, meaning at once his mind, the world, and Shakespeare's London stage. His final words to his uncle-father in 5.2 are another example of such wordplay. As he forces the goblet of poisoned wine down the king's throat, Hamlet rhetorically asks: *"Is thy union here?"*

For the term 'union' has three meanings. Firstly, it refers to the pearl with its secret poison which Claudius added to the wine goblet (*"And in the cup an union"*). Secondly, it describes the earthly marriage of Claudius and Gertrude (*"Father and mother is man and wife, man and wife is one flesh"*, 4.3). And thirdly, it anticipates the prospect of Denmark's royal couple remaining forever united in an afterlife of punishment to which old King Hamlet was condemned for only *"a certain term"* (1.5).

Whatever the actual nature and extent of Gertrude's guilt, Prince Hamlet's parting words to her (*"Wretched Queen, adieu"*) reveal that the prince is unwilling to extend to his mother the forgiveness a repentant Laertes granted to him (*"Mine and my father's death come not upon thee"*).

Sample 6.2
Gertrude's refusal to recognize the true character of the man she married leads to the destruction of her entire family.

Gertrude's self-deluding blindness to Claudius' villainous character is pathetically apparent in the final scene of 5.2. The *"all that is I see"* (3.4) queen believes she is about to watch a non-lethal fencing duel of honor. In reality, she will be the unknowing spectator to her husband's planned murder of her son. As Claudius says to his co-conspirator Laertes, the prince *"shall not choose but fall"* (4.7): a wound from a sharpened, poison-tipped sword if he loses; and, if he wins, a drink from a goblet of poisoned wine.

When her son scores two hits with his rapier against Laertes, she offers him her napkin to wipe his brow and, with the poisoned wine goblet, toasts his continued good luck: *"Here, Hamlet … The queen carouses to thy fortune."*

After she sips the deadly wine intended for the prince, she shouts out *"O my dear Hamlet—The drink, the drink! I am poisoned."* Her final words are more than a cry for help or a warning to her son. They are a damning exposure of her husband that is quickly followed by Laertes' confession of *"the King's to blame."* Prince Hamlet then by two means executes the man who twice schemed to murder him. He runs the king through with Laertes' poison-tipped sword. But Claudius' cry *"O, yet defend me, friends. I am but hurt"* reveals that the final, mortal blow will come from the same *"leperous distilment"* (1.5) that killed both his father and mother: *"Drink off this potion."*

Sample 6.3

Why does Gertrude drink down Hamlet's goblet of poisoned wine, despite her husband's direction not to? Prince Hamlet's farewell to his mother seems a harsh judgment on a woman who went to her death thinking her last act on earth was to save the life of her son.

In a play where almost every action can be interpreted in different ways, the queen's reaching in 5.2 for the goblet of poisoned wine leaves us wondering: why does she do that? Is she just yielding to thirst? Or is it because she suspects Claudius of devising a death-by-poison plot for her son—and is willing to sacrifice herself in his place?

Certainly, it is the first time we see her defy her husband's wishes. The queen who earlier responded to one of the king's requests with a deferential *"I shall obey you"* (3.1) now disobeys his direction of *"Gertrude, do not drink"* with the words *"I will, my lord. I pray you, pardon me."*

Moreover, she follows what seems like a small act of defiance with a devastating contradiction. As she falls to the floor, Claudius attempts to pass off her fainting as a reaction to the fencing duel: *"She swoons to see them bleed."* But Gertrude's warning cry of *"O my dear Hamlet—The drink, the drink! I am poisoned"* is also a damning accusation against her husband.

Her words prompt a conscience-stricken Laertes to confess all and bring the play to its conclusion: *"thy mother's poisoned ... the King, the King's to blame."* As she knew no more than did her son of Laertes' poison-tipped sword (*"treacherous instrument ... Unbated and envenomed"*), Prince Hamlet's words of *"Wretched Queen, adieu"* seem a harsh farewell to a mother went to her death in the belief her last act on earth was to save the life of her son.

8

The Relationship of Hamlet and Ophelia

"The canker galls the infants of the spring."

Prince Hamlet and his love interest the *"fair Ophelia"* (3.1) struggle to maintain their sanity against the contradictory demands of manipulative parents. Their relationship begins in uncertainty, descends into mutual deceit and rejection, and ends with their double surrender to death: she to the *"weeping brook"* (4.7); he to Claudius' *"he shall not choose but fall"* (4.7) rigged fencing duel.

8.1 – Introduction

Hamlet the play cannot end with the marriage of Hamlet and Ophelia because of the wedding that is celebrated at its beginning: the *"incestuous sheets"* (1.2) union of Prince Hamlet's *"uncle-father and aunt-mother"* (2.2). Neither the prince nor his love interest is free to follow the advice given to Ophelia's brother, Laertes: *"To thine own self be true"* (1.3). Instead, the story that unfolds is of two parallel tragedies: the revenge tragedy of Hamlet, and the love tragedy of Ophelia.

Sample 1-1

The first sample introduction characterizes Prince Hamlet and Ophelia as two figures selfishly manipulated by their fathers. Hamlet is trapped in a *"cursed spite"* conflict (1.5) between the murderous ambition of a living brother and the vengeful fury of an undead one. Polonius exploits Ophelia to gain favor with King Claudius. Yet both the prince and his love interest also fall victim to each's deception of the other.

> *"Still better, and worse"*—Ophelia's words in 3.2 to the title character of *Hamlet* carry a poignant echo of the vows exchanged at a traditional marriage ceremony. The prince who earlier wooed her *"With almost all the holy vows of heaven"* (1.3) is, like his boyhood mentor, *"a fellow of infinite mirth and most excellent fancy"* (5.1). And Ophelia, who fondly remembers his *"words of so sweet breath composed"* (3.1) is Hamlet's equal in punning wordplay, as shown by her teasing replies to her brother Laertes (*"No more but so? ... recks not his own rede"*, 1.3).
>
> However, the play in which the two characters find themselves is not a romantic comedy but a tragedy: it cannot end with their marriage because of the wedding that is celebrated at its beginning: the *"incestuous sheets"* (1.2) union of the couple Hamlet scornfully calls *"my uncle-father and aunt-mother"* (2.2). The Denmark ruled by King Claudius and Queen Gertrude, aided by Ophelia's meddlesome and manipulative father, Polonius, is a place

where all personal relationships are poisoned by self-interest and falsity.

Ironically, it is Queen Gertrude who reports Ophelia's death in the *"weeping brook"* (4.7) and who at her funeral later laments: *"I hoped thou shouldst have been my Hamlet's wife"* (5.1). For it was Gertrude's pre-play acceptance of Claudius' marriage proposal that helped set in motion the play's tragic chain of events. Hamlet's last words to the dying Claudius— *"Follow my mother"* (5.2)—are those of a *"scourge and minister"* (3.4) wedding celebrant who extends forever in a hell of *"sulphurous and tormenting flames"* (1.5) the marriage that blocked his path to his father's throne and his hopes of sharing it with his *"fair Ophelia"* (3.1).

Sample 1-2

Ophelia does not share the leading role occupied by the female title characters in other Shakespearean dramas such as *Romeo and Juliet* and *Anthony and Cleopatra*. However, both she and the prince illustrate one of *Hamlet*'s central themes: the struggle to remain true to oneself in a world of falsity.

In Shakespeare's *Hamlet*, the prince and his love interest the *"fair Ophelia"* (3.1) struggle to maintain their sanity against the contradictory demands of manipulative parents. Neither is free to follow the advice given to Ophelia's brother, Laertes: *"To thine own self be true"* (1.3). Instead, the story that unfolds is of two parallel tragedies: the revenge tragedy of Hamlet, and the love tragedy of Ophelia.

Hamlet's uncle-father King Claudius demands the prince's loyalty and that he *"think of us / As of a father"* (1.2). However, his undead ghost-father directs Hamlet to seek vengeance on the throne-stealing and brother-murdering Claudius: *"Revenge this murder most foul"* (1.5).

If the prince is trapped between the opposing male roles of a slavish subject to a tyrant (*"Am I a coward?"*, 2.2) and a rebellious if hell-bound avenger (*"Now could I drink hot blood"*, 3.2), Ophelia is successively cast by her cynical-about-love father Polonius (*"Affection? Pooh!"*, 1.3) into the female stereotypes of virgin and whore. First, she is to deny her romantic feelings for the prince (*"Think yourself a baby"*, 1.3); and then, to seductively exploit his feelings for her to protect the throne against the prince's politically *"dangerous lunacy"* (3.1).

Ophelia expresses helplessness about the tragic fate to which she eventually surrenders: *"Lord, we know what we are, but know not what we may be"* (4.5). Later, anticipating his own death is near, the prince adopts a similar tone of resignation when he tells his confidant Horatio: *"If it be not now, yet it will come—the readiness is all"* (5.2).

Sample 1-3

Sample introduction number three argues that the play cannot end with the marriage of Hamlet and Ophelia because of the wedding of Claudius and Gertrude that is celebrated at its beginning.

The relationship between Prince Hamlet and Ophelia is one of *"purposes mistook"* (5.2) that begins in uncertainty, descends into mutual deceit and rejection, and ends with their double surrender to death: she to the *"weeping brook"* (4.7); he to Claudius' *"he shall not choose but fall"* (4.7) rigged fencing duel.

Ophelia's uncertainty about the sincerity of Hamlet's *"many tenders / Of his affection to me"* (1.3) mirrors Hamlet's doubt about the truthfulness of the revenge-commanding Ghost who appears in the *"questionable shape"* (1.4) of his late father. Hamlet complains *"That one may smile, and smile, and be a villain"* (1.5), and Ophelia laments that *"There's tricks i'th'world"*, (4.5). However, both characters also practice deceit against one another. Ophelia mistakenly fears her rejection of the Hamlet has caused his insanity, and with it his *"rash and bloody"* (3.4) murder of her father.

Conversely, Hamlet allows Ophelia to believe his "*noble mind ... o'erthrown*" (3.1) is the cause of his cruelty to her.

Fearing that his revenge quest against the king could end in his trial and execution, Hamlet publicly distances himself from Ophelia to spare her from any guilt by association: *"I loved you not"* (3.1). She colludes in her father's manipulative ploy of the so-called 'nunnery scene' as her only way of seeing her prince again: *"How does your honour for this many a day?"* (3.1).

Hamlet's put-on *"antic disposition"* (1.5) is followed by Ophelia's very real insanity and apparent suicide. And her death is followed by Hamlet's expression of love and his duel with Laertes (*"I loved Ophelia ... I will fight with him upon this theme"*, 5.1) in which both Ophelia's brother and lover meet their deaths.

8.2 – Hamlet's wooing: *"I do not know what to think"*

From Ophelia's remark of *"'tis twice two months, my lord"* to the prince in 3.2, we can estimate the time span between old King Hamlet's funeral and the beginning of the play's timeline as two months. As to the extent and depth of the couple's relationship in that pre-play period, we can only speculate.

Sample 2-1

Indecision is a trait famously associated with Prince Hamlet. But in act one, it is Ophelia who is uncertain: of the sincerity of Hamlet's romantic interest; and of how she should respond to his overtures of *"almost all the holy vows of heaven"* (1.3). That word 'almost'!

In the period after his father's death and before the beginning of the play's timeline, what was Prince Hamlet doing? He was not in the company of Horatio, who the prince later professes to *"wear ... in my heart of heart"* (3.2). In 1.2, we learn that Horatio has been at Elsinore for old King Hamlet's funeral (*"'A was a goodly king"*) and afterward attended the wedding of Claudius and Gertrude (*"Indeed, my lord, it followed hard upon"*). But when Horatio meets Hamlet in the same scene, it is clearly for the first time since Wittenberg. The prince greets Horatio with questions: *"Horatio? Or I do forget myself? ... What, in faith, make you from Wittenberg?"* and *"But what is your affair in Elsinore?"*

In the court scene which precedes Hamlet's encounter with Horatio, the prince's attire (*"customary suits of solemn black"*) and demeanor (*"all forms, moods, shapes of grief"*) all suggest someone the grip of what Claudius describes as *"obstinate condolement"* and *"unmanly grief"* (1.2). As does the prince's *"this too too sullied flesh"* soliloquy afterward in which Hamlet admits that only God's *"canon 'gainst self-slaughter!"* stands between him and ending his life.

How probable is it that such an apparently grief-stricken young man who finds *"all the uses of this world ... weary, stale, flat, and unprofitable"* is also under the spell of romantic love? Yet in 1.3, Ophelia tells her father Polonius that Hamlet *"hath importuned me with love / In honorable fashion."* As to the prince's true state of mind and intentions, we the audience might wonder, as Ophelia confesses to her father: *"I do not know, my lord, what I should think."*

Sample 2-2
Sample response number two highlights the contrast between Hamlet's denied request of King Claudius in 1.2 and Ophelia's reported expression of his love in the next scene. Does the prince wish to return to Wittenberg University or remain with Polonius' daughter at Elsinore?

An ironic feature of Laertes' leave-taking from Elsinore is that the subject of his farewell conversation with Ophelia also wishes to depart Denmark. Ophelia's brother was successful in his request to return to his pleasure-seeking ways in Paris, later characterized by his father Polonius as *"drinking, fencing, swearing, quarrelling / Drabbing"* (2.2).

In contrast, the freedom of travel King Claudius grants to Polonius' son (*"What wouldst thou beg, Laertes, / That shall not be my offer, not thy asking?"*, 1.2) he withholds from his own nephew. The royal command of King Claudius (*"remain / Here in the cheer and comfort of our eye"*) is echoed by the plea of Queen Gertrude: *"Let not thy mother lose her prayers ... Go not to Wittenberg"* (1.2).

That Hamlet preferred his life at Wittenberg University in Germany to the company of Ophelia in Denmark suggests that Laertes has good reason for cautioning his sister against the prince's advances. Laertes construes any display of affection by Hamlet as *"trifling"* and *"not lasting"* (1.3). Moreover, he warns Ophelia that the prince's romantic choices are governed by his royal position: *"He may not ... as unvalued persons do, / Carve for himself"* for he is responsible for *"The safety and health of this whole state."*

Whatever relationship may have existed between the couple is summarily ended by Ophelia's father. Polonius commands his daughter never again to spend any time (*"slander any moment"*, 1.3) in the company of the prince.

Sample 2-3

In an aside in 2.2, Polonius admits that *"truly in my youth I suffered much extremity for love"* (2.2). But Ophelia's father now takes an entirely cynical and self-interested approach to romance and insists his daughter do the same.

We can only speculate about the nature of the relationship between Hamlet and Ophelia over the period following the prince's return to Elsinore from Wittenberg to attend his father's funeral.

Hamlet makes no mention of their relationship, either in conversation with his trusted confidant Horatio or in his first two soliloquies. Indeed, he will later deny ever sending Ophelia any letters or tokens of affection: *"No, not I. I never gave you aught"* (3.1), a claim she will immediately contradict: *"My honoured lord, you know right well you did; / And, with them, words of so sweet breath composed."*

It is only the three members of the Polonius family who refer to the couple's relationship. Ophelia tells her father that Hamlet *"of late made many tenders / Of his affection to me"* (1.3). To which Polonius responds: *"'Tis told me"* that Hamlet has *"Given private time to you; and you yourself / Have of your audience been most free and bounteous."* As for Laertes, his warning to his sister against yielding to Hamlet's advances (*"the perfume ... of a minute ... no more"*) is the main topic of their conversation before he departs for France.

Polonius' financial interpretation of the word 'tender' (*"Tender yourself more dearly"*) reveals his mercenary attitude towards romance (*"Affection? Pooh!"*). Hamlet's *"almost all the holy vows of heaven"* falls short of what Polonius would consider the *"true pay"* of a legally-binding marriage contract. The relationship her brother discouraged is ended by her father: *"from this time forth"* Ophelia is not to *"give words or talk with the Lord Hamlet"* (1.3).

8.3 – Ophelia's guilt: *"Mad for thy love?"*

Knowing nothing of the Ghost's appearance or Hamlet's *"antic disposition"* (1.5) ploy, Ophelia fears she that, by ending their relationship, she has driven insane the heir to Denmark's throne.

Hamlet, by acting in ways that leave her *"so affrighted"* (2.1), seeks to ensure Ophelia is not suspected as a throne-seeking co-conspirator should the prince actually assassinate the husband of his mother and the choice of his country's nobles as Denmark's monarch.

Sample 3-1
Hamlet's visit to Ophelia's closet and his inarticulate love letter foreshadow the disheveled appearance and fragmented speech that will characterize her mental breakdown later in 4.5.

> Following Hamlet's *"No hat upon his head"* (2.1) visit to her closet, Ophelia worries in 2.1 her father's interpretation of the prince's behavior (*"Mad for thy love?"*) may be correct: *"My lord, I do not know. / But truly, I do fear it."* By rejecting Hamlet's love at her father's command (*"I did repel his fetters and denied / His access to me"*), has she driven insane the prince on whom depends, in her brother's words, *"The safety and health of this whole state"*? (1.3).
>
> Assuming Ophelia did block any correspondence from the prince after she ended their relationship, the uncharacteristically inarticulate letter (*"I love thee best …"*) that Polonius shares with the royal couple in 2.2 must be one his daughter kept from an earlier time. It is unclear whether Ophelia is present on stage to endure the embarrassment of having her private correspondence read aloud by Polonius. Or to hear him tell the king and queen he regards his daughter as unworthy of her suitor's love: *"this I did bespeak: 'Lord Hamlet is a prince, out of thy star / This must not be'"* (2.2).

In my opinion, Hamlet's disheveled closet visit (*"he lets me go ... For out o'doors he went"*) is the prince's anguished expression of farewell to Ophelia. The *"dread command"* (3.4) of revenge demanded of him means he must forget about Polonius' daughter, just as he must set aside all *"trivial fond records"* of *"youth and observation"* so that the Ghost's *"commandment all alone shall live / Within ... my brain"* (1.5).

Sample 3-2

Sample response number two suggests that Hamlet's attitude towards Ophelia is both exploitative and protective. He intends his 'dumbshow' visit to her closet to spread the belief that her rejection of him is the cause of his madness. His other purpose is to ensure her safety; by pushing the *"so affrighted"* (2.1) Ophelia away from him, he seeks to ensure she is spared any blame should he kill Claudius.

Following his conversation with the Ghost, Hamlet's decision—made immediately and without explanation—to *"put an antic disposition on"* (1.5) makes Claudius more rather than less suspicious of his nephew. Yet I believe there is a *"method"* in the prince's *"madness"* (2.2).

In my view, Hamlet is setting in place a defense of temporary insanity should he kill the king and face a trial before Denmark's nobles for the crime of regicide. It is an excuse he later offers to Laertes for his murder of Polonius: *"His madness is poor Hamlet's enemy"* (5.1). Hamlet shares his ploy with Horatio and the guard Marcellus to assure them that his aberrant behavior is only an act, and that they should not doubt his fitness to rule as a future king capable of protecting the *"safety and health of this whole state"* (1.3).

The final element in his 'antic' ploy is to *"let belief take hold"* (1.1) that Ophelia's rejected love is the cause of *"the madness wherein now he raves"* (2.2). Hence, Hamlet's disheveled *"doublet all unbraced"* (2.1) visit to her closet, his teasing of Polonius (*"Have you a daughter?"*, 2.2), and his risqué banter at *The Murder of Gonzago* (*"Here's metal more attractive"*, 3.2).

I believe Hamlet's other, related purpose is to protect her reputation and safety. By acting in ways that leave her *"so affrighted"* (2.1), he seeks to ensure she is not suspected as a throne-seeking accomplice—or even punished as a co-conspirator—should the prince actually assassinate the husband of his mother and the choice of his country's nobles as Denmark's monarch.

Sample 3-3

Hamlet's love letter to Ophelia has puzzled audiences and critics. What is Hamlet trying to communicate? Is it even possible that someone other than the prince was the author?

"Came this from Hamlet to her?" Queen Gertrude's skeptical response in 2.1 to the letter Polonius reads aloud to her and the king is understandable: for its contents lack the usual sparkling eloquence of which her son is capable. For example, Ophelia will later speak of Hamlet's *"words of so sweet breath composed"* (3.1) and Gertrude of his *"golden couplets"* (5.1).

One explanation is that the prince simply cannot find the *"words, words, words"* (2.2) to express the sincerity and depth of his feelings for Ophelia; that he has not the *"art"* to *"reckon"* his *"groans"* (2.1). Another interpretation that the letter is not evidence of genuine love but a work of forgery. Did Polonius write the letter, motivated by the prospect of gaining for his daughter a marriage into Denmark's royal family?

Also puzzling is the ambiguity of the letter's content. In modern usage, *"Never doubt that I love"* means 'be certain always of my love.' In Shakespeare's time, however, the word 'doubt' had a second and opposite meaning. When Hamlet declares *"My father's spirit in arms! ... I doubt some foul play"* (1.5), he is expressing certainty rather than doubt.

So, the letter's words could equally mean 'Never suspect that I love.' Moreover, by including the line *"Doubt that the sun doth move"* in an era when opinion was still divided about whether the sun or the earth was at the center of the solar system, I believe Shakespeare's creation of ambiguity is intentional: it is to leave us wondering if Hamlet himself (assuming he is the letter's author) really knows whether he loves Ophelia or not.

8.4 – The double deception: *"No more marriages"*

The so-called 'nunnery scene' of 3.1 does not end well for either Ophelia or Hamlet. She is crushed by his verbal outburst (*"wise men know well enough what monsters you make of them"*). And, alarmed by what he has overheard (*"I am very proud, revengeful, ambitious ... Those that are married already, all but one, shall live"*), the king drafts his secret execution order for the prince (*"he shall with speed to England"*). Polonius too will come to regret this deceptive ploy. For on the next occasion when the prince suspects he is being spied upon, his will impulsively run his sword through the hidden eavesdropper.

Sample 4-1

Ophelia's conduct in the 'nunnery scene' reveals she still holds feelings for the prince. Her initial greeting, her production of his *"remembrances"* (3.1) and the patient silence with which she endures his ranting all point to this interpretation.

> Mirroring Polonius' submissiveness to Claudius (*"I hold my duty, as I hold my soul, / Both to my God and to my gracious King"*, 2.2), Ophelia willingly complies with her father's and the king's scheme to *"sift"* (2.2) Hamlet with the staged *"'twere by accident"* encounter of the so-called 'nunnery scene' in 3.1. The two *"lawful espials"* hope to discover, in the king's words, *"If't be the affliction of his love or no / That thus he suffers for"* (3.1).

Polonius seems sure that *"neglected love"* is *"The origin and commencement of his grief"* (3.1). A less certain Claudius seeks the advice of Gertrude (*"Do you think 'tis this?"*, 2.2), who in turns offers encouragement to Ophelia: *"I do wish / That your good beauties"* and *"virtues / Will bring him to his wonted way again"* (3.1).

Ophelia's opening remark to the prince suggests she misses him in her life: *"How does your honour for this many a day?"* Next—and on her own initiative—Ophelia says to her former suitor: *"My lord, I have remembrances of yours / That I have longed long to redeliver. / I pray you now receive them."* In my opinion, Ophelia is encouraging Hamlet to recall his past love for her (*"words of so sweet breath composed"*) in the hope that his so doing may also rekindle it.

The same apparent loss of mind (*"noble and most sovereign reason"*) Ophelia mistakenly suspected was caused by her rejection of him, she now sees as the reason for his verbal cruelty and rejection of her (*"Get thee to a nunnery"*). Her grief at Hamlet's seeming madness (*"O heavenly powers, restore him! ... O, what a noble mind is here o'erthrown!"*) foreshadows her own later descent into insanity when she will become *"Divided from herself and her fair judgement"* (4.5).

Sample 4-2

The second sample response focuses on Hamlet's sense of entrapment and feeling of rage brought on by his perception that Ophelia has exploited their former relationship as a weapon to be used against him. Having exposed his two old school friends Rosencrantz and Guildenstern as spies serving the king and queen (*"Were you not sent for? ... Come, come, deal justly with me"*, 2.2), Hamlet naturally reacts with suspicion on suddenly encountering the woman who has shunned his company. As the subsequent fate of Rosencrantz and Guildenstern will show, the prince does not treat lightly those he views as having betrayed him.

In staging the so-called 'nunnery scene' of 3.1, many *Hamlet* productions portray the prince's sudden and out-of-context question to Ophelia of *"Where is thy father?"* as the moment when he realizes their conversation is being spied upon, almost certainly by the meddlesome Polonius and very likely by his despised uncle and perhaps the queen too.

In my view, the prince's suspicion—and pained sense of betrayal—is present from the very beginning of the encounter. I interpret his opening question of *"Ha, ha! are you honest?"* as an echo of his earlier query to Rosencrantz and Guildenstern: *"Were you not sent for? ... Come, come, deal justly with me"* (2.2). Accordingly, I believe much if not all his verbal outburst is not for the ears of the *"fair Ophelia"* but for the benefit of the *"seeing, unseen"* observers.

The prince has three grounds for suspicion: after being mysteriously *"sent for"*, he encounters the woman who has for two months shunned his company; she happens to be holding *"remembrances"* to return to him; and lastly, her words of *"Rich gifts wax poor when givers prove unkind"* have the air of a prepared statement in the pompous verbal style of her father.

In the prince's tirade, there is anger at her perceived betrayal. But also, by pushing her away (*"I loved you not"*), a protective wish to shield her from any taint of involvement in the *"hot blood ... bitter business"* (3.2) action against King Claudius that may follow that evening's performance of *The Murder of Gonzago*. But in his rage, Hamlet blurts out his murderous intent towards Claudius (*"all but one, shall / live"*) that prompts the king to write the 'commission' that will see the prince dispatched *"with speed"* (3.1) to England. On overhearing the king's decision, Ophelia must surely feel any hope of restoring her relationship with the prince is forever lost.

Sample 4-3

The successive roles Polonius demands Ophelia play are not only manipulative but also contradictory. The Hamlet who once wooed her in *"honourable fashion"* (1.3) now rails against Ophelia in 3.1 as a representative of fickle womanhood.

The conflict of appearance versus reality is a central and continuous theme in *Hamlet*. From the nunnery scene of 3.1 onward, this theme is expressed in terms of female beauty and cosmetics concealing an interior of rottenness and decay, both physical and moral.

Polonius' cynical offering to Ophelia of a prayer book as a deceptive prop (*"that show ... may colour / Your loneliness"*) causes the king to admit in an aside: *"The harlot's cheek, beautied with plastering art, / Is not more ugly to the thing that helps it / Than is my deed to my most painted word."*

The verbal abuse which an at first suspicious (*"Ha, ha! are you honest?"*) and then hostile (*"To a nunnery, go, / and quickly too. Farewell"*) Hamlet directs at Ophelia echoes the contradictory roles her father has demanded of her: first, to be a coy maiden (*"a green girl"*, 1.3) and, then, an alluring temptress (*"Ophelia, walk you here ..."*) to uncover the source of the prince's *"lunacy"* which the Claudius fears may contain *"some danger."* The prince who once courted Ophelia *"In honorable fashion"* with *"holy vows of heaven"* now insults her: *"God hath given you one face, and you make yourselves another."*

After Hamlet's exit, Ophelia next endures the humiliation of hearing the king dismiss the theory that the prince's *"neglected love"* for her is the *"something in his soul"*, for *"his affections do not that way tend."* Her opinion unsought by her father (*"We heard it all"*), and holding her unreturned *"remembrances"*, the *"of ladies most deject and wretched"* Ophelia is left abandoned and uncomfortable: *"O, woe is me."*

8.5 – Two truth-tellers: *"Dangerous conjectures"*

In Hamlet's play-within-a-play of 3.2 and Ophelia's 'mad scene' of 4.5, the son and daughter of two murdered fathers break through the falsity of the Danish court. Unable to remain silent and repress their feelings any longer—but also lacking control over their circumstances—they can express their dilemmas only indirectly. One communicates through theater; the other through borrowed song lyrics and floral symbolism.

Sample 5-1

Hamlet's antics during *The Murder of Gonzago* suggest that the re-enactment of his father's murder and mother's seduction became much for the prince to endure passively. Rather than quietly observe the king's reaction, he instead delivers a provocative commentary that ends with a direct threat to Claudius' life. Similarly, Ophelia's later distribution of fennel and columbines to Claudius and Gertrude conveys accusatory messages that highlight the guilt of their recipients.

Hamlet, through theater, and Ophelia, through fragments of ballads and the symbolic language of flowers, each exposes Elsinore's dark secret: that the king and queen owe their position to a secret murder followed by a politically convenient marriage.

As they view *The Murder of Gonzago* in 3.2, which Hamlet has adapted so that it *"comes near the circumstance"* of his father's death, he informs the king that the play is *"the image of a murder done."* After which he adds sarcastically: *"but what of that? ... it touches us not."* And when the Player Queen vows never to remarry, the prince taunts his mother: *"Madam, how like you this play?"*

Later in 4.5, Ophelia will similarly direct accusations towards the royal couple. To the king, she presents fennel (representing flattery) and then columbines (adultery). To the queen and herself, Ophelia offers rue, the bitter-tasting symbol of sorrow and regret. But she adds that Gertrude must wear hers differently: as *"herb of grace o'Sundays"*, which carries the extra connotation of repentance-seeking for past sins.

Hamlet's play-within-a-play prompts Polonius to demand the queen chastise her son: *"Tell him his pranks have been too broad to bear with"* (3.4). In 4.5, Horatio cautions the queen that Ophelia's traumatized ramblings *"may strew / Dangerous conjectures in ill-breeding minds."* Hamlet's theatrical truth-telling is followed by his murder of Ophelia's father and his death sentence voyage across the sea to England. Ophelia's mad scene is followed by her own self-murder in the *"weeping brook"* (4.7) at Elsinore.

Sample 5-2

Sample response number two argues that, in different ways, the world of Elsinore has driven Hamlet and Ophelia mad: he to a feigned insanity; she to a madness that is all too real.

In her 'mad scene' of 4.5, I believe Shakespeare intends us to see Ophelia as a foil for Hamlet. Her disheveled appearance reminds us of Hamlet's *"doublet all unbraced ... And with a look so piteous"* closet visitation that left Ophelia *"so affrighted"* (2.2). In the Gentleman's account of her disjointed words that *"carry but half sense"* and *"doth move / The hearers to collection"* (4.5), we recall Hamlet's earlier teasing conversations with Polonius (*"Though this be madness, yet there is method in't"*, 2,2) and Guildenstern (*"Good my lord, put your discourse into some frame"*, 3.2).

Both characters have suffered devastating blows. The prince has lost his *"dear father"* (2.2); respect for his hastily-remarried mother (*"O God, a beast that wants discourse of reason / Would have mourned longer!"*, 1.2); and, on Polonius' command, *"fair Ophelia"* (3.1) too. On her part, Ophelia has lost her brother and confidant Laertes to Paris; her father, to death in an unmarked grave (*"At his head a grass-green turf"*, 4.5); and, to exile in England, Hamlet. There she imagines him as a pilgrim on a journey of repentance (*"cockle hat and staff / And his sandal shoon"*, 4.5).

Hamlet is sustained in part by his sense of self-worth; as he reminds Rosencrantz, he is *"the son of a king"* (4.2). And, as is shown in the very first scene, he enjoys the loyalty of Horatio and the palace sentries. For it is not to the king but to the prince they report the Ghost's appearance, *"As needful in our loves, fitting our duty"* (1.1). In contrast, Ophelia is entirely alone. Even Gertrude, the play's only other female character, refuses to offer her comfort in her distress: *"I will not speak with her ... What would she have?"* (4.5).

Sample 5-3

The third sample response contrasts the different ways that Hamlet and Ophelia deal with psychological pressure. The prince aggressively channels his distress outward towards others; Ophelia carries inside the pain that ultimately overcomes her.

When the prince decides *"to put an antic disposition on"* (1.5), I believe it is at least in part because such a talkative lover of *"words, words, words"* (2.2) cannot remain silent for very long. His feigned madness is an outlet for venting his rage at the royal couple and those who serve them. In the court scene of 1.2, he uses wordplay to defy both his uncle (*"I am too much in the sun"*) and mother (*"Ay, madam, it is common"*). Polonius, he calls a *"fishmonger"* (2.2); and Rosencrantz he insults as a toadying *"sponge"* (4.2). Although he berates himself that he can only *"unpack my heart with words / And fall a-cursing like a very drab"* (2.2), what would nowadays be called 'passive aggression' helps the prince cling to his sanity amidst the *"sea of troubles"* (3.1) that engulf him.

If Hamlet channels his distress outward in the form of verbal aggression, Ophelia carries the pain of her continual silencing and humiliation inside her, until, in 4.5, her sanity collapses under its weight. Put simply: Hamlet gets mad; Ophelia goes mad.

But Ophelia's madness is also a liberation. The *"green girl"* of 1.3 in 4.5 challenges the king and queen's condescending dismissals of her with a defiant *"Pray you, mark."* But, for so long unaccustomed to communicating her true feelings, she must borrow from popular ballads and the symbolism of flowers to express her truth. As her parting two lines demonstrate, her thoughts about Hamlet and Polonius commingle incoherently: firstly, she recalls her absent lover (*"For bonny sweet Robin is all my joy"*); and secondly, she then remembers her late father (*"They say he made a good end"*).

8.6 – Conclusion: *"All trivial fond records"*

Elsinore is a world where the old literally destroy the young. The self-serving motives of Ophelia's only parent and Hamlet's mother and two fathers lead inevitably to their children's deaths. For both Hamlet and Ophelia, Elsinore's graveyard was their only escape route from the *"prison"* (2.2) of Denmark.

Sample 6-1

The first sample conclusion details the two paths Ophelia and Hamlet follow to their deaths. In the era of the play, suicide was viewed as both a crime in law and a sin of despair. However, Shakespeare's portrayal of Ophelia's drowning elicits sympathy rather than condemnation. And Hamlet's self-sacrificing surrender to what he must surely recognize as Claudius' fatal ploy evokes our admiration and merits his *"like a soldier"* (5.2) funeral.

In Gertrude's lyrical account of 4.7, Ophelia's drowning contains elements of both accidental death and intentional suicide. She did not choose to fall into the brook, but an *"envious sliver"* broke beneath her feet, and into the *"weeping brook"* she tumbled. Once in the water, however, she made no attempt to save herself. Instead, she allowed *"her garments, heavy with their drink"*, to pull her down to her death.

In her final moments, Ophelia becomes a dramatic double for the absent-at-sea Hamlet. For her choice echoes in reverse order the dilemma expressed in the prince's *"To be or not to be"* (3.1) speech: the conflict between survival by passively accepting one's circumstances on the one hand; or, on the other, taking purposeful if life-threatening action.

Ophelia's choice of *"not to be"* recalls Hamlet's earlier despairing wish that his *"flesh would ... resolve itself into a dew"* (1.2). It also foreshadows the suicidal return of her *"bonny sweet Robin"* (4.5) to Denmark. For, as the prince must surely expect, the villainous king has some life-ending *"exploit"* (4.7) prepared for him. He returns without a plan of action; as he writes to Claudius. *"I am set naked on your kingdom"* (4.7).

Moreover, Ophelia's death leads to Hamlet's, for it is at her grave that the prince challenges Laertes: *"I will fight with him upon this theme ... I loved Ophelia"* (5.1). But in so doing, she also helps the prince achieve his goal of removing Claudius without his action tainted by personal ambition or private vengeance. For both Hamlet and Ophelia, Elsinore's graveyard was their only escape route from the *"prison"* (2.2) of Denmark.

Sample 6-2
The second sample conclusion argues that the destruction of the Hamlet and Polonius families followed inevitably from the *"o'erhasty marriage"* (2.2) of Claudius and Gertrude.

A central conflict running throughout *Hamlet* is the struggle between generations. Elsinore is a world where the old literally destroy the young. The self-serving motives of Ophelia's only parent and Hamlet's mother and two fathers led with dramatic inevitably to their children's deaths. Laertes' words to Ophelia as he leaves for Paris can be regarded as a summary of the play's storyline: *"The canker galls the infants of the spring"* (1.3).

Gertrude's speech in the final act about how *"I hoped thou shouldst have been my Hamlet's wife"* (5.1) comes too late, for, in the grave-digger's words, *"rest / her soul she's dead"* (5.1). But the same Gertrude, as a condition of accepting Claudius' proposal of marriage, could have insisted that both partners renounce any claim to Denmark's throne. Doing so would have cleared the path for the prince to gain his expected inheritance, perhaps with *"fair Ophelia"* (3.1) reigning as queen by his side. Instead, she selfishly prolonged through her second marriage the queenly role she enjoyed for thirty years as a result of her first.

Hamlet is correct to call Polonius a *"fishmonger"* (2.2) or pimp, for he exploits Ophelia as bait *"to find where truth is hid"* (2.2). Moreover, such is the control he exerts over her (*"This in obedience hath my daughter shown me ..."*, 2.2) that the prince cannot trust Ophelia to keep secret from her father and the king anything he might share about the Ghost's revelations or his feigned insanity. As befitting a tragedy, we the audience are left at the play's end with a sense of overwhelming loss. In the *"unweeded garden"* (1.2) of Elsinore, the unwed couple of Hamlet and Ophelia are united only in death.

Sample 6-3
The third sample conclusion asserts that *Hamlet* dramatizes the destructive impact of a maddening world on two otherwise sane characters.

Ophelia and Hamlet separately feature in the play's two visually iconic scenes. One happens offstage, but leaves us with an image of a drowning young woman, clutching a bouquet of wild flowers and singing songs of lost love as the water pulls her down. The other is of the prince, standing over a freshly dug grave, and holding in his hand the skull of his boyhood companion, the court jester Yorick. Unknown to the prince, who fondly recalls the cherished figure from his childhood (*"those lips that I have kissed I know not how oft"*, 5.1), the open grave over which he stands is for the young woman he had only months before *"importuned ... with love"* (1.3).

Old King Hamlet's son and Polonius' daughter can be seen as stereotypically gendered representations of mental distress: the melancholic male (*"I have of late ... lost all my mirth"*, 2.2) and the hysterical female (*"Divided from herself and her fair judgement"*, 4.5). The first, clad in his black *"inky cloak"* (1.2), broods alone (*"sometimes he walks four hours together / Here in the lobby"*, 2.2). The second, invariably portrayed with unkempt hair and wild gestures, can express herself only in disjointed words (*"Her speech is nothing"*, 4.5) that leave listeners struggling to understand.

Ophelia's bleak recognition of *"I cannot choose but weep"* (4.5) anticipates Claudius' later words about Hamlet before the rigged fencing duel: *"He cannot choose but fall"* (4.7). If the prince loses, he will die from a fatal wound; if he wins, a poisoned chalice is his prize. In the end, Ophelia's *"self-slaughter"* (1.2) is her revenge against everyone who silenced and manipulated her. And Hamlet's killing of Claudius is his against the villain who had *"Thrown out his angle for my proper life"* (5.1).

9

The Relationship of Hamlet and Horatio

"Tell my story" to the *"unknowing world."*

Horatio's relationship with Prince Hamlet is a genuine friendship in an Elsinore where other relationships are poisoned by deception and betrayal. Their companionship evokes the advice offered to Laertes: *"Those friends thou hast, and their adoption tried, / Grapple them unto thy soul with hoops of steel"* (1.3). Horatio is Hamlet's trusted confidant in life and vows to remain the keeper of his memory after the prince's death.

9.1 – Introduction
Hamlet's relationship with Rosencrantz and Guildenstern ends with him sending the two *"Good lads"* (2.2) to their deaths. His relationship with Horatio, however, remains one of loyal and trusting friendship throughout the play. Hamlet admires Horatio's Stoic detachment from the concerns of the world. But the prince's political position means he cannot merely be an observer of events.

Sample 1-1
The first sample introduction contrasts Hamlet's relationship with his pair of old school friends and his fellow scholar from Wittenberg University, Horatio. The first relationship quickly gives way to suspicion, then to hostility and finally to the prince's sending of Rosencrantz and Guildenstern to their deaths. Hamlet's relationship with Horatio, however, remains one of loyal and trusting friendship throughout the play.

"My excellent good friends! … Good lads, how do you both?" (2.2), Hamlet's greeting of Rosencrantz and Guildenstern is one of the title character's few unguarded moments in Shakespeare's play. Speaking earlier of her son's relationship with his unexpected guests, Hamlet's mother remarked: *"And sure I am two men there are not living / To whom he more adheres"* (2.2).

But the prince's spontaneous welcome quickly gives way to suspicion: *"Were you not sent for? … Come, come, deal justly with me"* (2.2). As Hamlet has correctly guessed, his *"two schoolfellows"* (3.4) have arrived as spies at the request of the king and queen under whose watchful eye the prince is unwillingly confined.

In contrast, Horatio is a trusted friend in whom Hamlet can confide without fear of betrayal. When, on their first meeting at Elsinore, Horatio introduces himself as *"your poor servant ever"*, the prince gently corrects him: *"Sir, my good friend, I'll change that name with you"* (1.2).

As the play progresses, Hamlet's distrust of Rosencrantz and Guildenstern evolves into undisguised contempt. The former, he derides as a *"sponge"* who *"soaks up the king's countenance, his rewards, his authorities"* (4.2). To his faithful companion Horatio, however, Hamlet says he will hold him *"In my heart's core, ay, in my heart of heart"* (3.2).

In the end, Hamlet sends the two *"Good lads"* to their deaths. But he saves the life of Horatio with his request that, rather than joining him in death from the king's poison, his loyal confidant live on so that he may tell the prince's story of *"How these things came about"* (5.2).

Sample 1-2

Sample response number two characterizes the personality of Horatio as a foil to Young Fortinbras of Norway. Each represents a different response to Hamlet's much-quoted *"To be or not to be"* question of 3.1.

In the most famous line from Shakespeare's *Hamlet*, the prince wonders in 3.1 which is *"nobler in the mind"*: to endure our current circumstances (*"To be"*) or to risk one's life by striving to remake the world more to our liking (*"not to be"*)? The character of Horatio represents the first response. At the other extreme is his foil, Young Fortinbras from Denmark's rival kingdom of Norway.

The prince is impressed by the latter's audacious spirit; he is a figure unafraid to risk *"To all that fortune, death, and danger dare"* (4.4). Yet Hamlet is also appalled at Fortinbras' senseless territory-grabbing: *"The imminent death of twenty thousand men"* for *"a little patch of ground / That hath in it no profit but the name"* and which is *"not tomb enough"* to bury *"the slain"* (4.4). And does not all human achievement lead only to the grave: *"Even Imperious Caesar, dead and turned to clay"* (5.1)?

Equally appealing to Hamlet is the blend of Stoic endurance and Christian forbearance represented by Horatio, his fellow scholar from Wittenberg University: *"As one in suffering all that suffers nothing"* (3.2). But although he values his friend's level-headed judgment, unlike Horatio, Hamlet cannot remain behind *"the pales and forts of reason"* (1.4), a detached observer of life. As Laertes says of the prince to Ophelia: *"his will is not his own ... for on his choice depends / The safety and health of this whole state"* (1.3).

In this essay, I will describe Hamlet's relationship with Horatio—the companion who remains loyally at his side in life; and after the prince's death, vows to be the keeper of Hamlet's memory: *"Good night, sweet Prince, / And flights of angels sing thee to thy rest!"* (5.2).

Sample 1-3

While Hamlet and Horatio share a genuine human connection, this third sample introduction emphasizes that each withholds certain information from the other. And what of the rescue-by-pirates tale that Hamlet reports to Horatio? Is it actually true?

Horatio's relationship with the title character Prince Hamlet—as friend, confidant and ultimately biographer—is a genuine human connection in a play where other relationships are corrupted by deception and betrayal.

Horatio empathizes with Hamlet's revulsion at his mother's remarriage so quickly after his father's funeral (*"Indeed, it did follow hard upon"*, 1.4). He shares with his friend the news of the Ghost's visitation and its similarity to the prince's deceased father (*"These hands were not more like"*, 1.2). If belatedly, Hamlet will in 3.2 inform Horatio of the Ghost's revelations. The prince values his friend's equanimity (*"Whose blood and judgement are so well commingled"*, 3.2) and is most generous in his praise for the friend whom he wears *"In my heart's core, ay, in my heart of heart"* (3.2).

However, each friend is selective in what he shares with the other. Horatio does not mention to the prince his interpretation of the Ghost as an *"omen"* that *"bodes some strange eruption to our state"* (1.1). Hamlet does not disclose to his friend why he puts on his *"antic disposition"* (1.5) and never discusses with Horatio his relationship with Ophelia.

In addition, we may with good reason wonder whether, at the play's end, Hamlet does not embellish with a self-glorifying yet improbable tale the memory which he wishes Horatio to preserve about him after his death. Is the prince exploiting Horatio's loyalty by asking him to *"report"* (5.2) a heroic adventure story that is, in fact, another *"forgery of shapes and tricks"* (4.7) in which the play abounds?

9.2 – Meeting Horatio: *"What brings you from Wittenberg?"*

Who is Horatio? And why is he at Elsinore? Section two of the sample essay provides some background on the character of Hamlet's trusted companion. Horatio's first role in the play is to verify that the Ghost is not a mere hallucination. Moreover, that he and the guards agree to report the spirit's visitation in secret to Hamlet suggests the newly-crowned King Claudius has only a limited claim on the loyalty of his subjects.

Sample 2-1

This first sample response records that Horatio has attended both old King Hamlet's funeral and the marriage ceremony of Claudius and Gertrude. In his first encounter with his friend the prince at Elsinore, Horatio has some astonishing news.

In the court scene of 1.2, Laertes seeks from King Claudius "Your leave and favour to return to France; / From whence though willingly I came to Denmark, / To show my duty in your coronation." Polonius' son makes no mention of attending the funeral of old King Hamlet, the monarch who served Denmark over Laertes' lifetime. Later in 4.5, the same Laertes will complain that his own father went unremembered after his death: "his obscure funeral—No trophy, sword, nor hatchment o'er his bones, / No noble rite nor formal ostentation."

In contrast, we learn from Horatio's conversation with Hamlet in the same scene that his *"fellow student"* (1.2) travelled from Wittenberg University to pay his respects to the late king (*"My lord, I came to see your father's funeral"*) and remained on to attend the royal wedding (*"Indeed, my lord, it followed hard upon"*). Strangely, we also discover that this is their first encounter since their time together at Wittenberg.

Hamlet's greeting suggests the prince is surprised to see his fellow scholar (*"Horatio—or do I forget myself?"*) and is puzzled at his presence (*"What, in faith, make you from Wittenberg?"* and *"But what is your affair in Elsinore?"*). The prince who will later bemoan Denmark's reputation for excessive drinking (*"They clepe us drunkards"*, 1.4) cordially insists Horatio join him for a boozy reunion: *"We'll teach you to drink deep ere you depart."* But, after some two months at Elsinore, Horatio has a very particular reason for seeking out the prince: *"My lord, I think I saw him yesternight ... the King your father"* (1.2).

Sample 2-2

The second sample response stresses Horatio's familiarity with Denmark's military history and current defensive preparations. The scholar from Wittenberg, who is clearly a Dane, even recognizes the Ghost's armor: it is the same as that worn thirty years before by old King Hamlet in a fatal duel with the rival king of Norway.

Although a *"fellow student"* (1.2) of Hamlet's at Wittenberg University in Germany, Horatio is unquestionably Danish. In 1.1, the guard Marcellus introduces Horatio as a *"liegeman to the Dane"*; that is, a man who owes allegiance to the state of Denmark as represented by the person of its ruler, the newly-crowned King Claudius. In the same scene, Horatio calls Denmark *"our state"* and refers to old King Hamlet as *"our last King."*

Moreover, so familiar is Horatio with Denmark's military history that when Ghost appears, he instantly recognizes the spirit's attire: it is *"the very armour"* (1.1) that was worn by the old King Hamlet, *"the majesty of buried Denmark"*, when he killed Norway's old King Fortinbras in a duel fought thirty years before.

From Marcellus, we hear of the hurried military preparations underway in Denmark, *"whose sore task / Does not divide the Sunday from the week."* Yet, it is the *"scholar"* Horatio rather than the guards who knows the reason for this *"sweaty haste."* It is because the son of Norway's late king now seeks *"to recover of us, by strong hand"* those lands his father gambled and lost along with his life in the fatal duel fought three decades before. Horatio's account, however, omits one detail later supplied by the grave-digging church sexton in 5.1: the duel took place on the day of Prince Hamlet's birth.

That Horatio suggests, with the guards' agreement, they reveal the Ghost's appearance only to Hamlet (*"As needful in our loves, fitting our duty"*, 1.1) indicates the loyalty of all three characters is to Denmark's prince rather than its king.

Sample 2-3
Horatio interprets the Ghost's appearance as foretelling a political upheaval in Denmark similar to the downfall of Julius Caesar in ancient Rome. But he does not later share his opinion with Hamlet.

In the play's opening scene of 1.1, a skeptical Horatio has agreed to join the Elsinore castle guards on their midnight watch so that he may *"approve our eyes"* by confirming that *"this dreaded sight"* they have previously witnessed is no mere hallucination. As Marcellus complains to his colleague Barnardo: *"Horatio says 'tis but our fantasy, / And will not let belief take hold of him."*

Horatio's disbelief (*"Tush, tush, 'twill not appear"*) quickly gives way to terror: *"it harrows me with fear and wonder."* Nevertheless, but without receiving a response, he repeatedly challenges the spirit *"so like the King that's dead"* to explain the purpose of its visitation, making the sign of the Christian cross as he does for his protection: *"I'll cross it, though it blast me ... Stay and speak."* To Horatio, a *"scholar"* and by temperament *"more an antique Roman than a Dane"* (5.2), the Ghost's appearance suggests parallels with the supernatural spirits (*"the sheeted dead"*) that appeared before the murder of Caesar (*"ere the mightiest Julius fell"*).

The opening scene both begins and ends with the suggestion of disorder in Denmark. The first line of *"Who's there?"* is asked by the relieving guard rather than, as is proper, the on-duty one. And when Horatio with his colleagues agree it is their *"duty"* to report the ghostly visitation, it will not be to the king but Prince Hamlet. Horatio does indeed share details of the sighting with the astonished prince (*"For God's love, let me hear ... I would I had been there"*, 1.2). But he does not mention his own interpretation that the Ghost's appearance is an *"omen"* that presages a political upheaval in Denmark: *"This bodes some strange eruption to our state"* (1.1).

9.3 – The Ghost: *"More things in heaven and earth"*
The third section of the sample essay discusses the reactions of Hamlet and Horatio to the Ghost's appearance. Although Horatio and the guards dutifully and in confidence reveal news of the spirit's visitation to the prince, Hamlet offers no explanation why he decides afterward to adopt his *"antic disposition"* (1.5). And he delays disclosing to Horatio the contents of his conversation with the *"apparition"* (1.1).

Sample 3-1
The first sample response focuses on how the Ghost's visitations create a shared conspiratorial secret between Elsinore's guards, Horatio and Hamlet. None of the characters feel it their duty to report the supernatural sighting in the form of old King Hamlet to his brother, the newly-crowned King Claudius.

Intended or not, the Ghost's successive visitations—first to the guards, next to the guards and Horatio, and then to the guards, Horatio and Hamlet—has the effect of creating among the subjects of King Claudius a shared conspiratorial secret.

"I know not seems"—Hamlet's words to his mother in the court scene of 1.2 suggest a man who is repulsed by the falsity of the world. But his conversation with Horatio later in the same scene reveals that the prince is just as conniving as any other character at Elsinore.

When Horatio, accompanied by "Marcellus and Bernardo … in dreadful secrecy", reports their encounter with the supernatural apparition, Hamlet makes this request: *"If you have hitherto concealed this sight, / Let it be tenable in your silence still."*

Hamlet will repeat this need for concealment in 1.5 after he has seen and spoken with the Ghost: *"Never make known what you have seen to-night … your fingers on your lips, I pray."* The ready agreement of Horatio (*"Propose the oath, my lord"*) and Marcellus to the prince's request and their swearing of the oath on his sword would have been regarded as a treasonous act in an era when such loyalty was due only to a king.

All the elements seem in place for a political uprising against King Claudius, with Hamlet as its leader and Horatio as the prince's intermediary with the soldiers. But, unlike Laertes who later leads a castle-storming mob, Hamlet ends the scene by announcing an entirely different strategy: he will pretend to be mad. Neither to Horatio nor to any other character does he ever offer an explanation for his decision.

Sample 3-2

Sample response number two argues that Hamlet's dismissal of the Stoic materialism (*"more things in heaven and earth"*, 1.5) he attributes to Horatio is not an entirely accurate representation of either character's philosophy. It is their different attitudes towards suicide rather than the supernatural that sets the two apart.

> *"There are more things in heaven and earth, Horatio, than are dreamt of in your philosophy"* (1.5). Hamlet's much-quoted remark is a gentle riposte from one friend and scholar to another. It is also more than a little misleading. For both characters represent the fusion of classical learning and Christian doctrine that was characteristic of educated Renaissance figures.
>
> For example, when Hamlet remarks that *"there is nothing either good or bad, but thinking makes it so"* (2.2), he is echoing the maxim of the ancient Greek philosopher Protagoras' that 'Man is the measure of all things.' But equally, the Gospel according to St. Matthew (10:29) is Hamlet's inspiration for his later expression to Horatio of how *"There's a special providence in the fall of a sparrow"* (5.2).
>
> Hamlet's *"more things in heaven and earth"* remark is made to Horatio following what his friend describes as their *"wondrous strange"* encounter with the Ghost. However, both characters reacted to the Ghost's appearance with

similar exclamations. Horatio said: *"Before my God, I might not this believe / Without the sensible and true avouch / Of mine own eyes"* (1.1). And Hamlet's first words were: *"Angels and ministers of grace defend us"* (1.5).

One critical distinction between classical and Christian philosophies that the play brings into sharp focus is their very different attitudes towards suicide. To the ancients, the taking of one's own life could be an honorable act. In Christianity, however, it represents the sin of despair. Hamlet, who is restrained from *"self-slaughter"* by the *"canon"* of the *"Everlasting"* (1.2), will later restrain the *"antique Roman"* Horatio from ending his life with a dying request for him to live on so that he can *"tell my story"* (5.2).

Sample 3-3

As sample response number three shows, it is Horatio in his warning to Hamlet who introduces the topic of madness, a subject which will become one of the play's central themes. The prince's courage—even recklessness—is also highlighted in this 1.5 scene.

Horatio performs two dramatic functions in the ghost scene of 1.5: he demonstrates that his friend the prince is not, as Hamlet later worries, a coward; and introduces into the play one of its central concerns—the theme of madness.

Twice Hamlet will soliloquize that his non-fulfillment of the Ghost's command for revenge may be due to the character defect of cowardice. After his first encounter with the Players, he rebukes his inaction with the words: *"Am I a coward? ... But I am pigeon-livered and lack gall / To make oppression bitter"* (2.2). And later again, as he faces exile to England, the prince reflects: *"A thought which, quartered, hath but one part wisdom / And ever three parts coward"* (4.4).

But, in 1.5, when the Ghost appears and *"with courteous action"* beckons Hamlet to follow him *"to a more removed ground"*, the prince displays no such fearfulness. It is rather Horatio and the guard Marcellus who urge caution. To

Horatio's insistence of *"Be ruled. You shall not go"*, Hamlet replies *"Unhand me gentlemen"* and threatens *"I'll make a ghost of him"* to either companion who might stand in his way.

Horatio's concern for his friend is not for his body or soul, but his sanity: *"What if it ... deprive your sovereignty of reason / And draw you into madness?"* What Horatio calls the *"wild and whirling words"* with which the prince speaks after his conversation with the Ghost must lead his friend to fear that his concern was well-founded. But the theater-loving Hamlet appears instead to be preparing his friends for a new role he has decided—without explanation—to adopt: the pretend madman.

9.4 – The Murder of Gonzago: *"Observe mine uncle"*

Section four of the sample essay covers Hamlet's staging of *The Murder of Gonzago* and Horatio's role as the prince's objective witness who agrees to scrutinize King Claudius' reaction *"Upon the talk of the poisoning"* for evidence of his *"occulted guilt"* (3.2). It seems that Hamlet has anticipated—correctly—he could not endure the Players' performance in silence.

Sample 4-1

The first sample response discusses how Hamlet recruits the level-headed Horatio as an objective witness in his scheme for testing Claudius' guilt: a performance by the Players that will include a reenactment of his father's murder and mother's seduction.

Both Hamlet and Horatio share a love and knowledge of the classical world. But the prince has one further passion in which his friend appears to have no interest: the theater. The prince's happiest moment in the play is his welcoming of the visiting Players (*"there did seem in him a kind of joy"*, 3.1), whom he greets excitedly as cherished acquaintances (*"Welcome, good friends"*, 2.2).

It is entirely in character, therefore, that the first positive action Hamlet takes against his antagonist King Claudius is in the form of a theatrical performance. As if following the advice of Polonius (*"Those friends thou hast, and their adoption tried, / Grapple them unto thy soul with hoops of steel"*, 1.3), Hamlet recruits Horatio as a second witness in his scheme for testing Claudius' guilt: a performance by the Players that, as he confides in Horatio, includes a scene that *"comes near the circumstance / Which I have told thee of my father's death"* (3.2).

After the play has sent a panicked Claudius fleeing the palace hall, an almost manically delighted prince boasts to Horatio: *"Would not this, sir … get me a fellowship in a cry of players?"* (3.2). But Horatio's response of *"You might have rhymed"* shows him to be too honest a friend to encourage the prince's interpretation. Hamlet's threatened assassination through the uncle-killing figure of Lucianus (*"nephew to the king"*) provided Claudius with a plausible excuse for abandoning the play, his guilt still *"occulted"* (3.2).

We the audience hear the king's later confession (*"a brother's murder"*, 3.3) but Hamlet never does. And we remain unsure what Horatio knows of his friend's *"rash and bloody"* (3.4) stabbing of Polonius.

Sample 4-2

At *The Murder of Gonzago*, Hamlet is effusive in his praise for his loyal companion. Is it because the prince fears this conversation with Horatio might be their last?

Both before and after *The Murder of Gonzago* in 3.2, the prince is effusive in his praise for his friend. *"Nay, do not think I flatter"*, Hamlet insists to Horatio when his friend replies humbly with *"O my dear lord"* after Hamlet addresses him with these words: *"Horatio, thou art e'en as just a man / As e'er my conversation coped withal."* By which he means, in contemporary language: 'In all the conversations we have shared and events with which we have coped, you have shown yourself to be fair-minded and wise.'

Later, after the Players' performance has been abandoned, the king *"marvelous distempered"* and the queen *"in most great affliction of spirit"*, Hamlet addresses Horatio as *"O dear Damon."* This is a reference to the relationship in Greek mythology of Damon and Pythias, which so completely exemplified the ideal model of friendship because one was willing to sacrifice his life for the other.

What has prompted this outpouring from the prince? In my view, Hamlet recognizes his play-within-a-play (*"'A poisons him i'th'garden for his estate"*) will reveal to Claudius his secret, Ghost-provided knowledge of old King Hamlet's murder. Consequently, Hamlet has every expectation of afterward finding himself either exiled to execution or committed to Elsinore's dungeon; in Polonius' ominous words of advice to the king: *"To England send him or confine him where / Your wisdom best shall think"* (2.2).

I hear the prince's words to Horatio as a farewell and an expression of gratitude for their past friendship. After Hamlet's fatal stabbing of Polonius, their paths separate: the prince is exiled to England; but Horatio, he of the *"truant disposition"* (1.2), does not return to Wittenberg and remains at Elsinore.

Sample 4-3

The third sample response contrasts the trust Hamlet places in Horatio with the prince's growing contempt for his two old school friends, Rosencrantz and Guildenstern.

"My lord, you once did love me"—Rosencrantz follows his plaintiff remark to Hamlet in 3.2 with a plausible sounding justification for why he and the prince might wish to rebuild their past relationship: *"You do surely bar the door upon your own liberty if you deny your griefs to your friend."*

But their conversation, which follows the abandoned performance of *The Murder of Gonzago,* finds Hamlet in no mood for a reconciliation. Moreover, to someone he calls the king's information-gathering *"sponge"*, the prince certainly will not reveal what Rosencrantz describes as *"your cause of distemper."*

In contrast, Hamlet has disclosed to Horatio the Ghost's account of old King Hamlet's poisoning by Claudius in the palace orchard. We can only speculate whether the prince shared this information with Horatio as one friend might unburden himself of a heavy secret to another; or whether Hamlet had a solely self-interested motive. Perhaps realizing—correctly—he would be unable to endure in silence a theatrical reenactment of his father's killing and mother's seduction, he needed his level-headed friend (*"Whose blood and judgement are so well commingled"*) to provide an objective assessment of whether the king's reaction betrayed his *"occulted guilt."*

As Hamlet requests, Horatio does *"observe mine uncle."* But his equivocal judgement (*"I did very well note him"*) reflects an opinion any objective observer would share: that the king's flight from the hall was as likely due to the prince's manic and threatening behavior as to any possible *"occulted guilt"* on Claudius' part for a secret murder.

9.5 – The pirate rescue: *"Thieves of mercy"*

Section five of this sample essay covers the events from Horatio's receipt of Hamlet's letter to the prince's fatalistic agreement, against his friend's warning, to enter the fencing duel with Laertes. In the famous graveyard scene which he shares with Horatio, Hamlet encounters through the words of the gravedigging sexton the *"wounded name"* (5.2) which he must fear is the memory he will leave behind: that of the mad-and-exiled-to-England prince.

Sample 5-1
The returned Hamlet's abandonment of solitary soliloquizing means that his conversations with Horatio become more expansive and offer a fuller insight into the prince's thinking.

The Hamlet who returns to Elsinore in 5.1 is a changed man, both on the outside and inside. Gone are his *"inky cloak"* (1.2) and *"antic disposition"* (1.5). And, as the prince has also abandoned his habit of solitary soliloquizing, Horatio now more than previously takes on the role of an exposition character with whom Hamlet shares out loud his innermost thoughts.

Also, we see that the prince is no longer possessed by vengeful anger; it is Polonius' grieving son who is now held in its grip. When in 5.1 Laertes challenges Hamlet *"The devil take thy soul!"*, the prince, who earlier asked *"shall I couple hell?"* (1.5), replies: *"Thou prayest not well."*

As his letter to Claudius shows (*"I am set naked on your kingdom"*, 4.7), the prince has returned to Denmark without a plan of action. In conversation with Horatio, Hamlet states he no longer feels impelled to devise failure-prone *"deep plots"* (5.2). He now believes the *"providence"* (5.2) to which attributes his escape from execution will provide the circumstances for him to complete the task for which *"my fate cries out"* (1.4): *"To quit (Claudius) with this arm"* (5.2).

Hamlet's choice of Elsinore graveyard as the venue for his reunion with Horatio suggests his fatalistic acceptance that Claudius *"will work him / To an exploit"* (4.7) the prince is unlikely to survive. Hamlet's response to Claudius' messenger (*"I am constant in my purposes, they follow the King's pleasure. If his fitness speaks, mine is ready"*) reveals that the prince shrewdly recognizes his real adversary will not be his hot-headed fencing opponent but his scheming uncle. But as he confesses to Horatio: *"thou wouldst not think how ill all's here about my heart. But it is no matter"* (5.2).

Sample 5-2
Horatio reacts with shock to the prince's arranged execution of Rosencrantz and Guildenstern in England. Later, he will ensure that King Claudius, although the play's villain, is not held responsible for what Hamlet's friend clearly regards as a callous act.

In a letter delivered by a sailor and which ends affectionately with *"He that thou knowest thine, / Hamlet"* (4.6), the prince announces to his friend his imminent return to Elsinore with the promise *"to speak in thine ear"* news that *"will make thee dumb."*

Of the many elements of his adventures at sea which Hamlet later shares with Horatio in 5.2, it is the prince's substitution of Rosencrantz's and Guildenstern's names for his own on the Claudius' written commission that most stuns his companion. Horatio does not hide his disapproval for what to him seems a callous act: *"So Guildenstern and Rosencrantz go to't."* Hamlet responds in justification: *"Why, man, they did make love to this employment. / They are not near my conscience."* But Hamlet's *"no shriving time allowed"* execution order for his pair of old school friends will remain so disturbing to Horatio that in his final *"All this I can truly deliver"* speech he will excuse Claudius from any blame for it: *"He never gave commandment for their death."*

Hamlet's ruminations with Horatio in the graveyard are of a man who is confronting his own death: *"If it be not now, yet it will come—the readiness is all."* When, on the king's behalf, Osrick asks Hamlet if he is ready to enter the fencing duel with Laertes *"or that you will take longer time"*, the prince's replies in the affirmative. Disregarding Horatio's caution (*"You will lose this wager, my lord ... I will say you are not fit"*), Hamlet is prepared for whatever *"providence"* brings. Moreover, in his words *"the interim is mine,"* the prince recognizes he has only a limited time before news arrives from England of the execution of Rosencrantz and Guildenstern.

Sample 5-3
Sensing his imminent death from some ploy by Claudius, does the prince exploit his friend's loyalty with his heroic if improbable tale of rescue by pirates with which the prince hopes to be remembered?

The tale with which Hamlet regales Horatio of his adventures at sea—first in his letter in 4.6 and later in more detail in their conversation in 5.2—is riven with improbable elements. So much so that we the audience may conclude that the prince's escape from execution in England and safe return to Elsinore was more likely the result of a pre-arranged rescue plan rather than the divinely-inspired intervention of friendly *"thieves of mercy"* (4.6) pirates.

At the end of 4.3, Hamlet expresses surprise at Claudius' order for his exile (*"To England?"*). But he already knows and has told Gertrude of the king's intentions (*"I must to England"*, 3.4). He is also aware of the sealed commission, drafted earlier that day by the king following the prince's encounter with Ophelia (*"I have ... set it down: he shall with speed to England"*, 3.1). The prince's remark to his mother of how *"'tis most sweet / When in one line two crafts directly meet"* (3.4) suggests a plan is in place with elements loyal to the prince for his rescue and return. As for the replacement commission, it is easier to believe it was written, sealed and substituted at Elsinore than aboard ship in the dark of night.

It is entirely consistent with the play's theme of remembrance, and with the theater-loving prince's own character, that he might stage-manage such an escapade. The graveyard scene he shares with Horatio reveals Hamlet's recognition of the possibility of survival after death through the memory of the living. In other words, is the self-glorifying adventure story the prince asks Horatio's to *"report"* (5.2) after his death just another *"forgery of shapes and tricks"* (4.7) in which the play abounds?

9.6 – Conclusion: *"All this I can truly deliver"*

At the play's end, Horatio appears to make no mention of Ghost's role in *"How these things came about"* (5.2). Yet, Hamlet's friend in life and appointed biographer after death was tragically correct in his interpretation of the Ghost's visitation as an *"omen"* of *"that bodes some strange eruption to our state"* (1.1). For the dynasty of the Hamlet family is destroyed and Denmark falls under the rule of the rival kingdom of Norway.

Sample 6-1

The first sample conclusion links Hamlet's thoughts of suicide at the beginning of the play with Horatio's same sense of life-ending despair at its end. The expiring-from-poison prince urges his friend in life to become his biographer after death: to *"tell my story … more and less"* to the *"unknowing world"* (5.2).

When in the final 5.2 scene Horatio hears Laertes' confession that the prince is only moments from death (*"Hamlet, thou art slain. / No medicine in the world can do thee good"*), his equanimity suddenly and poignantly deserts him.

No mention was ever made of Horatio's family, and his non-return to Wittenberg University suggests he had no social bonds there to draw him back. At different points in the play, we heard Hamlet address Marcellus, Barnardo, Rosencrantz and Guildenstern, and the visiting troupe of Players as 'friends.' But Hamlet appears to have been Horatio's only friend. Consequently, his loss of the prince's companionship must be all the more painful.

Horatio's reaction to his friend's imminent demise is an attempt to join him in death. Observing *"Here's yet some liquor left"*, he reaches to drink from the same goblet of poisoned wine that has just claimed the lives of both the queen and king. But Hamlet stays his hand: *"Give me the cup. Let go! By heaven, I'll ha't."*

> In his last moments, Hamlet urges his friend to live on so that he may *"set aright"* the prince's *"wounded name."* Hamlet's plea to Horatio (*"If thou didst ever hold me in thy heart"*, 5.2) echoes the command he received from the Ghost (*"If thou didst ever thy dear father love"*, 1.5).
>
> Horatio began the play by recounting the story (*"At least the whisper goes so"*, 1.1) of a fatal duel between two kings from two countries. He survives to tell another tale: of two kings from the same country—two brothers; one undead, one alive—who competed for the loyalty and ultimately doomed the life of Horatio's *"sweet Prince"* (5.2).

Sample 6-2

Hamlet comes to an abrupt and bloody end with the final catastrophe scene. As sample conclusion number two states, one task remains, and it is Horatio who is nominated by the dying prince to perform it: the telling of the true story of *"How these things came about."*

> The *"divinity that shapes our ends"* (5.2), to which Hamlet tells Horatio he has surrendered his fate, resolves all but one of the prince's concerns in a few short moments at the play's end. Laertes pardons him for his and Polonius' deaths; the villainous Claudius is exposed and punished; his nominated successor Young Fortinbras will protect the *"safety and health of this whole state"* (3.1); and, if at the cost of his life, Hamlet is granted his original wish: to leave the *"prison"* (2.2) of Elsinore.
>
> Only one task remains, for which the dying prince requires his now grief-stricken friend forswear his *"antique Roman"* impulse towards suicide: *"Horatio, I am dead / Thou livest."* The *"wounded name"* which Hamlet fears he leaves behind was expressed earlier by the grave-digging sexton: of *"he that is mad"* after *"losing his wits"* and *"sent into England"* (5.1). In place of this unflattering legacy, Hamlet's request to his friend is that he not surrender to despair but

live on to *"Report me and my cause aright / To the unsatisfied."*

Despite his promise of *"All this I can truly deliver"*, given his limited knowledge, Horatio's account can at best be only an incomplete one. The prince's appointed biographer knows nothing of Hamlet's soliloquies, his relationship with Ophelia, or his encounters with Claudius in his chapel and Gertrude in her closet.

That the prince believes an *"audience to this act"* will *"look pale and tremble"* at Horatio's story suggests the title of the tale he will tell and perhaps the Players may perform: 'The Tragedy of Hamlet, Prince of Denmark.'

Sample 6-3

As he stepped forward to confront the Ghost in 1.1, Horatio for a second time takes center stage in the final 5.2 scene. At Hamlet's request, he promises to restore the prince's *"wounded name"* and *"truly deliver"* an account of the events that have led to the play's bloody conclusion.

In both the first and last scenes of *Hamlet*, Horatio steps from the background to take a more central role. In 1.1, he demanded from the Ghost an explanation for its visitation: *"What art thou ... I charge thee, speak."* Now, in 5.2, in fulfilment of Hamlet's dying request (*"Report me and my cause aright / To the unsatisfied"*), and also in response to the arriving Young Fortinbras (*"You from the Polack wars"*) and the Ambassadors (*"you from England"*), Horatio volunteers to *"speak to th'yet unknowing world / How these things came about."*

Horatio offers a six-line summarized account, which we can only assume he will later elaborate on. The *"carnal, bloody and unnatural acts"* appear to refer to the incestuous marriage of Claudius and Gertrude, and to the former's killing of his brother and perhaps also to his attempted assassination of his nephew.

Gertrude's and Laertes' deaths would seem to be the subject of the line *"Purposes mistook / Fallen on th'inventor's heads."* The words *"Casual slaughters"* can be taken to include Hamlet's impulsive and fatal stabbing of Polonius, and maybe Ophelia's drowning too. As for *"deaths put on by cunning, and for no cause"*, this would seem to describe the executions in England of Rosencrantz and Guildenstern, engineered by Hamlet to his friend's previously expressed shock. *"All this"*, Horatio promises, *"I can truly deliver."*

Absent from Horatio's summary is any mention of the Ghost, whose *"dread command"* (3.4), as much as Claudius' *"ambition"* (3.3), set in motion the events that led to the final catastrophe.

10

The Relationship of Claudius and Gertrude

*"For 'tis a question left us yet to prove,
Whether love lead fortune, or else fortune love."*

A marriage of practical interest: he wanted something (the role of king) he did not have; she had something (the status of queen) she wanted to hold onto. Their *"incestuous sheets"* (1.2) royal union survives Hamlet's resentment, Polonius' stabbing, Laertes' rebellion, and Ophelia's madness and drowning. But it cannot escape a dark secret of murder that hides in the past.

10.1 – Introduction
The *"mirth in funeral ... dirge in marriage"* (1.2) union of Hamlet's *"uncle-father and aunt-mother"* (2.2) comes to an end when both die from the same *"juice of cursed hebenon"* (1.5) Gertrude's second husband used to murder her first.

Sample 1.1
Without Prince Hamlet at Elsinore, how different would life have been for Claudius and Gertrude? The first sample introduction poses this question as a way of exploring the prince's impact on the relationship of Denmark's royal couple.

I will begin my essay on the relationship between Claudius and Gertrude in Shakespeare's *Hamlet* by posing the question: how differently would the lives of Claudius and Gertrude have unfolded had Prince Hamlet departed Elsinore—perhaps eloping with Ophelia—after the court scene of 1.2?

In 'Hamlet without the Prince', I can imagine the middle-aged couple Hamlet derisively calls his *'uncle-father and aunt-mother'* (2.2) growing old together in settled contentment, untroubled by all the turmoil that followed from Hamlet's presence: Polonius' stabbing, Laertes' revolt, and Ophelia's drowning. As for the external threat from Norway's Young Fortinbras, the security of Denmark was more hindered than helped by the presence of the prince, absorbing as he did so much of the court's time and attention.

Hamlet's role in relation to his uncle and mother is, in the prince's own definition of drama, *"to hold a mirror up to nature"* (3.2). Old King Hamlet's son did succeed in bringing Denmark's false king to his knees in a moment of genuine repentance-seeking: *"O, what form of prayer / Can ... Forgive me my foul murder?"* (3.4). And it was through Hamlet that Gertrude could see the *"black and grained spots"* (3.4) in her soul.

Ultimately, it was Claudius' inability to give up *"those effects for which I did the murder"* (3.3) and Gertrude's refusal to act on her son's warning that her second husband was *"a murderer and villain"* (3.4) that undermined their shared throne and marriage, and doomed both their lives.

Sample 1.2

Sample response number two contrasts the Ghost's lurid description of the royal marriage with the couple's actual, onstage relationship.

From his unspeakable sufferings in the afterlife (*"O horrible, horrible, horrible"*, 1.5), the Ghost of Old King Hamlet returns after midnight to the Elsinore castle over which he reigned to lament in disgust that *"the royal bed of Denmark"* has degenerated into *"a couch for luxury and damned incest"* and how *"lust, though to a radiant angel linked, / Will sate itself in a celestial bed / And prey on garbage"* (1.5).

Coming as these words do from a man who by his brother's poison was *"Of life, of crown, of queen at once dispatched"* (1.5), Old King Hamlet's outrage is understandable. But his description of Claudius' and Gertrude's relationship suggests he may not be, in the prince's phrase, an entirely *"honest ghost"* (1.5). The royal relationship we see acted out on stage is far removed from the unrestrained sensuality which the Ghost luridly imagines. It more resembles that of a middle-aged, married couple which, of course, Claudius and Gertrude actually are.

But whatever the royal couple's present happiness and hopes for a shared future together, a dark secret of *"a brother's murder"* (3.3) hides in the past. As Hamlet says: *"Foul deeds will rise, / Though all the earth o'erwhelm them, to men's eyes"* (1.2). In this essay, I will discuss the relationship between Claudius and Gertrude—its likely origins, the evident mutual contentment it brings, and its fatal crumbling in a truth-revealing bloodbath.

Sample 1.3
The third sample introduction describes Claudius in theatrical terms as a usurping 'playwright-within-a-play' who stole a throne—and wife—that, in the original script, belonged to another character.

> Act one of Shakespeare's *Hamlet* presents audiences with a most unusual spectacle: a country ruled over by two monarchs, each of whom married their way to the throne: Queen Gertrude, by marriage first to one brother and then, after only *"A little month"* (1.2) of widowhood, to another; and King Claudius, *"In happy time"* (5.2), to his late brother's former wife and *"sometime sister"* (1.2). As Prince Hamlet, Gertrude's son from her first marriage, correctly predicts: *"It is not nor it cannot come to good"* (1.2).
>
> From a theatrical perspective, we can view Gertrude's new husband Claudius as a character that life has cast in a background role in the shadow of his brother, the fearsome warlord, Old King Hamlet. But through a secret murder performed offstage in the palace orchard—a 'play-outside-a-play'—the onetime supporting actor is able to recast himself as the star attraction and male lead: the king who shares the throne and bed of Gertrude, *"the beauteous majesty of Denmark"* (4.5).
>
> In this essay, I will explore the relationship between Claudius and Gertrude. External events trouble but do not destroy the royal marriage: it survives Hamlet's resentment, Polonius' murder and *"hugger-mugger"* (4.5) burial, Laertes' castle-storming, mob-leading insurrection, and Ophelia's madness and drowning. In the end, their relationship is doomed not from without but from within. Gertrude dies by the same means her second husband used to murder her first: poison. And Claudius is at the play's end, like his brother was at its beginning, *"Of life, of crown, of queen at once dispatched"* (1.5).

10.2 – The wedding: *"With mirth in funeral and with dirge in marriage"*

Claudius and Gertrude's union eased Claudius' path to the throne, a position we can imagine he jealously coveted during the long years he spent in his brother's kingly shadow; and it enabled Gertrude to continue living the life of a queen she had for three decades enjoyed.

Sample 2.1

Were Claudius and Gertrude having an affair before old King Hamlet's poisoning in the palace orchard? And was the queen an accomplice to the murder of her first husband?

Was the marriage of Claudius and Gertrude the culmination of an illicit love affair that began before old King Hamlet's murder? In 1.2, the Ghost does describe Claudius as *"adulterate beast"*—that is, a debased individual—but not, significantly, an adulterous one.

In *The Murder of Gonzago,* so adapted as to *"catch the conscience of the King"* (2.2), Hamlet presents the seduction of the Player Queen (*"you shall see anon how the murderer gets the love of Gonzago's wife"*) as following rather than preceding the murder of the sleeping Player King (*"A poisons him i'th'garden for his estate"*, 3.2). When the prince afterward in the 3.4 closet scene rages against his mother, he never suggests she is an adulteress. Finally, Hamlet's farewell words to King Claudius include no accusation of adultery: *"thou incestuous, murderous, damned Dane"* (5.2).

Gertrude's shocked reaction to Hamlet's accusation (*"As kill a king, and marry with his brother ... Ay, lady, 'twas my word."*, 3.4) strongly suggests Claudius alone was responsible for the crime which the conscience-haunted king will later confess to his private chapel: *"a brother's murder"* (3.3).

Yet, one line from the prince's rant at Ophelia—and, by extension, at all womankind—hangs over the relationship between Denmark's royal couple: *"wise men know well enough / what monsters you make of them"* (3.1). Would Claudius have turned his soul *"black as death"* (3.3) by disposing of Gertrude's first husband were he not confident that the *"all tears"* (1.2) widow would accept him afterward as her second—and with *"most wicked speed"* (1.2) at that?

Sample 2.2
With King Hamlet dead, why did Claudius propose marriage to the widowed Queen Gertrude? And why did she respond with 'I do'?

The order of words spoken by Claudius in the chapel scene (*"My crown, mine own ambition, and my queen"*, 3.3) suggests Gertrude has been *"taken to wife"* (1.2) by a man motivated primarily by the desire to gain the throne, and only to a lesser extent by love for his *"sometime sister"* (1.2). With the reigning queen as his wife and with her support, Claudius was afterward able to present himself to the nobles as the candidate for kingship who offered Denmark the prospect of continuity and stability.

For Gertrude, the death of old King Hamlet did not only leave her without a husband at her side. It also placed in jeopardy her royal status as *"the beauteous Majesty of Denmark"* (4.5). After the funeral of her first husband, whose coffin *"she followed ... all tears"* (1.2), we can imagine Gertrude's fear that her privileged, queenly life had too come to an end.

Responding 'I do' to Claudius' proposal held out for her the attractive prospect of retaining through a second marriage what she had for three decades enjoyed through her first: the position of Denmark's queen. And so, as the prince sarcastically notes, *"the marriage tables"* were *"coldly furnish(ed)"* with the *"funeral baked meats"* (1.2).

Nonetheless, we can also see genuine affection in their relationship. In *The Murder of Gonzago,* the Player King ponders: *"a question left us yet to prove"* of whether *"love lead fortune, or else fortune love"* (3.2). In the example of Hamlet's uncle and mother, I believe their love followed the shared good fortune that the mutually beneficial marriage brought to each spouse.

Sample 2.3
The third sample response focuses on the possibly incestuous nature of the marriage of Claudius to his *"sometime sister"* (1.2).

The Ghost once (*"a couch for ... damned incest"*, 1.5) and Hamlet twice (*"incestuous sheets"*, 1.2; *"thou incestuous ... damned Dane"*, 5.2) each clearly describe the marriage of Claudius and Gertrude as incestuous. Marriage between a brother and his brother's wife was condemned by the Bible as a sinful, "unclean thing" (Leviticus, 20:21). In the eyes of the Church and the law, a husband's brother was also a brother of the wife. And, for centuries, this prohibition was interpreted as continuing after the death of the husband.

When Claudius tells says he has *"taken to wife"* his *"sometime sister"* (1.2), he is admitting that, by marrying Gertrude, he has in effect incestuously married his own sister. Even more perversely, in Hamlet's mind, as *"man / and wife is one flesh"* (4.3), Claudius by so doing has also married his dead brother, old King Hamlet.

However, the prohibition on a man marrying his late brother's widow was removed in Shakespeare's era. So, strictly speaking, Gertrude's remarriage was not incestuous on religious or legal grounds. No other character in the play speaks of it as such. In 1.2, Claudius thanks the nobles *"have freely gone / With this affair along."*

Nevertheless, marriages between former in-laws were viewed with some suspicion. For the centuries-old prohibition was intended to prevent exactly the type of crime perpetrated on old King Hamlet by Claudius: the motivated-by-jealousy murder of one brother by another, and the theft of their inheritance from victim's rightful heir or heirs.

10.3 – The royal couple: *"I could not but by her"*

In my opinion, Claudius does love Gertrude, as much as a man of intricate schemes rather than sweeping passion can. And despite Hamlet's view that *"Frailty thy name is woman"* (1.2), Gertrude never wavers in her relationship with her second husband.

Sample 3.1
The first sample response emphasizes Gertrude's steadfast loyalty to her second husband. It further asserts that Claudius genuinely does love Gertrude—if only as far as his character allows him.

> One of the play's great ironies is that the person that Prince Hamlet most bitterly accuses of fickle disloyalty (*"Frailty thy name is woman … O God, a beast that wants discourse of reason / Would have mourned longer!"*, 1.2) is, in fact, the most loyal character in the entire play.
>
> Up until the very last scene, she remains steadfastly at the side of the man she married. When in 4.5 an angry mob shouts out *"Laertes shall be king!"*, she responds defiantly with: *"O, this is counter, you false Danish dogs!"* She even throws herself on an enraged, sword-wielding Laertes when she fears for the king's safety and defends her husband from any role in Polonius' death: *"But not by him."* This is hardly the behavior of a merely decorous trophy wife; rather they are the actions of a woman who fulfills the king's description of her as the *"imperial jointress to this warlike state"* (1.2).

Her husband Claudius is a man of intricate schemes rather than sweeping passion, a thinker rather than a feeler. I believe he does love Gertrude—if only as far as the limitations of his character allow him. He speaks of her in words that come directly from his heart (*"My virtue or my plague, be it either which / She's so conjunctive to my life and soul ... I could not but by her"*, 4.7) and turns to her for comfort as his troubles mount: *"O Gertrude, Gertrude, / When sorrows come, they come not single spies / But in battalions"* (4.5).

Sample 3.2

As this second sample response illustrates, Gertrude successively won the heart and hand of two brothers: the first, a triumphant warlord; the second, a Machiavellian schemer.

Queen Gertrude is clearly a woman of great personal magnetism. Prince Hamlet's first question to Horatio about the Ghost's demeanor (*"looked he frowningly?"*, 1.2) suggests his father was as an aggressive figure in the domestic sphere as he was combative in battle, when *"He smote the sledded Polacks on the ice"* (1.1). Yet the same Ghost later speaks to his son about Gertrude as *"a radiant angel"* (1.5), just as the prince recalls how old King Hamlet was *"so loving to my mother / That he might not beteem the winds of heaven / Visit her face too roughly"* (1.2).

As for the otherwise cold-hearted schemer Claudius, he talks of Gertrude to Laertes in sentimental terms: *"My virtue or my plague, be it either which / She's so conjunctive to my life and soul"* (4.7). I hear Claudius' observation of Prince Hamlet (*"Love! His affections do not that way tend"*, 3.2) as perhaps an even more accurate description of his own personal character. But such capacity as he does possess for romantic love, Claudius invests it all and fully in Gertrude.

Despite her promise to her son to no longer share her husband's bed, (*"Be thou assured"*, 3.4), there is no evidence in subsequent scenes to indicate the queen has distanced herself from the king. She will end the play as she began it: sitting by her second husband's side. Indeed, as Claudius and Gertrude appear onstage to oversee the fencing duel between Hamlet and Laertes, the prince remarks to his confidant Horatio of how the royal couple arrive together *"In happy time"* (5.2).

Sample 3.3
King and queen share their ceremonial duties with stately decorum and treat each other with mutual affection and respect.

In their royal marriage, Claudius is respectful towards Gertrude in public; and in their private scenes, they are comfortably at ease in each other's company. In 2.2, on hearing Polonius' claim that Ophelia's rejection of his romantic advances is the cause of Hamlet's 'antic' behavior, Claudius immediately seeks out his wife's opinion: *"He tells me, my dear Gertrude, he hath found / The head and source of all your son's distemper ... Do you think 'tis this?"* Later, in 3.1, when Claudius wishes to speak alone with Polonius and Ophelia, he does not order his wife away; instead, he requests politely: *"Sweet Gertrude, leave us too."* She responds with equal consideration: *"I shall obey you."*

In 4.1, Claudius' first reaction to Gertrude's report that her *"Mad as the sea and wind"* son has stabbed Polonius is not concern for his wife's distress but fear for his own safety (*"O heavy deed! / It had been so with us, had we been there"*, 4.1). Although by nature a Machiavellian schemer (*"I will work him / To an exploit"*, 4.7) and by his own admission a cold-blooded murder (*"O, my offence is rank"*, 3.3), Claudius does love Gertrude. For, as he tells Laertes: *"I could not but by her"* (4.7).

Even after all the challenges they have endured, among them a life-threatening, Laertes-led popular rebellion (*"Save yourself, my lord ... The doors are broke"*, 4.5), Claudius and Gertrude remain loyally at each other's side until the very end.

10.4 – The prince: *"My uncle-father and aunt-mother"*

Claudius fails to win over the bereaved prince with his lengthy rebuke spoken before the court in 1.2. After his *"rash and bloody"* (3.4) stabbing of Polonius, Gertrude must fear she has gained a husband and retained her throne at the cost of losing her son to unhappiness, insanity and exile.

Sample 4.1

The *"inky cloak"*-wearing (1.2) Prince Hamlet refuses to share in the evident happiness of Denmark's royal couple. Queen Gertrude is saddened; King Claudius grows fearful and plots a second murder.

Neither queen nor king succeeds in winning Prince Hamlet's support for their marriage. In 1.2, Gertrude implores her son not to *"Seek for thy noble father in the dust."* Although there is always a spontaneous tenderness in her love for him (*"Come hither, my dear Hamlet, sit by me"*, 3.2), her remarriage created a deep rift between son and mother. The prince's quest both to rescue his mother's soul (*"Confess yourself to heaven. / Repent what's past. Avoid what is to come"*, 3.4) and condemn his uncle's (*"as damned and black / As hell, whereto it goes"*, 3.3) reveals a son's longing to reunite in the afterlife his fractured-by-Claudius family of mother and father, so his two parents can again be as he fondly remembers them on earth (*"Why, she would hang on him"*, 1.2).

However, that the Ghost of old King Hamlet in the 3.4 closet scene is invisible to his former wife of thirty years (*"O gentle son ... Whereon do you look?"*) suggests that his memory is as dead to her as it is alive to the prince (*"Do you see nothing there? ... Nor did you nothing hear?"*).

Claudius' approach to his nephew begins with feigned benevolence (*"think of us / As of a father"*, 1.2), evolves into fearful suspicion (*"nor th'exterior nor the inward man / Resembles that it was"*, 2.2), and culminates in panic after Hamlet's play-within-a-play when, as Guildenstern reports, the king becomes *"marvellous distempered"* (3.2). But Hamlet engineers his escape from Claudius' execution plot in England and is greeted by an elated queen on his return. After their fraught conversation in 3.4, when she confessed *"thou hast cleft my heart in twain"*, she must have thought she would never see her *"dear Hamlet"* (3.2) again.

Sample 4.2

Will Claudius be able to contain any potential threat from the son of the man he murdered? As for Gertrude, why does she collude with her husband's decision to block Hamlet's return to Wittenberg?

As he plotted his three-step path to Denmark's throne—a murder, a marriage and an election—we can imagine the scheming mind of Claudius pondering the question: what to do with his victim's son?

It is only to be expected that Claudius would want to keep a watchful gaze (*"the cheer and comfort of our eye"*, 1.2) on his nephew. What is more difficult to understand is Gertrude's desire for Hamlet to remain at Elsinore: *"Go not to Wittenberg"* (1.2). She seems in no need of her son's company, and her interest in his well-being does not extend beyond colluding with the spying operations of Claudius and Polonius. His father's castle has indeed become Hamlet's *"prison"* (2.2) from where his *"uncle-king and aunt-mother"* (2.2) allow him no escape.

Both Claudius and Hamlet are deterred from striking openly against each other by the relationship they share with Queen Gertrude. As Claudius says to Laertes of Hamlet: *"The queen his mother / Lives almost by his looks"* (4.7). From the prince's perspective, he can see in the First Player's enactment of Hecuba's grief in 2.2 the heartbreak his mother would experience should he kill Claudius and make her a widow a second time in four months. Accordingly, both uncle and nephew *"stand in pause"* (3.3).

But following the prince's stabbing of Polonius, Claudius declares Hamlet must be removed from Elsinore, for *"His liberty is full of threats to all"* (4.1). Under the pretense of protecting his nephew (*"Yet must not we put the strong law on him"*, 4.3), he sends Hamlet to England and, unknown to the queen, to his execution.

Sample 4.3
The *"wicked speed"* (1.2) timing of Gertrude's *"o'erhasty marriage"* (2.2) deferred her son's financial inheritance from her first husband until such future time as her second husband dies.

It is not until the final act that Hamlet complains of how his uncle triumphed over him in the political contest for Denmark's throne; as he says to Horatio, Claudius *"popped between th'election and my hopes"* (5.2). However, in his very first soliloquy and regularly afterward, the prince bemoans his other loss: his financial inheritance.

According to the laws of inheritance under which Shakespeare's audience lived and died, a widow was entitled to at least one-third of her late husband's estate; the rest went to the couple's child or children. But the following condition applied: the widow could not remarry within forty days of her husband's death. If she did, the entire inheritance left by husband number one passed to the control of husband number two. Because of Gertrude's within *"A little month"* (1.2) remarriage, Hamlet now found himself financially ruined: a prince *"of shreds and patches"* (3.4).

On welcoming his two old school friends to Elsinore, the prince apologizes for being, literally, such a poor host: *"for, to speak to you like an honest man, I am most dreadfully attended"* (2.2). In responding to Rosencrantz's assuring reminder to him that he has *"the voice of the king / himself for your succession in Denmark"*, Hamlet will cite the first part of the *"something musty ... proverb"* (3.2) that runs: 'While the grass grows, the horse starves.'

Until such time as King Claudius dies, the prince was condemned to subsist on whatever allowance his uncle thought appropriate; confined in the *"prison"* (2.2) of Elsinore, he would remain the *"peasant slave"* son of a king *"Upon whose property and most dear life / A damned defeat was made"* (2.2). And if his *"uncle-father and aunt-mother"* (2.2) produced an heir, Hamlet's exclusion from both his father's throne and wealth could well be permanent.

10.5 – The descent: *"When sorrows come ..."*

To Gertrude, Ophelia's drowning allied with her son's exile represents the death of her future grandchildren who otherwise would have carried on the Hamlet dynasty at Elsinore.

For Claudius, there appears no escape from his enemies. His exile of one revenge-seeking son to England is followed only by the return of another from France. When Hamlet reappears from his death sentence, Claudius devises a plot to dispose of his nephew while appearing blameless.

Sample 5.1
The first sample suggests why Ophelia's death is a devasting blow to Gertrude. Claudius, unknown to the queen, devises a second murderous scheme to dispose of his returned nephew.

In 1.2, we saw the queen as a woman quick to move on from the past: *"All that lives must die, / Passing through nature to eternity."* Now in 5.1, Gertrude finds her future slipping away from her. Her eulogy at the funeral of Hamlet's onetime love interest expresses heartfelt sadness: *"Sweets to the sweet ... I hoped thou shouldst have been my Hamlet's wife."* To Gertrude, Ophelia's passing allied with her son's exile in England represents the death of her future grandchildren who otherwise would have carried on the Hamlet dynasty at Elsinore.

When her son reappears in 5.1, she exclaims, *"Hamlet, Hamlet!"* In this double-greeting, I hear both joy from a mother's heart and relief from a soul burdened with a measure of guilt for how events have unfolded so tragically since her *"o'erhasty marriage"* (2.2).

Claudius discovers his exile of one revenge-seeking son is followed only by the arrival and revolt of another. On learning of his father's death and 'hugger-mugger' burial, Laertes storms into Elsinore castle and holds Claudius responsible: *"O thou vile king, / Give me my father!"* (4.5). Hamlet's unexpected return to Denmark creates for Claudius the need to dispose of his troublesome nephew a second time, while again appearing blameless for his death. In 4.7, he channels Laertes' rage (*"I a noble father lost, / A sister driven into desperate terms"*) into a fatal duel with Hamlet disguised as a mere *"brother's wager"* (5.2). As the ever-duplicitous Claudius assures his co-conspirator, Laertes: *"even his mother shall uncharge the practice / And call it accident."*

Sample 5.2
Claudius plots to set the two revenge-seeking sons against each other. A traumatized Ophelia presents the queen with a gift of rue—a plant with uncomfortable associations for her.

When Gertrude is confronted by a traumatized Ophelia singing of lost love and offering her a gift of rue—a plant associated with sadness, regret and adultery—I suspect the queen was already reflecting ruefully: on her exiled son; on her dashed hopes expressed months previously to Ophelia (*"That your good beauties be the happy cause / Of Hamlet's wildness"*, 3.1); and perhaps too on how all such unhappiness has followed her remarriage when *"the funeral baked-meats / Did coldly furnish forth the marriage tables"* (1.2).

Although grief-stricken by Ophelia's apparent suicide, Gertrude is clearly overjoyed at Hamlet's unexpected reappearance and is protective of him. She orders Laertes to unhand him when the two men jostle in Ophelia's grave (*"For love of God, forbear him"*), and excuses her son's outburst as only a *"fit"* that will last merely *"awhile"* (5.1).

For Claudius, there appears no escape from his enemies. Unknown to him, old King Hamlet's spirit rose from the dead to 'ghost-write' the prince's play-within-a-play, which reenacted publicly the king's secret poisoning of his sleeping brother. Now, and again to his shock, the nephew he sent to execution in England is back on Danish soil. With his trademark cunning and with the collusion of an angry, bereaved Laertes, Claudius contrives a second plot to dispose of Hamlet. If the prince loses the rigged fencing duel, he will die from a fatal wound by sharpened, poison-tipped sword; if he wins, a poisoned chalice will be his prize. In the king's confident words: *"He cannot choose but fall"* (4.7).

Sample 5.3
Gertrude's cheerful nature gives way to despondency following the madness and death of Ophelia. Claudius' attention is absorbed by the return of Laertes and Hamlet. Has Denmark's king forgotten about the potential threat from Norway's Young Fortinbras?

Although I see her refusal in 4.5 to meet with a distressed Ophelia as typical of the queen's instinct to turn away from uncomfortable realities, I also believe something inside her has changed. I hear Gertrude's words at Ophelia's funeral (*"I hoped thou shouldst have been my Hamlet's wife … sweet maid"*, 5.1) as those of a woman who can no longer reconcile her optimistic view of life with all the calamities that have followed from her *"o'erhasty marriage"* (2.2) to Claudius.

Her lament, expressed in her only aside, that *"Each toy seems prologue to some great amiss"* (4.5) is echoed shortly afterward in the same scene by her husband's complaint: *"O Gertrude, Gertrude, / When sorrows come, they come not single spies / But in battalions."* Not least among the threats to their shared throne is evidence of simmering rebellion among their discontented subjects: *"the people muddied, / Thick and unwholesome in their thoughts and whispers."*

When in 2.2 Polonius brought news from Norway along with *"the very cause of Hamlet's lunacy"*, the king wished first to learn more of his nephew's state of mind (*"O, speak of that! / That do I long to hear"*) and only secondly about the menace to Denmark posed by Young Fortinbras' band of mercenaries. Now, in act four, the returned Hamlet again monopolizes all the king's attention. So much so that, for a second time, Claudius appears to have neglected Young Fortinbras, who is now leading an army of battle-tested men on their victorious return from *"the Polack wars"* (5.2).

10.6 – Conclusion: *"Is thy union here?"*

Gertrude is finally forced to confront the truth about her husband's character, acts to protect her son (*"O my dear Hamlet— The drink, the drink! I am poisoned"*, 5.2) and in doing so perhaps gains a measure of redemption. Claudius dies as he lived—a duplicitous and unrepentant villain.

Sample 6.1

The first sample conclusion stresses how the fates of Denmark's king and queen differ at the end. She is to some degree redeemed. Her husband, however, remains duplicitous and unrepentant to the very last.

Hamlet began the play in despair at his mother's within *"A little month"* (1.2) marriage to Claudius: *"It is not nor it cannot come to good, / But break, my heart, for I must hold my tongue"* (1.2). But the prince ends it, in his own mind at least, by extending forever into an eternity of *"sulfurous and tormenting flames"* (1.5) the incestuous union of his *"uncle-father and aunt-mother"* (2.2).

Distressed and confused in 1.5 by his encounter with his ghost-father, Hamlet used the triple pun of *"this distracted globe"*, meaning at once his mind, the world, and Shakespeare's London stage. His last words to his uncle-father in 5.2 are another example of such wordplay. As he forces the goblet of poisoned wine down the king's throat, Hamlet rhetorically asks: *"Is thy union here?"*

For the term 'union' has three meanings. Firstly, it refers to the pearl with its secret poison that Claudius added to the wine goblet (*"And in the cup a union shall be"*). Secondly, to the earthly marriage of Claudius and Gertrude (*"Father and mother is man and wife, man and wife is one flesh"*, 4.3). And thirdly, to the prospect of Denmark's royal couple remaining eternally united in an afterlife of punishment to which old King Hamlet was condemned for only *"a certain term"* (1.5).

Whatever the actual nature and extent of Gertrude's guilt, Prince Hamlet's parting words to her (*"Wretched Queen, adieu"*) reveal that the prince is unwilling to grant to his mother the forgiveness a repentant Laertes extended to him: *"Mine and my father's death come not upon thee."*

Sample 6.2

Sample conclusion number two argues that it is his mother's rather his father's death from Claudius' *"leperous distilment"* (1.5) that finally moves the *"tardy son"* (3.4) of a prince to action.

The self-deluding blindness to Claudius' villainous character that led to Gertrude to accept his proposal of marriage is most pathetically evident in the final 5.2 scene. The *"all that is I see"* (3.4) queen believes she is about to watch a sporting duel of honor. In reality, she is to be the unknowing spectator to the assassination of her son. When the prince scores two hits with his rapier against Laertes, she offers him her napkin to wipe his brow and raises the poisoned wine goblet in a toast to his continued good luck: *"Here, Hamlet ... The queen carouses to thy fortune."*

In response to the queen's reaching for the goblet, Claudius can utter only a half-hearted: *"Gertrude, do not drink."* It is a revealing moment that leaves us in no doubt Claudius places the wife he loves second to the mistress of kingly power he loves even more; he would rather lose her to death than risk losing his crown through exposure of his prince-murdering plot. Her final words (*"O my dear Hamlet—The drink, the drink! I am poisoned"*) are more than a cry for help or a warning to her son. They are a damning exposure of her husband who attempted to pass off her fainting as a response to the fencing duel: *"She swoons to see them bleed."*

I think it significant that when Hamlet finally kills Claudius he does so without making any reference to vengeance for old King Hamlet. It is his mother's rather his father's death from Claudius' poison that moves the *"tardy son"* (3.4) to action. Gertrude pays the ultimate price for her *"hoodman-blind"* (3.4) naivety, but not before she is finally forced to confront the true character of her second husband. Tragically, it is then too late for her, her son and Denmark.

Sample 6.3

Why does the queen, in defiance of her husband, drink down the goblet of poisoned wine (*"A chalice for the nonce, whereon but sipping ..."*, 4.7) Claudius intended for her son? The third sample response begins by posing this question and ends with the suggestion that Gertrude redeems herself as a mother.

In a play where almost every action can be interpreted in multiple ways, Queen Gertrude's behavior with the goblet of poisoned wine in 5.2 leaves us wondering: why does she do that? Is she just yielding to thirst? Or, when she hears Claudius say *"Gertrude, do not drink"*, does she suspect her husband of devising a death-by-poison plot for her son? And is willing to sacrifice herself in his place?

Certainly, it is the first time we see her defy her husband's wishes. The queen who earlier responded to one of the king's requests with a deferential *"I shall obey you"* (3.1) now disobeys his direction with the words: *"I will, my lord. I pray you, pardon me."*

Moreover, she follows what seems like a small act of defiance with a truth-revealing exposure that prompts Laertes' confession of guilt. As she falls from her royal throne to the floor, she undermines Claudius' attempt to explain her swooning as a reaction to the fencing duel with this damning accusation against her husband: *"O my dear Hamlet—The drink, the drink! I am poisoned."*

Hamlet's last words to Claudius in 5.2 (*"Follow my mother"*) suggest he believes it will be in the company of the prince's villainous uncle rather than his *"dear father murdered"* (2.2) that Gertrude will be eternally united. It seems a harsh judgement on a woman who in life admitted to him that her *"heart"* was *"cleft in twain"* (3.4) and who, in her death, perhaps earned a measure of redemption by acting as a self-sacrificing mother to her son.

11

The Themes of *Hamlet*

*"Lord, we know what we are,
but know not what we may be."*

A king murdered, an inhertance stolen, a family divided: Elsinore's older generation destroys its younger when two brothers—one living, one undead—battle in a *"cursed spite"* (1.5) over a crown and queen. The play ends in a *"feast"* of *"Death"* when the characters' *"deep plots"* all rebound back on their *"inventors' heads"* (5.2).

11.1 – Introduction
A theatrically-minded title character creates a play-within-a-play with a fictional avenging figure in order to motivate him to perform the stereotypical revenge hero role he believes fate has cast him in. But Prince Hamlet comes to accept that if *"providence"* (5.1) wishes him to remove Denmark's usurping king, it will provide the circumstances for him to do so—without him tainting his mind or damning his soul with the sin of revenge.

Sample 1-1
Sample introduction number one lists and summarizes the main themes of *Hamlet*, describes how they are expressed through the actions of its characters, and how they drive the play's storyline.

> Deception, revenge, madness, corruption, death, and destiny—in this essay I will explore what I regard as the main themes of Shakespeare's *Hamlet*.
>
> Appearance and reality drift ever further apart in a story of a secret murder concealed by deception (Claudius); of deception seducing willing self-delusion (Gertrude); exploiting vengeful grief (Laertes), corroding vulnerable innocence (Ophelia), and ultimately rebounding back on itself (Polonius, Rosencrantz and Guildenstern). As the play unfolds, the poison Claudius poured into his sleeping brother's ear metaphorically spreads outward until the *"whole ear of Denmark / Is ... rankly abused"* (1.5), and the natural human relationships of friendship and romantic love are corrupted by mistrust.
>
> Revenge and remembrance are present in legacies of three fathers to their sons: a reckless lust for territorial conquest (Young Fortinbras); an overvaluing of social rank and reputation (Laertes); and a soul-damning command for vengeful murder (Prince Hamlet).
>
> *Hamlet* also offers a poignant portrayal of the limits of human choice. Prince Hamlet can neither return to the university life he loved nor move forward to claim his

expected kingship. His *"fair Ophelia"* (3.1) too is trapped in a situation over which she has no control. But even the *"dread lord"* (1.2) Claudius and his *"seeming-virtuous queen"* (1.5) must in the end submit to a power greater than that of earthly monarchs. For as the play's tragic prince declares: *"Foul deeds will rise, / Though all the earth o'erwhelm them, to men's eyes"* (1.2).

Sample 1-2

Although this second introduction does not use the word 'meta-theatricality', it does suggest that *Hamlet* is at its core a play about play-acting—in politics, in theater and in life.

Shakespeare's *Hamlet* is fundamentally a story about story-telling: the stories we tell others (the murderously deceitful Claudius: *"a little shuffling"*, 4.7); the stories we tell ourselves (the opportunistically delusional Gertrude: *"All that is I see"*, 3.4); and also about seeking life's meaning and guidance for proper action in stories (Prince Hamlet: *"The play's the thing"*, 2.2).

The theatrically-minded, sparklingly eloquent Prince Hamlet struggles to discover what type of story destiny has cast him in. Is it a ghostly tale with a *"goblin damned"* (1.4) luring his soul to hell? A romantic comedy where his overtures to *"fair Ophelia"* (3.1) are thwarted by her meddlesome father? A black farce where he lugs about the remains of his murder victim whose final words are *"I am slain"* (3.4)?

And if he has been cast him as a stereotypical 'revenge hero', why does Hamlet need to create a play-within-a-play with a fictional avenging nephew Lucianus (*"Thoughts black, hands apt, drugs fit, and time agreeing"*, 3.2) to motivate him to do the deed the script expects?

The story Shakespeare has written for Prince Hamlet is, of course, a tragedy. No more than fictional characters can rewrite their author's script, Hamlet the character is not free to *"carve for himself"* (1.3) his own destiny. And just as he comes to recognize *"There is special providence in the fall of a sparrow"*, the fall of princes too is set by *"heaven ordinant"* (5.2). He is *"Hamlet the Dane"* (5.2), born a prince but fated to kill a king rather than become one.

Sample 1-3

Hamlet—a play where almost everything comes in twos. Sample introduction number three outlines how such pairs and contrasts express the play's underlying theme of dualism: appearance and reality, truth and falsehood, free will and destiny, and life and death.

For over four hundred years audiences and literary critics have sought to understand and explain Shakespeare's play *Hamlet*. From the beginning of the last century, they have been joined by psychologists who have tried to 'cure' its title character. On one point there is general agreement: almost everything in *Hamlet* appears in twos.

Two ambassadors travel between two kings, each one a childless uncle to a fatherless son; two of Hamlet's old school friends spy on him; and two gravediggers debate Ophelia's drowning. A pair of swapped fencing swords causes the death of two duelers. Each of Hamlet's parents loses their life to Claudius' poison. And when he eventually kills the usurping king who twice plotted his own death, Hamlet does so by two means.

In my view, such pairs and contrasts symbolize what I see as the play's core theme which draws together all its other concerns—deception, revenge, madness, death, free will, and destiny: dualism. *"What a piece of work is man?"* (2.2), declares the play's title character. *"How noble in reason"* but yet also the *"quintessence of dust."*

We are free to choose between truth and falsehood. But if we pretend to be someone we are not, we might suffer the ironic fate of Polonius: killed because we were mistaken for someone else. We are also free to choose between good and evil. But our evil acts—even the seemingly perfect crime of murdering a sleeping king—will eventually surface for *"There's a divinity that shapes our ends, / Rough-hew them how we will"* (5.2).

11.2 – Appearance versus reality: *"Who's there?"*

When *"The actors come hither"* in 2.2 of *Hamlet*, they arrive at an Elsinore where two theatrical performances are already in progress: a throne and queen-grab, directed by and starring the usurping Claudius; and a one-man show of madness, written and performed by his nephew, Prince Hamlet. Both the on-stage characters and we the audience struggle to tell the difference between what 'seems' and what 'is.'

Sample 2-1
Hamlet the play is a sequence of theatrical performances by characters who themselves are performing theatrically—they are continually deceiving one another as to their true natures and motives.

> The Denmark of *Hamlet* is a place where appearance and reality are as maddeningly far apart as the twin-like pair of Rosencrantz and Guildenstern are comically similar. *"He that plays the king shall be welcome"*, Prince Hamlet remarks in 2.2 on hearing of the Players' arrival. But *Hamlet* the play reveals what tragic consequences follow for people and country when the royal role is seized by a man who is driven by only amoral ambition continually concealed by *"a little shuffling"* (4.7).

What Claudius gained through a secret murder, he seeks to retain through a false show of grief (*"our whole kingdom / To be contracted in one brow of woe"*, 1.2) and legitimate monarchy (*"There's such divinity doth hedge a king"*, 4.5). His duplicitous advisor Polonius sends a spy Reynaldo after Laertes to Paris in a convoluted scheme that will include spreading malicious rumors about his own son (*"Your bait of falsehood takes this carp of truth"*, 2.1). And he exploits Ophelia's relationship with Prince Hamlet in an attempt to uncover the cause of the prince's aberrant behavior.

While others present false faces to the world, the *"hoodman-blind"* (3.4) Queen Gertrude deceives only herself. She is forced to confront the true character of her second husband only when it is too late. Her cry in 5.2 of *"The drink, the drink! I am poisoned"* prompts Laertes' exposure of Claudius: *"the King's to blame."*

Bernardo and the other castle lookouts of act one were watching in the wrong direction. In the end, Denmark was not conquered by an invading foreign army; it collapsed under a domestic web of deception.

Sample 2-2

It is not only *Hamlet* audience members who may be confused by a play in which there is so much uncertainty, ambiguity, and dramatic irony. The on-stage characters too are often unsure of what is really going on.

Although Shakespeare entitled his play a 'tragedy', to its characters *Hamlet* seems more like a baffling mystery. With Denmark's borders under threat from Norway, Polonius' irritation at what he describes to Gertrude as her son's *"pranks"* (3.4) is understandable. A plainly hurt Rosencrantz, who sees himself as dutifully carrying out the wishes of a legitimate monarch, asks of his old school friend, the prince: *"My lord, you once did love me ... what is your cause of distemper?" (3.2). Laertes has genuine cause for grief after Polonius' murder, but he is never told of the circumstances surrounding his father's death. Most poignantly, Ophelia is mystified why her prince's *"noble and most sovereign reason"* has become *"Like sweet bells jangled, out of tune and harsh"* (3.1).

It is not merely that the above characters do not know what Hamlet knows; even the prince himself cannot be sure of the difference between what 'seems' and what 'is'. Is the Ghost (*"I am thy father's spirit"*, 1.5) really a *"goblin damned"* (1.4)? Does his uncle rush *"marvelous distempered"* (3.2) from *The Murder of Gonzago* because the adapted play has caught *"the conscience of the King"* (2.2)? Or is his panic a result of the threat to his life implicit in Hamlet's revelation that on-stage murderer Lucianus is, like him, a king's nephew?

On his return to Elsinore, Prince Hamlet no longer struggles Polonius-like to *"find where truth is hid"* (2.2). He has accepted the Everlasting as the playwright of his life and death; whatever is destined to happen, will happen: *"There's a special providence in the fall of a sparrow ... the readiness is all"* (5.2).

Sample 2-3

The prince's adaptation of *The Murder of Gonzago* is just one of the many 'plays-within-a-play.' In almost every scene of *Hamlet*, one or more characters are either planning a theatrical performance or acting out one.

"Who's there?" Barnardo's opening line addresses an underlying theme of the play: the difficulty of distinguishing between appearance and reality in the character of others. For nothing is quite what it seems in *Hamlet*, and not even the dead may be who they claim to be.

Both the opening and final court scenes are themselves theatrical performances—'plays-within-a-play'—with the villainous king as playwright and lead actor. In the first, Claudius falsely acts out the role a grieving brother and, to the prince, offers himself as caring stepparent (*"think of us / As of a father"*, 1.2). In the second, Queen Gertrude thinks she is watching a sporting fencing duel (*"Here, Hamlet ... The queen carouses to thy fortune"*, 5.2). In reality, she is an unknowing spectator to the planned murder of her son. As the king earlier says to Laertes, *"even his mother shall ... call it accident"* (4.7).

At various points Shakespeare uses the motif of painting to reinforce the underlying theme of false outward appearances concealing hidden inner truths. Claudius compares his masquerading as a rightful monarch with the make-up worn by a prostitute: *"The harlot's cheek, beautied with plastering art, / Is not more ugly to the thing that helps it / Than is my deed to my most painted word"* (3.1). When he greets the First Player in 2.2, Hamlet begins a speech which he then asks him to continue; the words are from a character in Virgil's *Aeneid*, the Claudius-like *"painted tyrant Pyrrhus."* But Hamlet too will soon commit a murder, leaving behind a woman, like Hecuba, broken by grief.

11.3 – Revenge and remembrance: *"Where is thy father?"*

Dead fathers cast a shadow over the children of the Hamlet, Polonius and Fortinbras families. Revenge destroys the three children of the first two—Prince Hamlet, Laertes and Ophelia. And the son of Norway's old King Fortinbras succeeds to Denmark's throne.

Sample 3-1

This first sample summarizes the play's three revenge plot lines and describes how they interweave at the end. The final act can be regarded as a restaging of the duel fought on the day of the prince's birth—but with Norway's Fortinbras triumphing over old King Hamlet.

Although *Hamlet* addresses a wide range of themes, the play's storyline is driven by three sub-plots centered on a single topic: revenge. Prince Hamlet struggles with the burden placed on him by a vengeful Ghost who resembles *"the same figure like the King that's dead"* (1.1). But the prince realizes *"the devil hath power / T'assume a pleasing shape"* (2.2) and never hears Claudius' confession of guilt. Given that Claudius' fratricide (*"A brother's murder"*, 3.3) preceded his marriage to his victim's widow, the order of words spoken by the prince in 5.2—*"thou incestuous, murderous, damned Dane"*—suggests Hamlet revenges his own poisoning by Claudius rather than his father's.

Hamlet's blind, impulsive stabbing of the king's advisor Polonius sets in motion a second revenge plot which recasts the prince as a target rather than an agent of revenge. As Hamlet says of Laertes, *"For by the image of my cause I see / The portraiture of his"* (5.1). The manipulative king entices Polonius' angry son into a rigged fencing duel with Hamlet: *"show yourself in deed your father's son / More than in words"* (4.7). But the supposed non-lethal *"brother's wager"* (5.2) culminates in the death of the Hamlet and Polonius families.

On arriving at this bloodbath scene, Norway's Young Fortinbras receives Hamlet's *"dying voice"* (5.2) as his successor. The interwoven revenge stories end with the son of old King Fortinbras, who had been killed by old King Hamlet in a duel over a patch of land on the day the prince was born, recovering not just that territory but now inheriting the entire nation of Denmark.

Sample 3-2

Prince Hamlet, whose father's spirit commands him to commit revenge, himself becomes Laertes' target of revenge. Although the two characters respond in contrasting ways to their fathers' deaths, in the end the burden of vengeance-seeking claims both their lives.

Commanded to seek revenge by King Hamlet's Ghost— *"The serpent that did sting thy father's life / Now wears his crown"* (1.5)—Prince Hamlet, half-way through the play and with tragic irony, kills the wrong man. His blind, through-a-curtain stabbing of Polonius (*"I took thee for thy better"*, 3.4) creates a second fatherless son bent on vengeance. Always quick to see theatrical parallels, the prince later says to Laertes: *"I'll be your foil"* (5.2).

Hamlet's response to the Ghost's accusations (*"O my prophetic soul. My uncle?"*, 1.5) reveals he suspected Claudius of murdering his father. Yet the prince had still chosen to depart Elsinore and resume his life at Wittenberg. In contrast, news of Polonius' demise brings Laertes immediately home from Paris in search of answers—*"How came he dead?"* (4.5). The Ghost's revelations send Hamlet retreating inward into untrusting isolation. Polonius' son instead reaches outward to lead an angry, castle-storming mob against Claudius, which shouts, *"Choose we! Laertes shall be king!"* (4.5).

Cunningly, Claudius sets the two avengers against each other in the rigged fencing match of 5.2. But a providential swapping of swords is followed by a real exchange of forgiveness. Claudius is *"justly served"* by a *"poison tempered by himself"* and the cycle of vengeful violence—the *"cursed spite"* (1.5), as Hamlet earlier described it—is finally broken. In the end, it is not an impassioned avenger but an opportunistic adventurer who triumphs. With Denmark's two noble families of Hamlet and Polonius now wiped out, Young Fortinbras of Norway succeeds to the country's throne.

Sample 3-3
Ophelia's living father hides behind Elsinore's pillars and curtains. Hamlet's undead father conceals himself too, but is also continually and watchfully present. The spirit of old King Fortinbras lives on in his son's reckless territory-grabbing.

"Where is thy father?" Had Ophelia asked the same question of Hamlet as he does of her in 3.1, would his answer have been any less dishonest? Ophelia replies *"at home"*, when in fact Polonius and the king are eavesdropping nearby, *"seeing, unseen."* As for the prince's late father, his spirit has returned Elsinore to issue a *"dread command"* 3.4 that would damn his son's soul to hell forever. He even tinges his request with emotional blackmail: *"If thou didst ever thy dear father love"* (1.5).

Throughout the play, dead fathers cast a dark shadow over the children of the Hamlet, Polonius and Fortinbras families. Laertes' complaint to Claudius regarding Polonius' passing (an *"obscure funeral ... No noble rite nor formal ostentation"*, 4.5) are those of a son raised to prize social rank above all else. His father's duplicity is too apparent in Laertes' eagerness to join in Claudius' scheme of the murderous fencing duel.

Thirty years previously, Norway's King Fortinbras, *"pricked on by a most emulate pride"* (1.2), recklessly threw away his life in a duel with old King Hamlet over a parcel of land. Young Fortinbras, also with *"divine ambition puffed"* (4.4), arrives at Elsinore in the final scene after gaining *"a little patch of ground / That hath in it no profit but the name"* (4.4).

In 5.2, a dying Prince Hamlet too wants to be remembered, but not with revenge, social rank or territory. All he wants is his story to be told. *"Report me and my cause aright"*, he asks of Horatio. It is a tale of revenge and *"purposes mistook. / Fallen on th'inventors' heads."*

11.4 – Madness: *"Taint not thy mind"*

Hamlet claims to Laertes that he, the prince, was by *"madness ... from himself be ta'en away"* (5.2). But was Denmark's ever-theatrical prince ever really insane? But neither the play's characters nor we the audience can question Claudius' description of Polonius' daughter: *"Poor Ophelia / Divided from herself and her fair judgement"* (4.5).

Sample 4-1

Is Hamlet ever really mad – or is he just pretending to be? Whatever the answer, the prince's acting out of his "antic disposition" drives the unfortunate Ophelia into real insanity.

> *"How came he mad?"* Hamlet's question about himself to the grave-digger yields only the unhelpful response: *"On account of losing his wits ... here in Denmark"* (5.1). But is Hamlet's *"antic disposition"* (1.5) just an act by the theatre-loving prince?
>
> Although the prince is clearly traumatized by his circumstances – the father he idolized, dead (*"I shall not look upon his like again"*, 1.2); respect for his hastily remarried mother gone too (*"A beast would have mourned longer"*, 1.2); his succession hopes crushed (*"I lack advancement"*, 2.2); and his old school friends and love interest manipulated against him (*"It hath made me mad"*, 3.1) – I believe Hamlet's madness is entirely feigned. The prince uses what the king calls his *"turbulent and dangerous lunacy"* (3.1) to help him cling to his sanity – and avoid immediate execution for Polonius' murder, a crime described by Laertes as *"so capital in nature"* (4.7).
>
> With tragic irony, Hamlet's pretend insanity – and the very real rage it both conceals and reveals – is the cause of actual madness in his love interest, Ophelia. Already distraught at her prince's behavior (*"Oh, what a noble mind is here o'erthrown!"*, 3.1), Hamlet's stabbing of her only parent sends her first into madness (*"Her mood will needs be*

pitied", 4.5) and then to an apparently suicidal drowning. Gertrude's words at Ophelia's funeral (*"I hoped thou shouldst have been my Hamlet's wife ... sweet maid"*, 5.1) poignantly describe what has been lost in the unfolding tragedy.

Sample 4-2

One of the reasons *Hamlet* is Shakespeare's longest play is that its title character talks so much. Is his madness just a means for him to vent his anger at Elsinore's cast of corrupt and duplicitous characters? While Hamlet speaks in puns and riddles, Ophelia finds her own way of expressing what she really feels.

> *"But break, my heart, for I must hold my tongue"*, an anguished Hamlet declares in 1.2 when he remembers his widowed mother's wedding to Claudius only a *"little month"* after *"she followed my poor father's body ... all tears."* When he later decides after meeting the Ghost to put on an *"antic disposition"* (1.5), I suspect it is at least in part because such a talkative lover of *"words, words, words"* (2.2) cannot remain silent for very long. His feigned madness provides him with the perfect outlet for venting his rage at the falsity of Claudius, the willful self-delusion of Gertrude and the duplicity of those who serve them.
>
> Polonius he calls a *"fishmonger"* (2.2) or pimp for exploiting Ophelia as bait *"to find where truth is hid"* (2.2). Rosencrantz, he insults as a toadying *"sponge ... that soaks up the king's ... rewards"* (4.2). To Queen Gertrude, he spits out: *"would it were not so—you are my mother"* 3.4. And in 4.3, Claudius' request for the whereabouts of his advisor's dead body is met with the scornful reply: *"In heaven. Send hither to see. If your messenger find him not there, seek him i' th' other place yourself."*

When *"driven to desperate terms"* (4.7) by Elsinore's false world, Ophelia too finds a way to speak her truth: in songs of lost love and the symbolic language of flowers: fennel (flattery and deceit) for Claudius and rue (sorrow and regret) for Gertrude. Her surrender to the water and death foreshadows the suicidal return of her *"bonny sweet Robin"* (4.5) to Elsinore where, as he must know, Claudius has some fatal *"exploit"* (4.7) planned for him.

Sample 4-3

Prince Hamlet is presented with a maddening dilemma. Does it drive him mad—or is his acted-out madness his way of clinging to his sanity? Horatio never doubts his friend's sanity. And no one doubts Ophelia's poignant descent into very real madness.

> The vengeful Ghost of 1.5—*"I am thy father's spirit"*—sets Prince Hamlet a potentially maddening dilemma: how can he remove his uncle from the throne without himself becoming another Claudius—villainous in this life and damned to hell in the next? The Ghost offers no practical guidance (*"howsoever thou pursuest this act*), only a warning (*"Taint not thy mind"*).
>
> I believe Hamlet's *"antic disposition"* (1.5) is a coping mechanism for the theatrically-minded prince. He plays the role of a madman to avoid actually becoming one. Certainly, his confidant, the ever-skeptical Horatio, never doubts Hamlet's sanity. Neither does the prince ever lose his sharp awareness of other's duplicity. He sees through Rosencrantz's claim that he and Guildenstern have arrived unprompted at Elsinore: *"There is a kind of confession in your looks which your modesties have not craft enough to colour"* (2.2). Of Ophelia, he inquires, *"Where is your father?"* (3.1), suspecting correctly that the king's advisor is eavesdropping nearby.

It falls to Gertrude, to whom Hamlet has admitted *"I essentially am not in madness / But mad in craft"* 3.4, to deliver the graveside eulogy for Ophelia, who has been driven to very real and apparently suicidal insanity by the loveless, manipulative and treacherous world of Elsinore. In her so-called 'mad scene' of 4.5, Polonius' daughter hands out a range of symbolism-laden flowers—except the one that represents faithfulness: *"I would give you some violets, but they withered all when my father died."*

11.5 – Corruption, decay and death: *"An unweeded garden"*

The prince's description of Elsinore as an *"unweeded garden"* is sometimes seen as evidence of a depressed state of mind. But then the prince has a lot to be depressed about. King Hamlet's castle is now Prince Hamlet's prison, where he is surrounded by human nature at its worst. *"Fie on 't, ah fie!"*, indeed.

Sample 5-1

This first sample suggests the play's graveyard scene is just one example of its focus on the inevitability of death. The relationship between falsity and corruption in individuals and in politics is also highlighted.

> Significantly for a play that features so much discussion of decay and death, the only scene that occurs outside the castle is set in Elsinore graveyard. When Hamlet asks of the clownish sexton *"How long will a man lie i'th'earth ere he rot?"*), the reply suggests that some are already diseased in life: *"if he be not rotten before he die—as we have many pocky corses now-a-days, that will scarce hold the laying in"* (5.1).

At a time when a country's health and security were seen as linked with the moral legitimacy of its monarch, Hamlet's description in 1.2 of Denmark as *"an unweeded garden"* reflects his opinion of Claudius as a bestial *"satyr"*, a lustful half-goat and half-man. While it is not only Hamlet who doubts Claudius fitness to rule—Norway's opportunistic Young Fortinbras senses the king's weakness, Horatio fears some *"eruption to our state"* (1.1) and Marcellus famously opines *"Something is rotten in the state of Denmark"* (1.4)—the prince's obsessive speaking of decay and death reflects a deeper disgust at the falsity of life in Elsinore.

In 3.1, Hamlet chastises Ophelia—and, more generally his mother and all womankind—when he declares: *"I have heard of your paintings too, well enough. God has given you one face and you make yourselves another."* But, as the prince observes in the graveyard scene of 5.1, death will inevitability triumph over all painted makeup and disguises. Speaking to Yorick's skull, he declares: *"Now get you to my lady's chamber, and tell her, let her paint an inch thick, to this favor she must come."*

Sample 5-2
Hero and villain regard each other as contagious illnesses that can be cured only by their death.

Both Hamlet and Claudius speak of each other in similar terms. To Claudius, his troublesome nephew is *"like the hectic in my blood"* (4.3). Of the king, Hamlet asks of Horatio: *"And is't not to be damned / To let this canker of our nature come / In further evil?"* (5.2). It is the language of sickness, disease and death that is all-present throughout the play.

In 4.5, Claudius describes Ophelia's madness as *"the poison of deep grief"* and worries that rumors of Polonius' death are spreading plague-like in *"pestilent speeches"* among a restless populace. In his conversation with a revenge-seeking Laertes in 4.7, the king declares, *"But, to the quick o' the ulcer"*, referring to Hamlet. Laertes tells Claudius of his purchase of a poisonous *"unction of a mountebank"* and that news of the prince's return *"warms the very sickness in my heart."*

When Claudius, in his attempt at prayer, admits *"O, my offence is rank, it smells to heaven"* (3.3), his words echo the prince's earlier description of Denmark as an *"unweeded garden / That grows to seed; things rank and gross in nature / Possess it merely"* (1.2).

Nor does the succession of Young Fortinbras at the play's end offers much hope that the Denmark, and by extension *"this distracted globe"* (1.5), will ever be free of rulers afflicted what Hamlet calls *"some vicious mole of nature"* (1.4). For the Norwegian prince's reckless territorial conquest is yet another example of *"the imposthume of much wealth and peace, / That inward breaks and shows no cause without"* (4.4).

Sample 5-3

Prince Hamlet's first traumatic loss was not of his father, his respect for this mother or even of his throne to his uncle. It was the death of Yorick, who passed away when the prince was just seven years old. But just as the tragic prince lives on in Shakespeare's play, the fellow of 'infinite jest' survives too as part of the prince's character. There would be no *Hamlet* without Hamlet, and Hamlet would never have been Hamlet without Yorick.

If the title character's *"To be or not to be"* is the play's most famous line, its most iconic visual image is that of the prince holding a skull in the Elsinore graveyard: *"Alas, poor Yorick!"* I do not believe Shakespeare included the graveyard scene of 5.1 merely to remove from Hamlet any fear of death. As we saw in 1.5, the prince does not lack bravery. He rushed towards the Ghost despite the protective efforts of Horatio and Marcellus to restrain him; *"Unhand me, gentlemen. / By heaven, I'll make a ghost of him that lets me" (1.4)*. Nor, as his response to Claudius' request for the location of Polonius' remains revealed, does the prince need any reminding of human mortality: *"At supper ... Not where he eats, but where he is eaten ... worms are e'en at him ... we fat ourselves for maggots"* (4.2).

Instead I see the graveyard scene as a reminder that while death comes even to emperors like Alexander and Caesar, some leave behind to an often *"sterile promontory"* (2.2) of a world a life-affirming legacy of happy memories. In his only soliloquy that speaks of real human connection, Hamlet recalls the court jester Yorick as a nurturing father-figure (*"He carried me on his back a thousand times"*) and mother-figure too (*"those lips that I have kissed I know not how oft"*). Where now are those *"flashes of merriment that were wont to set the table on a roar"*, asks Hamlet? In his final moments, Hamlet will too seek to be remembered, and, thanks to the long-dead character the gravedigger calls a *"whoreson mad fellow"*, Denmark's melancholic prince lives on as literature's only tragic hero with a sense of humor.

11.6 – Conclusion: *"The fall of a sparrow"*

Elsinore's grave-diggers will be busy after the play's final act. Off-stage characters too receive their comeuppance. An ambassador brings news of Rosencrantz's and Guildenstern's execution in England. And it is old King Fortinbras rather than the revenge-seeking King Hamlet who has won this duel. Prince Hamlet does kill Claudius—but is it in revenge for his father's murder? The prince is death is as he was in life: a puzzle.

Sample 6-1

This first sample conclusion summarizes the eventual fate of the play's main characters. Two are damned, two find redemption, and all except one are revealed for the characters they really are.

"Who's these?" The question posed by Barnardo in the play's opening line is answered in the final 5.2 for all but one of the main characters.

Characteristically duplicitous to the very last, Claudius attempts to pass off Gertrude's fainting as a reaction to the fencing duel (*"She swoons to see them bleed"*). By the same means of his own poison, but by Hamlet's hand, Claudius is *"Of life, of crown, of queen at once dispatched"* (1.5).

That Gertrude did not make it a condition of her marriage to Claudius that Ophelia's *"rose and expectancy of the fair state"* (3.1) accede to the throne suggests to me her *"shameful lust"* (1.5) was in fact for the queenly role she had for three decades enjoyed. Hamlet's words to the dying Claudius (*"Follow my mother"*) indicate that she too is damned to hell.

Showing himself to be a more honorable figure than his father, Laertes achieves redemption by exposing Claudius' plot (*"the King's to blame"*), and by seeking and receiving Hamlet's pardon (*"Exchange forgiveness with me, noble Hamlet"*).

As for the prince who never said why he put on his antic disposition and admitted he did not know why he delayed his revenge, he is in death as much a puzzle as he was in life. With his final words, Hamlet requests Horatio to *"To tell my story."* But the fast-acting poison in his body means that we, *"the audience to this act"*, will hear only an incomplete version: *"Things standing thus unknown, shall live behind me!"* We can only guess what the *"sweet Prince"* would have revealed to us had he lived.

Sample 6-2
Sample conclusion number two focuses on the exposure to the court and the downfall of the play's antagonist. There is comeuppance too for his late brother's death-demanding Ghost. But no one in the play kills more people than Providence's *"scourge and minister"* (3.4), Prince Hamlet.

As is typical of revenge tragedies, *Hamlet* concludes with the exposure and comeuppance of the villain; in this case, King Claudius. His lust for *"My crown, mine own ambition, and my queen"* (3.3) drove him to commit one murder only to find that he must plot a second to cover up the first (*"His liberty is full of threats to us all"*, 4.1). When this plan failed, his next scheme of the poisoned wine goblet (*"a chalice for the nonce"*, 4.7) leads to the death of the woman he loves (*"Gertrude do not drink"*, 5.2). King Hamlet ruled his country for at least three decades. His usurping brother lasted only about six months, and ended up losing Denmark to a foreign power.

But, ironically, is not the villain but the hero Prince Hamlet who by the play's end has taken the most lives: Polonius, mistakenly (*"I took thee for thy better"*, 3.4); Ophelia, indirectly (*"He is gone, he is gone"*, 4.5); Rosencrantz and Guildenstern, deliberately (*"they did make love to this employment"*, 5.2); and Laertes, unknowingly

("*Hamlet, … The treacherous instrument is in thy hand, / Unbated and envenomed*", 5.2).

Another of the play's many ironies is that Denmark's throne passes to a ruler who is exactly the type of militarist figure old King Hamlet would have wanted and admired. But that young man is the son of his old rival, Norway's King Fortinbras. Like a poisoned Laertes, who guiltily confesses he is like *"a woodcock"* trapped in *"mine own springe"*, the blood-thirsty, revenge-obsessed Ghost, who would have damned his son's soul to hell, too receives his comeuppance.

Sample 6-3

Shakespeare's play *Hamlet* has been described as a life-affirming play in which everyone dies at the end. The title character's killing of Claudius might seem like a much-delayed fulfillment of the Ghost's *"dread command"* by his *"tardy son"* 3.4. But is it really?

Deception unmasked, comeuppance for all, and death everywhere. In the play's final scene four dead bodies lie on the stage, fatally stabbed, poisoned or both. A shocked Young Fortinbras exclaims on his arrival in 5.2: *"O proud Death, / What feast is toward in thine eternal cell."*

Claudius' manipulative schemes finally catch up with him when Gertrude—*"I could not but by her"* (4.7)—reaches for the goblet of poisoned wine. His need to conceal his plot against her son means Claudius can only manage to utter a half-hearted and ineffective *"Gertrude, do not drink"* (5.2). The queen's cry of *"O my dear Hamlet—The drink, the drink! I am poisoned"* prompts a conscience-stricken Laertes to expose Claudius for the villain he really is. With control of Denmark passing to Norway, the assembled nobles too receive their comeuppance for their choosing of brother to succeed brother rather than son to succeed father.

Hamlet's killing of Claudius is commonly described as a delayed revenge-taking for his father's murder. Personally, I am not convinced. The prince's suspicions of Claudius' involvement in old King Hamlet's death (*"O my prophetic soul. My uncle?"*, 1.5) were not enough to keep him at Elsinore. In contrast, Hamlet's discovery on board ship of the king's order for his execution in England brought him directly back to Denmark. When Hamlet kills his villainous uncle, who had *"Thrown out his angle for my proper life"* (5.2), I believe his motive is best expressed by a variation of a famous line from the movie, *"The Godfather*: 'This is not revenge. This is personal.'

12

The Theme of Revenge

"Thou prayest not well"

Two bereaved sons of Denmark journey from vengeance, through obsession and anger, to forgiveness. An opportunist from the rival kingdom of Norway succeeds to an empty throne. And the revenge sought by the Ghost of old King Hamlet on his brother in act one becomes in act five the revenge of old King Fortinbras on old King Hamlet.

12.1 – Introduction

Prince Hamlet's and Laertes' pursuit of vengeance claims both their lives, but not before they exchange forgiveness in their dying moments. The last act of Old King Hamlet's son is to reverse the outcome of the duel fought thirty years before on the day of his birth. By restoring Young Fortinbras' inheritance and adding to it the entire kingdom of Denmark, he atones for his father's sins and so ends his afterlife torment *"in fires"* (1.5).

Sample 1-1

The pursuit of revenge rebounds on the two avengers, Prince Hamlet and Laertes. As this first sample introduction asserts, their mutual destruction leaves Denmark's vacant throne to be claimed by Young Fortinbras from the rival kingdom of Norway.

Shakespeare's *Hamlet* dramatizes the journeys of two young men, Prince Hamlet and Laertes, from revenge to forgiveness. Hamlet's quest for revenge (*"I, the son of a dear father murdered, / Prompted to my revenge by heaven and hell"*, 2.2) ends halfway through the play and triggers the second revenge storyline, that of Laertes (*"I'll be revenged / Most thoroughly for my father"*, 4.5). However, each character's pursuit of vengeance rebounds on the avenger himself, like two *"purposes mistook"* that fall *"on th'inventors' heads"* (5.2).

In a *"rash and bloody deed"* (3.4), Hamlet blindly murders the wrong man—Claudius' advisor Polonius rather than the king himself: *"For this same lord, / I do repent"* (3.4). So rather than avenging the murder of his father, old King Hamlet's son succeeds only in creating in Polonius' son Laertes a second vengeance-seeker like himself. And Laertes' devious revenge plot against Hamlet ends with him losing his own life as well as causing the death of the prince. As he confesses: *"Why, as a woodcock to mine own springe ... I am justly killed with mine own treachery"* (5.2).

The play ends with the two avengers exchanging forgiveness in their dying moments, and leaves Denmark's vacant throne to be claimed by Norway's Young Fortinbras. He too had lost his father to a violent death. But his preference for patient opportunism over revenge is rewarded when the kingdom ruled for three decades by his father's killer, old King Hamlet, falls into his grasp: *"I embrace my fortune ... to claim my vantage"* (5.2).

Sample 1-2

This second introduction suggests that *Hamlet* the play is the journey of Hamlet the character towards the acceptance that *"providence"* (5.1) will provide the morally justifiable circumstances for him to remove Denmark's usurping king —without the prince tainting his mind with madness or damning his soul for the sin of revenge.

In the final 5.2 scene of Shakespeare's *Hamlet*, a messenger from the king asks the title character if he is ready to enter the fencing duel with Laertes or if he *"will take a longer time."* Prince Hamlet's response is both affirmative and shrewd. He recognizes his real adversary will not be Polonius' hot-headed son but the scheming King Claudius. Hence his reply: *"I am constant in my purposes, they follow the King's pleasure. / If his fitness speaks, mine is ready."*

After being torn for so long between the urge to avenge or not his father's death (*"In my heart there was a kind of fighting"*, 5.1), the prince has come to accept that if *"providence"* (5.1) wishes him to remove Denmark's usurping king, it will provide the morally justifiable circumstances for him to do so. He no longer feels the need to devise failure-prone *"deep plots"* (5.2). All the prince need do is be prepared to act when the moment comes, for *"the readiness is all"* (5.2). The final scene brings not just comeuppance but forgiveness too. Laertes, the father-avenger Hamlet's obsession with revenge created, is also the man who both kills the prince and pardons him: *"Mine *and my father's death come not upon thee, / Nor thine on me"* (5.2).

In the play's final irony, Denmark's crown passes to the type of figure old King Hamlet would have admired: a reckless territory-grabber who would risk his and other's lives over *"a little patch of ground / That hath in it no profit but the name"* (4.4). However, that young man is not his own *"tardy son"* (3.4) Prince Hamlet; it is the father-emulating offspring of his old rival, Norway's King Fortinbras.

Sample 1-3
This third sample introduction contrasts the responses to their fathers' violent deaths of Hamlet and Laertes on the one hand and, on the other, Norway's Young Fortinbras. It also makes the connection between the play and the biblical story of Cain and Abel. The parallels are to be found in the direct references by Claudius (*"my offence ... hath the primal eldest curse upon't"*, 3.3;) and the prince (*"as if it were Cain's jawbone, that did the first murder"*, 5.1), and in the number of lives lost in Hamlet's and Laertes' pursuit of revenge.

"Purpose is but the slave to memory" (3.2)—the words of the Player King in Shakespeare's *Hamlet* can be regarded as a summary of the three subplots that drive the play's tragic storyline. For *Hamlet* describes how the lives of three sons are overshadowed by the memories of their three fathers' violent deaths.

Of the three, Prince Hamlet and Laertes succumb to the temptation of seeking vengeance for their fathers' deaths. But first Hamlet and then Laertes fall victim to their mind-tainting obsession with revenge. In a fit of blind rage, the prince kills the wrong man: *"Is it the King? ... I took thee for thy better"* (3.4). And Laertes, following an accidental swapping of swords, in effect murders himself: *"The foul practice / Hath turned itself on me"* (5.2). The third bereaved son, Young Fortinbras of Norway, makes his move only when the man who killed his father is himself dead. His patient opportunism is rewarded when he gains for Norway the vacant throne of Denmark.

Linking the fates of the three sons is the play's antagonist, Claudius. His jealous ambition drove him to murder Prince Hamlet's father, a crime he compares to that of Cain, the first murderer in the Bible: *"My offence ... hath the primal eldest curse upon't, / A brother's murder"* (3.3). God protected Cain from human vengeance with a sevenfold curse on anyone who was tempted to seek revenge against him, for vengeance belonged only to God. Excluding that of Claudius himself, who at the end is killed in justice rather than revenge, seven is the number of deaths that follow Hamlet's and Laertes' ultimately self-destructive pursuit of revenge.

12.2 – Hamlet and his ghost-father: *"Thy dread command"*

Why doesn't Hamlet simply walk up to Claudius and run the villainous usurper through with his sword? This first set of three sample responses covers those scenes, extending over a period of two months, from the Ghost's appearance in 1.5 up to Hamlet's delivery of his *"To be or not to be"* speech in 3.1.

Sample 2-1

This first sample text suggests one answer to the question: Why does Hamlet delay his Ghost-commanded pursuit of revenge against King Claudius?' The prince is certainly capable of killing in a rage (Polonius) and with cold-blooded calculation (Rosencrantz and Guildenstern). The first sample offers one response to the question of Hamlet's famed 'delay.'

"*However thou should accomplish this act*"—the Ghost's demand of Prince Hamlet in 1.5 for revenge against Claudius is unaccompanied by any practical guidance on how this deed is to be carried out. In my opinion, the prince delays murdering King Claudius because what *"apparition"* (1.1) presents Hamlet with is a *"Cudgel thy brains"* (5.1) dilemma.

We, the audience, twice hear Claudius' confession—*"O heavy burden!"* (3.1) and *"a brother's murder"* (3.3)—and are so certain of the king's guilt. But what if, like Hamlet, we had not? Claudius' alleged crime left behind neither witnesses nor evidence. What would we do? The king he has been asked to assassinate has been duly elected as Denmark's monarch by his country's nobles in their *"better wisdoms"* (1.2). Moreover, he is also to man to whom the prince's mother is very happily—if incestuously—married. How cruel would it be to make her a widow a second time?

Hamlet responds to his ghost-father in 1.5 as he did earlier to his uncle-father in 1.2—with verbal evasion. Then he replied to Claudius' request to *"think of us / As of a father"* with *"I am too much in the sun."* The oath the prince swears on the castle battlements after midnight is not to avenge the Ghost but only never to forget him: *"Now to my word. / It is 'Adieu, adieu. Remember me.' / I have sworn't."* Trapped between feelings of inadequacy in this world (*"Am I a coward?"*, 2.2) and fear of damnation in the next (*"The spirit that I have seen / May be the devil"*, 2.2), Hamlet takes refuge in a put-on *"antic disposition"* (1.5) that both hides and expresses his inner turmoil.

Sample 2-2

This second sample response suggests that Hamlet's feigned madness is a cunning plan to escape execution on the grounds of temporary insanity should the prince actually murder the king and face a trial for the crime of regicide.

After his conversation with the Ghost, Hamlet declares he will *"put an antic disposition on"* (1.5). What Claudius later describes as the prince's *"transformation"* (2.2) makes the king more rather than less suspicious of his nephew. Yet I believe there is a *"method"* in Hamlet's *"madness"* (2.2).

In my opinion, the prince is setting in place a defense of temporary insanity should he face a trial before Denmark's nobles for the murder of Claudius. After Ophelia's rejection of him at Polonius' command, he further pretends it is *"The pangs of despised love"* (3.1) that is the cause of *"the madness in which he now raves"* (2.2). Hence, his *"doublet all unbraced"* (2.1) visit to Ophelia's closet, his teasing of Polonius (*"Have you a daughter?"*, 2.2), and his risqué banter at *The Murder of Gonzago* (*"Here's metal more attractive"*, 3.2).

But, beset by doubts of the Ghost's truthfulness (*"the devil hath power / To assume a pleasing shape"*, 2.2), Hamlet delays performing the part of the *"Mad as the sea and wind"* (4.1) assassin, a role he later adopts with Laertes to excuse his *"rash and bloody"* (3.4) murder of Polonius: *"His madness is poor Hamlet's enemy"* (5.1).

Tragically, the prince's feigned madness leads to Ophelia's very real and suicidal insanity. Hamlet shares his 'antic' ploy with Horatio and the guard Marcellus, so they should not lose confidence in him as a future king, however *"strange or odd soe'er I bear myself"* (1.5). But the prince comes to be regarded as *"he that is mad, and sent into England"* (5.1). In summary, I see Hamlet's pretend insanity as one example of the play's many *"purposes mistook"* that in the end fall *"on th'inventors' heads"* (5.2).

Sample 2-3
Even after he has made up his mind to follow a course of action, Hamlet can't seem to resist falling back on some intellectual speculation as to the dilemma that confronts him. This third sample response focuses on the prince's *"To be or not to be"* speech.

"To be or not to be" (3.1)—it is significant that Hamlet delivers the speech that begins with these words after he has already committed to a course of action: of using the visiting Players to *"catch the conscience of the King"* (3.2). It tells us that the *"thinking too precisely on th'event"* (4.4) prince is still struggling with the question: what is the right thing to do? For Hamlet, the alternative to life is the suicide mission of assassinating Denmark's legitimately elected monarch at the request of an *"apparition"* (1.1). I believe Shakespeare's audience would have regarded regicide on such dubious grounds as a crime punishable by immediate and merited execution.

More generally, Hamlet's dilemma is the timeless and universal choice between acceptance (*"To be"*) and action (*"not to be"*). Should we passively endure the *"calamity of ... life"* with all its *"slings and arrows"*? Or take on *"a sea of troubles"* by seeking to change the world for the better? For doing the latter may damn our souls if we are tempted into committing a wrong to achieve a rightful goal.

Both the classical and Christian worldviews each offer different responses. The Players remind us in 2.2 of how the Greek warrior Pyrrhus savagely avenged his father's death. But the character Horatio, *"more an antique Roman than a Dane"* (5.2), provides a contrary example of stoic endurance. For Christians, vengeance belonged only to God, but as Hamlet asks Horatio, might a Christian not also *"in perfect conscience"* take a life to prevent *"further evil"* (5.2)? The scholar Hamlet, a man of reason, cannot reason his way to a solution. He is trapped in a tragic storyline in which, as Claudius observes later, *"he shall not choose but fall"* (4.7).

12.3 – Hamlet and his aunt-mother: *"Up, sword ... My mother stays"*

In the chapel and closet scenes of act three, we see that Hamlet has added a second quest to the Ghost's command for revenge. The prince's parallel aim is part demonic and part poignant: to damn his uncle's soul to hell, and to reunite in the afterlife of heaven his fractured family of father and mother.

Sample 3-1

The Ghost's directions to Hamlet were clear: kill Claudius and ignore your mother, Queen Gertrude: *"let thy soul contrive / Against thy mother aught. Leave her to heaven"* (1.5). But, as this first sample response argues, the prince cannot so easily abandon his mother to her fate. *"Like a man to double business bound"* (3.3), Hamlet's revenge mission is complicated by his wish to rescue his mother's soul as well as damning his uncle's to hell.

> If Hamlet struggles with the Ghost's command regarding Claudius (*"Revenge"*, 1.5), he defies completely his direction about Gertrude (*"Leave her to heaven"*, 1.5). In 3.2, the prince shares with Horatio his motive for requesting the visiting Players to stage *The Murder of Gonzago* with additional content that *"comes near the circumstance ... of my father's death."* As he soliloquized earlier, it is to *"catch the conscience of the King"* (2.2).
>
> But as the performance unfolds, it becomes clear that the conscience-catching target of the Players' show is as much Hamlet's *"seeming virtuous"* (1.5) mother as his uncle. The spoken play shows a soon-to-be-widowed Player Queen vowing she will never remarry: *"Both here and hence pursue me lasting strife / If, once a widow, ever I be wife!"* (3.2). It is then that Hamlet pointedly questions his mother: *"Madam, how like you this play?"* (3.2). Later, in her closet, he confronts her directly with the accusation: *"As kill a king and, marry with his brother"* (3.4).

I believe Hamlet seeks to separate his mother from Claudius to minimize the devastation she will feel at her second husband's death. Hamlet's words over Polonius' lifeless body are a clear statement that he intends his next victim to be the king: *"Thus bad begins and worse remains behind"* (3.4). Moments earlier, the prince deferred striking Claudius because of his wish to murder the king's soul as well as his body. The double irony is that Hamlet's delay both extended the king's earthly life and spared his still unrepentant soul. For Claudius' attempts at prayer were unsuccessful: *"My words fly up, my thoughts remain below"* (3.3).

Sample 3-2

On his knees in his private chapel, the usurping King Claudius is an easy target for the prince's sword: *"Now I might do it pat, now he is praying"* (3.3). But Hamlet wonders would the king's soul ascend to heaven rather than fall to hell if the prince murdered him while he is at prayer.

Hamlet's staging of *The Murder of Gonzago* does indeed cause Claudius to be *"struck so to the soul"* and sends him to his knees to *"proclaim"* his *"malefactions"* (2.2). Unfortunately for the prince, his uncle confesses his crime in his private chapel rather than publicly in front of the court. Such an admission to the *"general ear"* (2.2) would have relieved Hamlet of the burden of revenge and virtually assured his succession to the throne.

Torn between repenting his sins or retaining *"My crown, mine own ambition, and my queen"* (3.3), Claudius feels *"like a man to double business bound"* (3.3) The man he is like is, of course, Hamlet. The prince defers striking the kneeling-in-prayer Claudius. His states he will wait until he catches the king in a state of sin (*"some act / That has no relish of salvation in't"*, 3.3).

> But perhaps another and more poignant reason for Hamlet's delay is contained in the prince's words: *"Up, sword ... My mother stays"* (3.3). For it reveals that the prince seeks to rescue his mother's soul (*"Repent what's past. Avoid what is to come"*, 3.4) as well damning his uncle's (*"as damned and black / As hell, whereto it goes"*, 3.3). In other words, Hamlet's quest has evolved beyond Ghost-commanded revenge to a second, more poignant quest: to reunite in the afterlife of heaven his fractured-by-Claudius family of mother and father.
>
> But, in his mother's closet, Hamlet blindly and impulsively kills the wrong man. For the second half of the play Hamlet's role changes from avenger to the target of revenge, as Polonius' angry, bereaved son Laertes seeks to murder the man who murdered his father.

Sample 3-3

The Claudius we see in the chapel scene of 3.3 is no smiling villain, but an imperfect man tortured by a troubled conscience. As for Prince Hamlet, in his wish to murder both Claudius' soul and body, the prince resembles the politician he later condemns in the graveyard scene because he *"would circumvent God"* (5.1).

> Just as Claudius knows nothing of the Ghost's revelations, he is also unaware of Hamlet's plan to use the Players' performance to test his *"occulted guilt"* (3.2). But when the play-within-play begins, the prince abandons his scheme of scrutinizing the king's countenance in favor of a provocative running commentary. It is when Hamlet identifies the stage murderer Lucianus as the *"nephew to the king"* (3.2) that a panicked Claudius flees the hall and Polonius calls out *"Give over the play"* (3.2).

Swept up with *"the motive and cue for passion"* (2.2) that the reenactment of his father's murder and mother's seduction has provided, Hamlet is no longer paralyzed by *"my weakness and my melancholy"* (2.2) but is ready to *"do such bitter business"* (3.2). When he encounters the kneeling-in-prayer Claudius, I suspect Hamlet's speculation about the king's soul is just one reason why he defers striking until a more opportune time.

In my opinion, Hamlet at some level recognizes that were he to succeed to the throne by means of such a cowardly murder, he might find himself struggling Claudius-like with a tormented conscience and *"limed soul"* (3.3). And like the king, he could find forgiveness only by giving up *"those effects for which (he) did the murder"* (3.3).

It is in his mother's closet that the rage which has been building inside him finally explodes. Hamlet's blind, through-a-curtain stabbing of Polonius sends the play's storyline on its tragic, downward course. It drives Ophelia into suicidal madness, and in Laertes creates a second fatherless son whose obsession with revenge will end both his and Hamlet's lives.

12.4 – Laertes: *"I'll be your foil"*

The contrast between Laertes and Hamlet is not between action and delay but between reason and passion. Laertes too is delayed: first by Gertrude (*"But not by him"*, 4.5); then by Claudius (*"I pray you, go with me"*, .4,5); and later, at his sister's funeral, by the king, queen, Horatio and the prince himself (*"Hold off thy hand"*, 5.1). Cunningly, Claudius sets the two sons of murdered fathers against each other in the rigged fencing duel of the final scene.

Sample 4-1
The first sample response notes the similarity between the Ghost and King Claudius in that each seeks to lure a bereaved son into seeking revenge for the murder of their father.

"Was your father dear to you?" (4.7)—King Claudius' manipulative question of a grieving and angry Laertes reminds us of old King Hamlet's emotional blackmailing of his son: *"If thou didst ever thy dear father love ..."* (1.5). The Ghost wanted revenge against the brother he claims stole his throne and wife. Now, that same brother Claudius plots the death of the prince who threatens his hold on each.

Laertes' words of how he has *"a noble father lost, / A sister driven into desperate terms"* (4.7) echo Hamlet's appraisal of his own situation: *"a father killed, a mother stained"* (4.4). However, the prince evaded Claudius' offer to *"Think of us / As of a father"* (1.2) by replying only to the queen that *"I shall in all my best obey you, madam"* (1.2). Laertes, after an initial rebellious outburst, is converted by Claudius' *"witchcraft of his wit"* (1.5) from adversary to ally, and submits to the king's invitation: *"Will you be ruled by me?"* (4.7).

Laertes' revelation to Claudius of his purchase of an *"unction from a mountebank"* (4.2) reveals he has few scruples about how he might achieve his revenge. Earlier, Hamlet restrained from striking a kneeling-in-prayer Claudius in his private chapel. Laertes declares himself ready *"To cut his throat i'th'church"* (4.7). Claudius, who was unaware of Hamlet's intrusion into his private chapel, ironically concurs with Laertes that *"No place, indeed, should murder sanctuarize. / Revenge should have no bounds"* (4.7). Cunningly, Claudius devises a ploy to set the two sons of murdered fathers against each other in the rigged fencing duel of the play's final scene.

Sample 4-2

Sample response number two illustrates some of the ways that Polonius' son Laertes provides a dramatic contrast in personality and action to Prince Hamlet.

Half-way through the play and with tragic irony, Prince Hamlet's sword finds the wrong target: the man who helped put Claudius on the throne rather than Claudius himself. The prince's blind, through-a-curtain stabbing of Polonius (*"Take thy fortune ... Thou intruding fool, farewell"*, 3.4) creates a second grieving son of a murdered father.

The role of Laertes in the play is to provide a dramatic contrast to the title character. Always quick to see theatrical parallels, Hamlet says of Polonius' son to Horatio: *"For by the image of my cause I see / The portraiture of his."* And later to Laertes himself: *"I'll be your foil"* (5.2).

Hamlet's response to the Ghost's accusations (*"O my prophetic soul. My uncle?"*, 1.5) reveals he suspected Claudius of murdering his father. Yet the prince had still chosen to depart Elsinore and resume his former life at Wittenberg University. In contrast, rumors (*"pestilent speeches"*, 4.5) of Polonius' death brought Laertes immediately home from Paris in search of answers from the king: *"How came he dead?"* (4.5).

The Ghost's revelations sent Hamlet retreating inward into untrusting isolation. Polonius' son instead reaches outward to lead a rebellion against Claudius: *"Choose we! Laertes shall be king!"* (4.5). Hamlet reflects that conscience makes *"cowards of us all"* (3.1). Laertes, however, consigns *"Conscience and grace, to the profoundest pit!"* (4.5). And the question which Hamlet asked of himself in his self-berating soliloquies, Claudius now asks of Laertes: *"What would you undertake / To show yourself in deed your father's son / More than in words?* (4.7).

Sample 4-3

Horatio in 1.1 tells us how Young Fortinbras' inheritance was lost by his father in a fatal duel. Hamlet's inheritance, the kingdom of Denmark, is stolen by Claudius. But what of Laertes' inheritance?

"Dead"—Claudius' single-word response to Laertes' question of *"Where is my father?"* (4.5) may seem callous. But Shakespeare's audience would have understood that the king's public acknowledgment of Polonius' death would also come as a relief to his son. For had his father simply disappeared, Laertes' inheritance would have passed to the crown rather than to him. Already in possession of the inheritances of both Prince Hamlet and Young Fortinbras, the usurping Claudius would then have acquired Laertes' inheritance as well.

In common with Hamlet, Laertes lacks reliable information about the circumstances of his father's death. For as Claudius states in 4.5, Polonius' secret (*"hugger-mugger"*) burial was followed by widely circulating rumors (*"pestilent speeches"*) not based on fact (*"of matter beggared"*) as to the nature of his demise.

But unlike Hamlet and in response to Claudius' manipulative urging, Laertes unreservedly assumes the role of the stereotypical avenger in which the Ghost wished to cast Hamlet. Whereas the prince soliloquized about *"the dread of something after death"* (3.1), Laertes unhesitatingly declares *"I dare damnation"* (4.5).

In 4.7, the king exploits Laertes' vanity as a swordsman (*"a quality / Wherein, they say, you shine"*, 4.7) to draw him into his scheme to dispose of Hamlet, with the assurance that not *"even his mother shall uncharge the practice / And call it accident."* However, Claudius seems to have little confidence in Laertes' ability, either to keep their plot a secret (*"keep close within your chamber"*) or to win the fencing contest (*"If this should fail … I'll have prepared him / A chalice"*).

12.5 – Young Fortinbras: *"Lands lost by his father"*

No one in the play delays longer than Young Fortinbras of Norway. Thirty years lapse before he makes his move against Denmark, and then only when his father's killer is himself dead. That Young Fortinbras's uncle can so easily bribe him into diverting his troops into attacking Poland is proof that what drives Fortinbras is not revenge but the prospect of land and military glory.

Sample 5-1

The first sample response compares and contrasts the characters and actions of Denmark's Prince Hamlet with those of his princely counterpart in the neighboring kingdom of Norway. Hamlet's one act in his few moments as Denmark's monarch is to give his *"dying voice"* (5.2) to the son of the man his father killed on the day of the prince's birth.

> Horatio may be Hamlet's confidant who the prince holds in his *"heart of heart"* (3.2). But he never forgets his inferior rank to old King Hamlet's son and always addresses him as 'My lord.' Only one character in the play is Prince Hamlet's political and social equal. That he is introduced to us through Horatio as *"young Fortinbras"* in the same scene he speaks of *"young Hamlet"* (1.1) suggests we are to compare their characters, situations, and actions.
>
> Both are princes who attempt to deceive their respective uncle-kings. Hamlet pretends to be insane; under the guise of attacking Poland, Fortinbras seeks to *"recover lands lost by his father"* (1.1) to Denmark thirty years previously. Moreover, Fortinbras' hired mercenaries—*"a list of lawless resolutes, / For food and diet"* (1.2)—mirror the role of the Players who will, on Hamlet's command, be *"well bestowed"* (2.2) in exchange for performing the adapted play-within-a-play, *The Murder of Gonzago*.
>
> The similarly-named Polonius and Poland serve as diversions in the tragedy's unfolding storyline—but with entirely opposite results. Hamlet and Ophelia will never

rule as king and queen because the prince's mistaken murder of Laertes' father sets him up as a victim of revenge and sends Ophelia to apparent suicide. Although forced by his uncle *"never more / To give th'assay of arms"* (2.2) against Denmark, Fortinbras' diversion into Poland becomes a stepping-stone to Denmark's kingship. In the play's final irony, Prince Hamlet's one act in his short moment as his country's monarch is to give his *"dying voice"* (5.2) to the son of the man his own father killed on the day of his birth.

Sample 5-2

Sample response number two stresses the key difference in motivation between Young Fortinbras and the play's other two fatherless sons, Prince Hamlet and Laertes. Fortinbras' aim is military glory not personal revenge against his father's murderer.

I do not see Norway's Young Fortinbras as the play's third revenge-seeking son. Hamlet declares he will *"sweep to my revenge"* (1.5) and Laertes rants about how *"I'll be revenged / Most thoroughly for my father"* (4.7). But Fortinbras never speaks of revenge; nor does any other character describe him as an avenger.

Unlike the fathers of Hamlet and Laertes, his died in honorable combat—a fatal duel with a mutually agreed prize of territory set out in *"a sealed compact / Well ratified by law"* (1.1). After a lapse of thirty years, Fortinbras makes his move against Denmark only after his father's killer is himself dead. No one in the play delays longer than Fortinbras.

Nor does his character demonstrate qualities of military leadership supposedly absent in the scholarly Hamlet and hot-headed Laertes. In 1.5, Elsinore's guards unhesitatingly swear an oath on the prince's sword before departing in a soldier-like band of brothers, *"come, let's go together."* Laertes inspires an unarmed crowd to rebellion against Claudius' Switzers. In contrast, Fortinbras' only followers are hired mercenaries (*"lawless resolutes"*, 1.2) and, later, soldiers directed to do so by his uncle. His Polish adventure is regarded by one of his own captains as a purposeless quest for *"a little patch of ground / That hath in it no profit but the name"* (4.4).

Fortinbras' sole insight was his recognition that Claudius would prove an inferior king to the man he succeeded. His good fortune was to be in the right place and time when Denmark's royal family of Hamlet self-destructed.

Sample 5-3

As this third sample response states, Prince Hamlet and Young Fortinbras never actually meet. But Hamlet's encounter with one of his captains halfway through the play prompts yet another of the prince' self-berating soliloquies.

Halfway through the play, Prince Hamlet and Young Fortinbras pass each other without actually meeting: one is dispatched to England in a secret execution plan; the other is diverted into Poland after agreeing *"never more / To give th'assay of arms"* (2.2) against Denmark.

Both young men share the names of their respective dead fathers and hold equivalent positions as princes in countries ruled by their uncle-kings. But their motivations could not be more different. While Hamlet is revenge-obsessed, Fortinbras is an opportunist who is stirred to action by the death of Hamlet's father rather than his own. That for *"three thousand crowns in annual fee"* (2.2) he is willing to divert his plundering troops from Denmark to Poland makes clear his motivation: the prospect of land and military glory.

As his meeting with the Players did earlier, the sight of Fortinbras army prompts Hamlet to berate himself for his inaction. Then he was astonished at how an actor could be so moved by the plight of a fictional character: *"And all for nothing ... For Hecuba!"* (2.2). Now he marvels at how men would for *"a fantasy and trick of fame ... fight for a plot ... Which is not tomb enough ... To hide the slain"* (4.4). Hamlet's musings that *"A thought which, quartered, hath but one part wisdom / And ever three parts coward"* (4.4) reveals he is still unsure whether to attribute his inaction to the presence of conscience or a lack of willpower: *"I do not know."* He ends this speech with the words *"My thoughts be bloody."* But his two months of murderous *"imaginations ... as foul / As Vulcan's stithy"* (3.2) have not been enough to unseat Claudius from the throne.

12.6 – Conclusion: *"Exchange forgiveness with me"*
Elsinore's world of deception collapses in a truth-revealing final scene. Laertes exposes the villainy of the king who is then murdered by a dying Prince Hamlet. And it is not the son of old King Hamlet but the son of his rival, old King Fortinbras of Norway, who succeeds to the throne of Denmark.

Sample 6-1
With Polonius and Ophelia already dead, the final scene adds six other victims—Gertrude, Hamlet, Laertes, Claudius, Rosencrantz and Guildenstern—to the play's list of lives lost. The first sample conclusion asks the question: which of the play's characters is ultimately responsible for this carnage?

Showing himself to be a more honorable man than his father, a conscience-stricken Laertes brings the play to its conclusion with his truth-revealing declaration that *"The King's to blame"* (5.2). But which king?

Claudius is the obvious candidate to blame for the bloodbath that confronts the arriving Fortinbras. For the *"arrant knave"* (1.5) is exposed as responsible, if indirectly, for Gertrude's and Laertes' deaths, and vicariously for Prince Hamlet's: *"In thee there is not half an hour of life"* (5.2). Hamlet's killing of the villainous Claudius is not the Ghost's sought-for *"Revenge"* (1.5), but his own spontaneous response to the king's revealed guilt. Thus, Hamlet never actually carries out the revenge he never vowed to perform.

But what of old King Hamlet, *"the King that's dead"* (1.2)? Perhaps the blame lies ultimately with him? What if the Ghost not returned from the grave? Or had asked instead for prayers to end the suffering of two souls: his in the *"sulfurous and tormenting flames"* (1.5) of purgatory; and his brother's in Elsinore's chapel, *"limed"* and *"struggling to be free"* (3.3)?

The third candidate for blame is the play's title character, who on his return from his sea voyage introduced himself with the kingly title of *"Hamlet the Dane"* (5.1). Had he heeded Horatio's advice against conversing with the Ghost, lest it *"tempt you toward the flood, my lord"* (1.4), perhaps Polonius would yet be alive, Laertes still in France, and his *"fair Ophelia"* (3.1), to whom he made *"made many tenders / Of his affection"* (1.3), would not have become *"Divided from herself"* (4.5) and surrendered to despair and death in the *"weeping brook"* (4.7)?

Sample 6-2

Gertrude's reaching for the poisoned wine goblet intended for Hamlet and the swapping of the two fencing swords are the catalysts that expose Claudius' corruption and transform private vengeance into public justice. Are they evidence for the intervention of *"providence"* (5.2) in the play's final scene?

In 5.1, Hamlet's exchange with Laertes in Ophelia's grave reveals how the prince has left behind the vengeful anger that now holds Polonius' son in its grip. When Laertes exclaims *"The devil take thy soul!"*, Hamlet, who earlier asked *"shall I couple hell?"* (1.5) replies: *"Thou prayest not well."*

As his letter to Claudius (*"I am set naked on your kingdom"*, 4.7) shows, the prince has returned to Denmark without a plan of action. In conversation with Horatio, he believes the *"providence"* (5.2) to which attributes his escape from execution will provide morally justifiable circumstances for him to complete the task for which *"my fate cries out"* (1.4): *"To quit (Claudius) with this arm"* (5.2). Hamlet no longer feels the need to devise failure-prone *"deep plots"* (5.2); all the prince need do is be prepared, for *"the readiness is all"* (5.2).

In a final 5.2 scene, Elsinore's world of deception collapses in a truth-revealing resolution. Gertrude dies after drinking from the poisoned wine goblet Claudius intended for her son. An accidental swapping of swords leaves Laertes dying from his own poison, but only after he has fatally stabbed Hamlet. Following Laertes' public exposure of Claudius' guilt (*"The King's to blame"*), the prince twice strikes his villainous uncle: he stabs him with the poisoned sword (for his own death); and then forces down his throat the poisoned wine (for this mother's). It is more public execution than private vengeance.

But has villainy been *"justly served"* through the intervention of *"the divinity that shapes our ends"* (5.2)? Or has the ending been just another turn of the *"wheel"* of *"fortune"* (2.2) of which the Players spoke?

Sample 6-3

So much commentary on *Hamlet* focuses on the theme of revenge. But what of revenge's opposite: forgiveness? At the play's end, Laertes extends the hand of forgiveness to Hamlet. And Hamlet's concession of Denmark to Young Fortinbras can be seen as an expression of atonement for his father's sins that might shorten his soul's suffering the flames of purgatory. Thus, the son who struggled with the Ghost's other commands—kill Claudius in revenge, ignore your mother and preserve your sanity—in his final act breaks the last one: *"Pity me not"* (1.5).

Hamlet the play is commonly regarded as containing three interrelated stories about revenge. There is revenge debated (Hamlet); revenge impulsively pursued (Laertes); and revenge deferred for decades in favor of timely opportunism (Fortinbras). But to the extent that it is a revenge play, *Hamlet* is also a forgiveness play: forgiveness, withheld (old King Hamlet); forgiveness, refused (Claudius and Gertrude); and, in the end, forgiveness both offered and accepted (Laertes and Hamlet).

On his knees in his private chapel, Claudius recognizes he cannot attain forgiveness while he remains *"possessed / Of those effects for which I did the murder"* (3.3). As for Gertrude, we see no evidence that she heeds the *"guilt"* in her *"sick soul"* (4.5) but instead remains at Claudius' side on Denmark's throne.

Speaking of the conflict between his father and uncle, Hamlet declared, *"O cursed spite that I was born to set it right"* (1.5). But in the final scene it is not the prince but Laertes who ends the cycle of violent retribution with the words: *"Exchange forgiveness with me, noble Hamlet. / Mine and my father's death come not upon thee, Nor thine on me."* (5.2).

As for old King Hamlet (*"Alas, poor Ghost"*, 1.5), by surrendering Denmark to his rival's son perhaps the prince granted his *"dear father murdered"* (2.2) something more than the revenge he demanded: forgiveness for his land-grabbing, *"Extorted treasure in the womb of earth"* (1.1) sins committed *"in his days of nature"* (1.5)—and with it escape from his suffering in the *"sulfurous and tormenting flames"* (1.5) of purgatory.

13

The Theme of Appearance Versus Reality

"I know not seems"

Echoing the grave-digger's comment that *"an act hath three branches"* (5.1), *Hamlet* the play can be regarded as an extended triple pun on the verb 'to act': to take action, to behave deceitfully, and to perform in theater. The conflict between appearance and reality poisons the characters' relationships until the guilty and innocent are both destroyed. Even the *"green girl"* (1.3) Ophelia does *"not escape calumny"* (3.1).

13.1 – Introduction

Who's there?— the play's opening question is one the characters of *Hamlet* ask of each other in a world where outward appearances cannot be trusted.

Even the virtuous Horatio is drawn into Elsinore's web of deception when he agrees to Prince Hamlet's request to keep secret the Ghost's midnight visitations: *"If you have hitherto concealed this sight, / Let it be tenable in your silence still"* (1.2). As for the returned-from-the-grave apparition (*"I am thy father's spirit"*, 1.5), is he really who he claims to be?

Sample 1.1

When *"The actors come hither"* in 2.2 of *Hamlet*, they arrive at an Elsinore where two theatrical performances are already in progress. The first sample introduction suggests that Shakespeare's play can be regarded as an extended triple pun on the verb 'to act.'

> Play-acting did not begin at Elsinore with the arrival of the *"tragedians of the city"* (2.2), as the prince's old school friend Rosencrantz describes them. The visiting troupe of fictional actors—played, meta-theatricality, by a troupe of real actors—comes to a castle where two performances are already in progress.
>
> One is a charade of legitimate kingship, directed by and starring a villainous usurper. In secret, Claudius poisoned his brother and predecessor, old King Hamlet. In public, he acts out the role of a grieving family member (*"our whole kingdom ... in one brow of woe"*, 1.2) and benevolent monarch (*"What wouldst thou beg, Laertes, / That shall not be my offer, not thy asking?"*, 1.2). The second work of theater is a one-person show of madness, conceived and performed by his nephew, Prince Hamlet. So convinced is Ophelia by Hamlet's role-playing that she declares: *"Oh, what a noble mind is here o'erthrown!"* (3.1).

Echoing the grave-digging sexton's comment that *"an act hath three branches"* (5.1), *Hamlet* can be regarded as an extended triple pun on the verb 'to act': to take action, to behave deceitfully and to perform in theater.

In this essay, I will explore the challenges faced by the play's major characters as they struggle to distinguish between appearance and reality in the duplicitous world which, through their own deceptive actions, each helps to create. *Hamlet* ends with a truth-revealing resolution when, as Horatio phrases it, the characters' deceptive ploys—including *"carnal, bloody, and unnatural acts"*—all fall on *"th'inventors heads"* (5.2).

Sample 1.2

As this second sample introduction asserts, *Hamlet* is a play where everything comes in twos. Such pairs and contrasts remind us that Elsinore is a two-faced world where every major character leads a double life.

In 2.2 of Shakespeare's *Hamlet*, the king and queen recruit two of the prince's old school friends in an effort to uncover the source of what Claudius describes as Hamlet's *"transformation."* As they depart on their mission, they are thanked with the following words:
Claudius: Thanks, Rosencrantz and gentle Guildenstern.
Gertrude: Thanks, Guildenstern and gentle Rosencrantz.

That the royal couple seems unable to tell one old school friend from the other is more than a comic moment; it is an expression of an underlying theme of the play: the difficulty of correctly identifying the true, authentic selves of others—and by extension, of distinguishing between reality and appearance, between what actually 'is' and what merely 'seems.'

Almost everything in *Hamlet* appears in twos: two ambassadors travel between two kings, each one a childless uncle to a fatherless son; two clownish grave-diggers debate Ophelia's drowning; two swords are accidentally swapped between two sons of murdered fathers, causing both their deaths. Both of Hamlet's parents lose their lives to Claudius' poison. And when he eventually kills the usurping king, the prince does so by two means.

Such pairs and contrasts reinforce the fact that almost everyone in the play leads a double life: their public face is a mask behind which they hide their true thoughts and motives. In this essay, I will explore the actions of the major characters in Elsinore's two-faced world, both as practitioners of deception, and, ultimately, as victims of it.

Sample 1.3

The third sample introduction describes Shakespeare's *Hamlet* as 'meta-theatrical'—that is, as a play about play-acting. *Hamlet* is a work of fiction in which actors play characters who themselves are acting fictitiously.

For example, the role of King Claudius is played by an actor. The person we see on stage or in a film adaptation isn't actually (in 'real life') the King of Denmark; he is just someone pretending to be. And, meta-theatrically, the King of Denmark in the play is not Denmark's true king either, but a murderous usurper who masquerades as a legitimate monarch.

> 'It's so meta.' That's what a modern critic might say when describing a self-referential moment on stage or screen; for example, when one character states to another: "This isn't some make-believe story, this is real life." With this remark, the first character is attempting to convince the second of the situation's realism. On hearing the same remark, however, the audience is reminded that neither is a 'real person'—the two are characters in a fictional story.

Shakespeare's *Hamlet* can be regarded as a play about play-acting that is rich in such meta-theatricality—that is, theater about theater.

For example, Claudius' kingship is both real and at the same time false. Hamlet's 'antic disposition' is a put-on pretense; yet, it also reveals his genuine inner turmoil. The king's murderous command for *"The present death of Hamlet. Do it, England"* (4.3) is spoken to a London audience in the Globe theater which the prince punningly referred to earlier as *"this distracted globe"* (1.5). The Hamlet who bitterly contrasts his inaction with the Player's *"in a fiction"* (2.2) performance of Hecuba's grief is himself only a fictional character.

At the mid-point of *Hamlet*, the prince stages a 'play within a play' in an attempt to distinguish what is fictionally true from what is fictionally false. So delighted is Hamlet with the reaction of one audience member to *The Murder of Gonzago* (*"O good Horatio, I'll take the ghost's word for a thousand pound"*, 3.2) that he fancies he would enjoy success in a career as a playwright and actor: *"Would not this, sir ... get me a fellowship in a cry of players?"*

13.2 – Claudius: *"He that plays the king"*

The *"something ... rotten in the state of Denmark"* (1.4) which is sensed by the guard Marcellus is the web of corruption that spreads outward from the false kingship of the play's antagonist, Claudius. His *"ambition"* (3.3) for Denmark's throne leads him to commit one murder only to find that he must plot a second to cover up the first.

Sample 2.1

Every deceitful performance at Elsinore originates with Claudius' *"painted word"* (3.1) triple masquerade: of a grieving brother to old King Hamlet; a caring father-figure to Prince Hamlet; and a legitimate monarch of Denmark. Although a deceitful manipulator of others, Claudius is undeniably honest with himself.

> In the opening court scene of 1.2, the newly-crowned Claudius assumes the role of chief mourner for his deceased brother: *"That we with wisest sorrow think on him."* To Prince Hamlet, he offers himself as a kindly step-parent: *"think of us / As of a father ... remain / Here in the cheer and comfort of our eye ... our son."* Later in 4.5, in response to Laertes' mob-leading, castle-storming rebellion, Claudius adopts the pose of a divinely-appointed ruler: *"Let him go, Gertrude. Do not fear our person."* Laertes, at *"the riotous head"* of a *"rabble"* may have overpowered the king's personal bodyguards (*"O'erbears your officers"*), but a serene Claudius exudes the confidence of a man who enjoys divine protection: *"There's such divinity doth hedge a king"* (4.5).
>
> In reality, so *"unnatural"* (1.5) were Claudius' brother-murdering, *"sometime sister"*-marrying (1.2) and kingdom-stealing crimes that Shakespeare's audiences would not have been surprised to see them followed by a breach in the natural boundary between this world and the next. A *"dreaded sight"* (1.1) was released from beyond the grave with this command to the rightful heir to Denmark's stolen throne: *"Bear it not"* (1.5).
>
> Although a deceitful manipulator of others, Claudius is undeniably honest with himself. On his knees in his private chapel, the usurping king recognizes he can achieve redemption only by giving up *"those effects for which I did the murder"*: his *"crown"* and *"queen"* (3.3); this he never does. In the play's final scene, Claudius will die as he lived—an unrepentant villain.

Sample 2.2

The storyline of *Hamlet* begins and ends with a murder disguised as an accident. In both instances, the perpetrator is the play's villain, Claudius; and in each case, his chosen weapon is the same: poison. The first victim is old King Hamlet; the second is his son, Prince Hamlet.

What Claudius gained through a secret, pre-play murder, he seeks to retain through a false show legitimate kingship. In 1.2, the usurper addresses the assembled court as an actor might an audience. Although his lines are forced and awkward—*"with a defeated joy ... mirth in funeral and with dirge in marriage"*—his performance wins the approval of Denmark's nobles who, in their *"better wisdoms"*, have chosen brother to succeed brother rather than son to succeed father.

In the *"hasty sending"* (2.2) for Hamlet's two old school friends, Gertrude's concern may have been only for the welfare of her *"too much changed son"* (2.2). For his part, however, Claudius is more interested in protecting his stolen throne from what he calls Hamlet's *"turbulent and dangerous lunacy"* (3.1). Later, with Polonius murdered and fearing for his own life (*"It had been so with us, had we been there"*, 4.1), Claudius exiles his nephew to England with these departing words: *"Hamlet, this deed, for thine especial safety ... we ... must send thee hence ... Thy loving father"* (4.3). But in an aside, Claudius reveals he is, in fact, dispatching the prince to his execution: *"Do it, England, / For like the hectic in my blood he rages"* (4.3).

However, much like his father's Ghost, Hamlet returns from the dead—or at least from a death sentence in England. But unlike Claudius' brother-poisoning crime in the palace orchard, his Hamlet-poisoning ploy of the final 5.2 scene is publicly exposed to the court. As the prince remarked in 1.2: *"Foul deeds will rise, / Though all the earth o'erwhelm them, to men's eyes."*

Sample 2.3

The playwright of Providence cast Claudius as a secondary character in the shadow of his brother, old King Hamlet. But Claudius rewrote the script so that it is he who now occupies center stage at Elsinore.

From a theatrical perspective, Claudius can be viewed as a man who was cast by destiny—by *"heaven ordinant"* (5.1), to borrow Hamlet's expression—to play a minor role in the shadow of his brother, old King Hamlet. But Claudius rewrote the script to recast himself as the male lead—the king who shares the throne and bed of Gertrude, *"the beauteous majesty of Denmark"* (4.5).

Claudius' role-stealing performance on the Elsinore stage convinces everyone—except his harshest critic, the prince: *"one may smile, and smile, and be a villain"* (1.5). Claudius responds to Hamlet's own act of an *"antic disposition"* (1.5) by stage-managing three plays-within-a-play. But the first two fail in their purpose, where the aim of theater is, in the prince's words, *"to hold a mirror up to nature"* (3.2). Neither the false show of concern by Rosencrantz and Guildenstern nor the *"'twere by accident"* (3.1) encounter with Ophelia yield a satisfactory insight into Prince Hamlet's true state of mind. Worse, the third ploy in the queen's closet, as suggested by Polonius, proves to be his advisor's final performance.

Claudius next resorts to dealing with Prince Hamlet as he dealt with his father: by writing him out of the drama. But fate (*"the divinity that shapes our ends"*, 5.1) interferes with his two murderous schemes. A pirate attack saves the prince from execution in England. And Gertrude's unintended drinking from the poisoned wine goblet, along with an accidental swapping of swords, leads to Laertes' conscience-stricken confession (*"The King's to blame"*, 5.2) and ultimately to Claudius' *"justly served"* death from *"a poison tempered by himself"* (5.2).

13.3 – Polonius: *"Seeing, unseen"*

In every scene in which he appears, Polonius is either planning or performing some act of deception. The man who claims to have been *"accounted a good actor"* (2.2) in his youth even deploys his duplicitous schemes against his own son and daughter.

Sample 3.1

It takes a lot to shock Prince Hamlet's antagonist and the play's villain, King Claudius. But this is what his unscrupulous henchman Polonius succeeds in doing. Here is the first sample description of the deceitful character of Polonius.

Whereas King Claudius twice voices feelings of guilt, his advisor Polonius never displays any qualms about his own manipulative conduct. If the usurping king is the originator of the falsity at Elsinore, his Lord Chamberlain, Polonius, father to Laertes and Ophelia, is his chief instrument.

Foreshadowing Hamlet's later directions to the Players before *The Murder of Gonzago* (*"Speak the speech, I pray you … let your own discretion be your tutor. Suit the action to the word, the word to the action"*, 3.2), Polonius in 3.1 gives acting instructions to his daughter, Ophelia, on how to stage a most convincing performance for deceiving Prince Hamlet (*"And pious action we do sugar o'er / The devil himself"*). King Claudius willingly colludes in Polonius' scheme to *"sift"* (2.2) Hamlet with this *"'twere by accident"* encounter. Yet, he is also so appalled by his advisor's unscrupulous use of Ophelia as bait (*"I'll loose my daughter to him"*, 2.2) that, speaking in an aside, the king is for the first time prompted to reveal his moral crisis: *"How smart a lash that speech doth give my conscience!"* Even for a man who has poisoned his own brother and will soon plot his nephew's execution, Polonius' conduct seems to Claudius as beyond the bounds of acceptable behavior.

However, Polonius will regret his eavesdropping scheme of the so-called nunnery scene. For on the next occasion when the prince suspects he is being spied upon, his will, in *"a rash and bloody deed"* (3.4), impulsively run his sword through the hidden eavesdropper. With deadly irony, Polonius, who in life so enjoyed acting as someone he was not, dies because he is mistaken for someone else: *"Is it the King?"*

Sample 3.2
Like Claudius' kingship and Hamlet's madness, Polonius' bumbling behavior is both real and at the same time a self-serving pretense. Here is the second sample response.

The king's chief advisor Polonius is both a *"tedious old fool"* (2.2), as Hamlet describes him, and also a man, again in the prince's words, who likes to *"play the fool"* (3.1)—a cynical hypocrite who hides his duplicity behind the mask of a bumbling buffoon.

When directing his spy Reynaldo to monitor Laertes in Paris, Polonius loses himself in mid-sentence: *"what was I / about to say? By the mass, I was about to say / something. Where did I leave?"* (2.1). Yet Claudius' remark to Laertes at the court scene makes clear the debt the king feels towards the counselor he later describes as *"faithful and honorable"* (2.2): *"The head is not more native to the heart, / The hand more instrumental to the mouth, / Than is the throne of Denmark to thy father"* (1.2).

It is hardly surprising that a senior political operator such as Polonius is a manipulative individual. What is shocking, however, is how as a father he behaves towards his daughter. With the king, he directs Ophelia to stumble across Hamlet *"as 'twere by accident"* (3.1) while he and Claudius will lurk behind a curtain, *"seeing, unseen"* (3.1). For added theatrical effect (*"such an exercise may colour /*

Your loneliness", 3.1), he hands Ophelia a prayer book as a stage prop to deflect Hamlet's suspicions.

Appropriately, Polonius dies as he lived, hiding behind a curtain in an act of eavesdropping. He is quickly buried *"hugger-mugger"* (4.5), without ceremony in an unmarked grave. His expression while alive that *"the apparel oft proclaims the man"* (1.3) serves as an ironic comment on his final resting place in death.

Sample 3.3

Sample response number three describes the meta-theatrical aspect of Polonius' role. The character who is actually stabbed to death in *Hamlet* was theatrically stabbed in a play he performed in his youth.

Like Hamlet's two old school friends, the king and his closest advisor operate as a double act. Claudius masquerades as a legitimate monarch; in reality, he is a murderous usurper. Polonius presents himself as an honorable if sometimes bumbling old man; in fact, he is a cynic devoid of either moral scruples or human feeling.

Not even his own family is safe from Polonius' duplicitous ploys. He sends a spy Reynaldo after Laertes to Paris in a convoluted *"bait of falsehood"* to catch the *"carp of truth"* scheme that will include spreading false and malicious rumors about his son: *"put on him / What forgeries you please ... gambling ... drinking, fencing, swearing, / Quarreling, drabbing—you may go so far"* (2.1).

We learn in 3.2 that the man Claudius calls *"faithful and honorable"* (2.2) shares with the prince a university education and a love of the theater. Polonius boasts he was *"accounted a good actor"* and that that he *"did enact Julius Caesar ... (who) was killed i'th'Capitol."* Playing the role of Caesar, Polonius would have met his death by stabbing. Playing himself in *Hamlet*, the 'real' Polonius suffers the same fate; he is stabbed by Hamlet while eavesdropping behind a curtain in Gertrude's closet.

In his immediate reaction, the prince expresses little remorse for what he has done; instead, he regards the interfering busybody as having brought his death on himself, finally and fatally the deserving victim of his own deceitful nature: *"Take thy fortune. / Thou find'st to be too busy is some danger"* (3.4).

13.4 – Hamlet: *"I know not seems"*

A lover of acting in theater, Hamlet claims to be a hater of falsity in life: *"Ay, sir; to be honest, as this world goes, is to be / one man picked out of ten thousand"* (2.2). But the prince is just as duplicitous as any of the play's other characters.

Sample 4.1

The first sample response argues that Prince Hamlet is more successful at detecting deceitful behavior in others than he is in practicing it himself.

>Prince Hamlet is *"free from all contriving"* (4.7), Claudius assures Laertes as he manipulates him into the rigged fencing duel against his nephew. On the contrary, Hamlet is as contriving as any other character in the play. In my opinion, however, the prince is more successful at detecting deceit than at practicing it.
>
>Hamlet sees through Rosencrantz's claim that he and Guildenstern have arrived unprompted at Elsinore: *"To visit you, my lord; no other occasion"* (2.2). To which the prince responds: *"Come, come ... There is a kind of confession in your looks which your modesties have not craft enough to colour"* (2.2). Of Ophelia in the nunnery scene, he inquires *"Ha, ha! are you honest? ... Where is your father?"* (3.1), suspecting correctly that the king's advisor is eavesdropping nearby.

The prince is rightly suspicious of the *"letters sealed"* (3.4) his two old school friends are to deliver to the English king; as he later discovers on their voyage, they contain the prince's death warrant: *"My head should be struck off"* (5.2).

But Hamlet's own two subterfuges— his *"antic disposition"* (1.5) ploy and the play-within-a-play—both rebound on the prince. Ophelia blames herself for Hamlet's apparent insanity and descends into real madness. And rather than disclose Claudius' *"occulted guilt"* (2.2) to the court, *The Murder of Gonzago* instead reveals Hamlet's secret knowledge of his father's poisoning to Claudius. Like Polonius' son in the final scene (*"as a woodcock to mine own springe"*, 5.2), Hamlet is caught in his own 'Mousetrap.'

Sample 4.2

Prince Hamlet is a harsh critic of other characters' insincere performances. But words alone will not unseat Claudius from Denmark's throne or detach his mother from her husband's side.

"(A)s good as a chorus" (3.2)—Ophelia's comment on Hamlet's behavior during *The Murder of Gonzago* aptly describes the prince's role for much of the first half of the play. Hamlet responds to the insincere performances of other characters much as a harsh theater critic might deliver unsparingly negative reviews. He calls Polonius a *"fishmonger"* (2.2) or pimp for offering up Ophelia as bait in the king's spying plans. He insults Rosencrantz as a toadying *"sponge ... that soaks up the King's ... rewards"* (4.2). Queen Gertrude, he addresses as *"your husband's brother's wife"*; and her *"marriage-vows"* he condemns for being *"As false as dicers' oaths"* (3.4).

At *The Murder of Gonzago* in 3.2, Hamlet delivers a provocative running commentary intended to goad his uncle and humiliate his mother. Claudius' questioning about the play is met with the prince's response that it is *"the image of a murder done"*, after which he adds sarcastically: *"but what of that? ... we that have free souls, it touches us not."* (3.2). After the Player Queen vows to the dying Player King never to remarry (*"Both here and hence pursue me lasting strife / If, once a widow, ever I be wife!"*), Hamlet pointedly questions his mother: *"Madam, how like you this play?"*

Although Hamlet berates himself that he can only *"unpack my heart with words / And fall a-cursing like a very drab"* (2.2), his rage-filled outbursts help the prince cling to his sanity. In contrast, Ophelia carries inside her—and is ultimately crushed by— the pain of her continual silencing and humiliation.

Sample 4.3
Sensing his imminent death from some ploy by Claudius, Hamlet's thoughts in the graveyard scene of 5.1 turn to how the dead can afterward live on in the memory of the living. Does Hamlet invent the improbable tale of divinely-inspired rescue by pirates with which he hopes to be remembered?

Does the returned-from-sea Hamlet seek to exploit Horatio's loyalty with his heroic story of rescue by pirates with which the prince hopes to be remembered? Certainly, the tale with which Hamlet regales Horatio of his adventures at sea—first in his letter in 4.6 and later in more detail in their conversation in 5.2—is riven with improbable elements.

At the end of 4.3, Hamlet expressed surprise at Claudius' order for his exile (*"To England?"*). But he already knew and has told Gertrude of the king's intentions (*"I must to England"*, 3.4). He is also aware of the sealed commission, drafted earlier that day by the king following the prince's encounter with Ophelia (*"I have ... set it down: he shall with speed to England"*, 3.1). The prince's remark to his mother of how *"'tis most sweet / When in one line two crafts directly meet"* (3.4) suggests a plan is in place with elements loyal to the prince for his rescue and return. As for the replacement commission, it is easier to believe it was written, sealed and substituted at Elsinore than aboard ship in the dark of night.

We the audience may wonder whether the prince's escape from execution in England and safe return to Elsinore was more likely the result of a pre-arranged rescue plan rather than the divinely-inspired intervention of friendly *"thieves of mercy"* (4.6) pirates. In other words, is the self-glorifying adventure story the prince asks Horatio's to *"report"* (5.2) after his death just another *"forgery of shapes and tricks"* (4.7) in which the play abounds?

13.5 – Gertrude: *"Paint ... an inch thick"*

Do Queen Gertrude and Ophelia contribute to the web of deception at Elsinore? And how does the repeated use of the motifs of painting and cosmetics reinforce the play's theme of physical and moral rottenness concealed behind a *"painted"* and *"beautified"* (3.1) exterior?

Sample 5.1
While others in the play put on acts of 'seeming' to conceal their true selves, this first sample response argues that Gertrude fools only one person—herself. The queen who claims that *"all that is I see"* (3.4) hides from herself the true nature of the man she married. When subjected to Hamlet's *"speak daggers"* (3.2) tirade, however, she can offer no defense against his charge that her second husband is a *"murderer and a villain"* (3.4).

Was Gertrude carrying on a secret affair with Claudius while old King Hamlet was still alive? Was she even an accomplice to his murder? In 1.5, the Ghost calls Claudius an *"adulterate beast"*—that is, a debased individual—but not, significantly, an adulterous one. When Hamlet rages against Gertrude in her closet in 3.4 (*"Mother, you have my father much offended"*), he never suggests she was an adulteress. And in the final 5.2 scene, the prince's farewell taunt to the king—*"thou incestuous, murderous, damned Dane"*—makes no mention of adultery.

Gertrude's shocked reaction in 3.4 to Hamlet's accusation of *"As kill a king, and marry with his brother"* convinces me she had no part in old King Hamlet's death. But equally revealing is her non-response to Hamlet's accusation that Claudius is *"A murderer and a villain."* When Gertrude speaks of the *"black and grained spots"* in her *"very soul"*, I believe she is admitting to her opportunistic self-deception. Tempted by the prospect of continuing the queenly role she had for three decades enjoyed, Gertrude hides from herself the true character of her second husband. It is this inner wall of *"hoodman-blind"* (3.4) self-delusion that Prince Hamlet seeks to breach when he demands of her: *"Have you eyes?"*

Although she promises Hamlet she will no longer share her bed with Claudius (*"be thou assured"*), Gertrude afterward shows no sign of wavering in her relationship with the *"king of shreds and patches"* (3.4). Her final act in the play is to drink from the same *"leperous distilment"* (1.5) her second husband previously used to take the life of her first: *"O my dear Hamlet—The drink, the drink! I am poisoned"* (5.2).

Sample 5.2
Hamlet and Ophelia's encounter in the so-called nunnery scene of 3.1 contains a double deception, but *"Who is the more deceived?"*

Ophelia's complaint that *"There's tricks i'th'world"* (4.5) echoes the prince's earlier remark: *"That one may smile, and smile, and be a villain"* (1.5). However, in the so-called nunnery scene of 3.1, both characters practice deceit against one another—but for reasons that are not entirely exploitative.

Ophelia worries her father's interpretation of the prince's antic behavior (*"Mad for thy love?"*) may be correct: *"My lord, I do not know. / But truly, I do fear it"* (2.1). At least in part, her motivation for participating in the staged *"'twere by accident"* encounter is the hope expressed in the queen's words of encouragement to her: *"I do wish / That your good beauties"* and *"virtues / Will bring him to his wonted way again."*

Moreover, Ophelia's opening remark to Hamlet (*"How does your honour for this many a day?"*) suggests she misses the prince whom her father Polonius has blocked her from seeing. Through her offer to return *"remembrances of yours"* I believe Ophelia is encouraging Hamlet to recall his past love for her (*"words of so sweet breath composed"*) in the hope that so doing may also rekindle it.

In the prince's tirade, there is anger at her perceived betrayal. But, strongly suspecting that Polonius and the king are eavesdropping on their conversation, I believe the Hamlet is also protecting her. His denial of feelings for her (*"I loved you not"*) is intended to shield Ophelia from any accusation that she is a throne-seeking co-conspirator in the event that the evening's performance of *The Murder of Gonzago* is followed by *"hot blood ... bitter business"* (3.2) against King Claudius.

Sample 5.3

The third sample response analyses Shakespeare's repeated use of the motifs of painting and cosmetics to reinforce the play's theme of inner realities hidden behind false outward appearances.

At various points in *Hamlet*, Shakespeare uses the motifs of painting and cosmetics to reinforce one of the play's central themes: how benign or attractive outward appearances can disguise inner moral or physical rottenness.

In an aside in 3.1, Claudius compares his masquerade as a legitimate monarch with the make-up worn by a prostitute: *"The harlot's cheek, beautied with plastering art, / Is not more ugly to the thing that helps it / Than is my deed to my most painted word."* It is an admission that echoes the First Player's reference to the *"painted tyrant Pyrrhus"* (2.2).

Shortly afterward in the 3.1 scene, Hamlet uses similar language to excoriate Ophelia—and by extension, his mother and all womankind: *"I have heard of your paintings too, well enough. / God has given you one face and you make yourselves another."*

Later in 4.5, Claudius continues the paint metaphor when manipulating Laertes into his scheme to dispose of his troublesome nephew: *"Laertes, was your father dear to you? / Or are you like the painting of a sorrow, / A face without a heart?"*

Speaking to Yorick's skull in the 5.1 graveyard scene, Hamlet observes how death will inevitability triumph over all painted makeup and disguises: *"Now get you to my lady's chamber, and tell her, let her paint an inch thick, to this favour she must come."* Tragically, the open grave over which the prince declares *"make her laugh at that"* is intended for *"One that was a woman, sir; but, rest her soul, she's dead"*— the *"fair Ophelia"* (3.1) whom the prince had once *"importuned ... with love / In honorable fashion"* (1.3).

13.6 – Conclusion: *"Who's there?"*

The watchful castle guards of act one were looking in the wrong direction. Denmark as an independent nation was not conquered by an external military campaign; it collapsed under a web of domestic deception. Claudius (*"He that plays the king"*, 2.2), fooled everyone—except Hamlet (*"one may smile, and smile, and be a villain"*, 1.5). Gertrude (*"all that is I see"*, 3.4) fooled only herself.

Sample 6.1
The first sample conclusion asserts that Denmark, and the families of Hamlet and Polonius, were destroyed from the inside not from without. The watchful sentinels Barnardo and Francisco of 1.1 were looking in the wrong direction.

> *Hamlet* is a play that begins with a question and ends with much left unrevealed. *"Who's there?"* asks the guard Barnardo on the Elsinore castle battlements as midnight approaches in 1.1. With his dying breath at the end of 5.2, Hamlet utters: *"Had I but time—as this fell sergeant, Death, / Is strict in his arrest—O, I could tell you."*
>
> Barnardo's opening question does not receive an answer but is met with a counter-demand: *"Nay, answer me. Stand and unfold yourself."* It is a tense exchange between two anxious guards in which uncertainty about identity is accompanied by a disruption in the proper social order; it is the role of the on-duty guard Francisco to ask such a question, not his colleague Barnardo who has come to relieve him.
>
> With his final words, Hamlet requests Horatio to *"To tell my story."* But the fast-acting poison in the prince's body means that we, *"the audience to this act"*, will hear only an incomplete version: *"Things standing thus unknown, shall live behind me!"*

We will never know what the *"sweet Prince"* would have revealed to us had he lived. And we *"mutes"* in the audience cannot speak to Hamlet about what we know but which he could only suspect: that Claudius did indeed kill his father: *"O, my offence is rank ... A brother's murder"* (3.3).

Ironically, the watchful lookouts Barnardo and Francisco were looking in the wrong direction. The menace that doomed Denmark as an independent nation came from inside the walls of Elsinore itself. Denmark was not conquered by an external military campaign; it collapsed under a web of domestic deception.

Sample 6.2

In Shakespeare's time, the security and well-being of a nation were seen as linked to the God-fearing righteousness of its monarch. Sample conclusion number two focuses on what disastrous consequences follow when the role of king is played by a morally unfit man.

"He that plays the king shall be welcome", the prince remarks in 2.2 on hearing of the Players' arrival. But *Hamlet* the play reveals what tragic consequences follow for people and country when the royal role is seized by a man who is driven only by amoral ambition cloaked in a web of deceit.

Shakespeare gives us no hint that Polonius knew of Claudius' pre-play murder of old King Hamlet. Rosencrantz and Guildenstern believed they were serving a legitimate monarch who, in that era, would have been regarded as God's representative on earth. Given his lack of knowledge, Polonius' irritation at what he describes to Gertrude as her son's *"pranks"* (3.4) is understandable. So too is Rosencrantz's plea to his old school friend, the prince: *"My lord, you once did love me ... what is your cause of distemper?"* (3.2).

Although Laertes has genuine cause for anger, he is not told of the circumstances of his father's death. Moreover, his assertion to Claudius—*"I'll not be juggled with"* (4.5)—is cruelly twisted against him by the manipulative king. Directly and indirectly, all the above characters lose their lives as a result of Claudius' false kingship—and their country forfeits its independence to Norway. The Ghost's words regarding his brother's poison and deceit are proven by events to be more than a metaphor: *"the whole ear of Denmark / Is by a forged process of my death / Rankly abused"* (1.5).

Most poignantly, a traumatized Ophelia surrendered to despair and death in the *"weeping book"* (4.5) never knowing why her prince's *"noble and most sovereign reason"* had become *"Like sweet bells jangled, out of tune and harsh"* (3.1).

Sample 6.3

The final sample conclusion portrays Claudius' crimes as offenses against the theater of life, as scripted by the cosmic playwright of destiny, *"the Everlasting"* (1.2). He successfully stole two roles. It was his third attempted role-grab as Prince Hamlet's father that led to his undoing.

Two lines from Shakespeare's *As You Like It*—*"All the world's a stage. / And all the men and women merely players"*—echoed the then widely-believed concept of *Theatrum Mundi*: that life is a play and, at our story's end, we are judged on our performance of the roles assigned to us by the *"divinity that shapes our ends"* (5.1). With the *"witchcraft of his wit"* (1.5), Claudius successfully stole two roles that rightfully belonged to another: husband and king. For her part in the first, Gertrude forfeited her life. For colluding in the second, the country's nobles lost their political power to Norway.

Claudius' third role-grabbing attempt was directed at his nephew: *"think of us / As of a father"* (1.2). But Hamlet could and did not. In 5.1, the prince recounts to Horatio how he altered the king's sealed orders for his execution on arrival in England: *"Ere I could make a prologue to my brains, / They had begun the play."* While he could rewrite the fatal 'play' Claudius had scripted for him, Prince Hamlet cannot rewrite the tragic tale that bears his name. For, as Laertes said earlier in 1.3, *"He may not ... carve for himself"* his own fate.

Claudius' disruption of Providence's divinely-ordered roles is foreshadowed in 1.1. Describing the frenzied defense preparations, Marcellus notes how the natural distinctions of everyday life had become blurred—the work *"Does not divide the Sunday from the week"* and *"make the night joint laborer with the day."* When Hamlet finally kills the usurping king, his words—*"thou incestuous, murderous, damned Dane"* (5.2)—summarize Claudius' three thefts: a wife, multiple lives, and the kingship of Denmark.

14

The Theme of Madness

*"Mad call I it; for, to define true madness,
What is't but to be nothing else but mad?"*

"Your noble son is mad" (2.2), Polonius tells Denmark's king and queen. But is Hamlet ever really insane? If he is not, why is he pretending to be? Is the prince's behavior the cause of Ophelia's mental collapse?

And was his loss in childhood of his surrogate parent Yorick the trauma that shaped the dual aspects of Hamlet's personality: his artistic temperament and his near-sociopathic cruelty?

14.1 – Introduction

Is Shakespeare's *Hamlet* a play about insane characters? Or about what follows when normally sane individuals are subjected to maddening life situations? The portrayal of insanity, as expressed in irrational, manipulative and self-destructive behaviors, extends beyond the figures of Hamlet and Ophelia. It may even be argued that they are the two sanest characters in the play.

Sample 1.1

This first sample introduction focuses on the so-called 'madness' of Prince Hamlet. Is it all only an act by the theater-loving prince? Or does his feigned *"antic disposition"* (1.5) descend into real insanity?

> *"My wit's diseased"*, Hamlet tells Guildenstern in 3.2 following his old school friend's complaint to the prince: *"put your discourse into some frame and / start not so wildly from my affair."* But is the title character of Shakespeare's play really insane? If so, is it because of some psychological defect in his personality? Or has the prince lost his reason as the result of the stress that has come with being *"benetted round with villainies"* (5.2)?
>
> And if Hamlet is not as *"Mad as the sea and wind, when both contend / Which is the mightier"* (4.1), why is the prince pretending to be? The motive for his put-on *"antic disposition"* (1.5) cannot be to protect his life from Claudius. As the king explains to Laertes, he is prevented from striking openly against Hamlet for two reasons: *"The queen his mother / Lives almost by his looks"* and the prince enjoys the *"great love the general gender"* (4.7). Having no reason to suspect Hamlet knows the true cause of his father's death, Claudius instead attempts to win the prince's support by offering himself as a caring step-parent: *"think of us / As of a father"* (1.2). If anything, what the king calls Hamlet's *"turbulent and dangerous lunacy"* (3.1) makes him more rather than less suspicious of his nephew. So, given all this, what is the *"method in (Hamlet's) madness"* (2.2)?

As for Ophelia, no one doubts her poignant descent into very real trauma. But was Hamlet's feigned insanity the cause of actual madness in Polonius' daughter? In this essay, I will explore the play's theme of madness, chiefly as it affects the characters and actions of Hamlet and his *"fair Ophelia"* (3.1).

Sample 1.2

The second sample introduction summarizes the responses of Hamlet and Ophelia to the maddening circumstances in which they find themselves. He lashes outward, first verbally and then violently with his *"rash and bloody"* (3.4) stabbing of Polonius; she retreats inward and ultimately surrenders in despair to death.

"The canker galls the infants of the spring" (1.3)—in this essay, I will argue that this line from Laertes can be viewed as a summary of the underlying theme of Shakespeare's *Hamlet*. It is a play where the older generation destroys the younger—first, by driving them into maddening circumstances (*"he shall not choose but fall"*, 4.7; *"I cannot choose but weep"*, 4.5), and, then, into the grave.

Over the past century, psychologists have offered clinical diagnoses of Hamlet and Ophelia as if Shakespeare's dramatic characters were patients afflicted by some mental disability. In my opinion, although Hamlet and Ophelia respond in opposite ways to their dilemmas, there is nothing in either's behavior that differs significantly from how a mentally well, 'normal' person would react had they been subjected to similar stresses.

Hamlet's put on *"antic disposition"* (1.5) provides him with an outlet to vent his rage and enables the prince to cling to his sanity amidst the *"sea of troubles"* (3.1) that engulf him. In contrast, the submissive and isolated Ophelia carries the pain of her continual silencing and humiliation inside her until her sanity collapses under its weight and she surrenders to death in a *"weeping brook"* (4.7).

In summary, I see *Hamlet* as not so much a play about mad characters; rather it is a portrayal of characters who struggle to endure in a maddening world of deception and betrayal where neither is free to follow the advice given to Laertes: *"To thine own self be true"* (1.2).

Sample 1.3

Is everyone at Elsinore mad? And are Hamlet and Ophelia the two sanest characters in the play?

"How came he mad?", Hamlet inquires about himself to the grave-digging sexton who is unaware it is with the prince with whom he is speaking. *"On account of losing his wits"* (5.1) is the unhelpful reply he receives. As for the likelihood that Hamlet may *"recover his wits"* in England, the grave-digger adds *"if he do not, it's no great matter ... there the men / are as mad as he."*

Focus on the theme of insanity in Shakespeare's *Hamlet* has tended to center on only two figures: the prince and Ophelia, the young woman to whom he *"hath importuned ... with love in honourable fashion"* (1.3). An alternative perspective is that Hamlet and Ophelia are the sanest characters in a play where so many others are in the grip of irrational, self-destructive behaviors. To borrow the words of Denmark's corrupt and corrupting king, the whole play seems *"a document in madness"* (4.5).

So deranged is the Ghost's desire for revenge he demands the sacrifice of his son's soul to satisfy it. A delusional Gertrude blinds herself to the villainous character of the second husband. As for Claudius, he sinks into a depression (*"When sorrows come, they come not single spies / But in battalions"*, 4.5) on reflecting how his winning of the crown has brought only the threat of a foreign invasion, a popular rebellion and a haunted conscience (*"O heavy burden"*, 3.1). It is little wonder he pines for *"an hour of quiet"* (5.1).

In the end, the only major character to survive is the prince's level-headed confidant, Horatio. But even he needs to be restrained from *"self-slaughter"* (1.2) by Hamlet's insistence that Horatio live on so he may *"speak to th'yet unknowing world / How these things came about"* (5.2).

14.2 – Hamlet's performance: *"An antic disposition"*

Following his encounter with the Ghost in 1.5, why does Hamlet decide to feign (*"put ... on"*) episodes (*"perchance hereafter shall think meet"*) of insanity (*"antic disposition"*)? Hamlet never explains his motive for so doing, either to his trusted colleagues or in soliloquy. As a result, we are left to hunt for clues in search of an answer.

Sample 2.1

This first sample response explores one theory to explain Hamlet's *"antic disposition"* (1.5). Is it a ploy by the prince to disguise his real—and kingship-disqualifying—mental fragility?

> Is Hamlet's put-on *"antic disposition"* (1.2) a strategy by the prince to conceal some actual psychological disability by hiding it in plain sight?
>
> In his second soliloquy, Hamlet acknowledges a feature of his character that, as he must surely realize, might disqualify him from replacing Claudius should his uncle no longer sit on Denmark's throne: his mental fragility (*"my weakness and my melancholy"*, 2.2). Moreover, we have Gertrude's words that her son is prone to manic episodes (*"a while the fit will work on him"*, 5.1).
>
> If Hamlet's motive is to mask a genuine and underlying mental disability, why does he not keep to himself his plan to put on periodic performances of feigned insanity? Why does he decide instead to share his ploy—but not its motive—in confidence with his trusted colleagues (*"your fingers on your lips, I pray"*, 1.5)?

Perhaps it is because, should he later need proof he was never really insane, the prince can release from their oath of secrecy two credible witnesses: Marcellus, a representative of Elsinore's soldiers, and Horatio, a man trusted by them (*"thou art a scholar"*, 1.3)?

Each will be able to testify that the prince had indeed planned to feign eccentric behavior. And that, at his request (*"As you are friends, scholars and soldiers, / Give me one poor request ... Consent to swear"*, 1.5), they had agreed to keep his intention a secret (*"Propose the oath, my lord"*, 1.5).

However, in a play of *"purposes mistook / Fallen on th'inventors' heads"* (5.2), the reverse happens. The prince comes to be regarded not as an entirely sane man who only occasionally pretended to be otherwise; but as a complete lunatic (*"he that is mad"*, 5.1) who was banished from Denmark in the hope he might *"recover his wits"* (5.1).

Sample 2.2

An alternative explanation for the *"antic disposition"* (1.5) charade is that it is a forward-thinking plan by the prince to prepare a defense of temporary insanity should he actually assassinate the king.

One interpretation of Hamlet's unexplained decision to adopt *"an antic disposition"* (1.5) is as follows: the *"Looking before and after"* (4.4) prince is setting in place a defense of temporary insanity should he assassinate King Claudius and face a trial before Denmark's nobles for the capital crime of regicide. In support of this theory, one can note it is exactly this excuse of 'my madness made me do it' that the self-admitted *"indifferent honest"* (3.1) prince later offers to Laertes as a defense for his murder of Polonius: *"I here proclaim was madness. / Was't Hamlet wronged Laertes? Never Hamlet ... Who does it, then? His madness"* (5.2).

In this view, the prince shares his intent to feign episodes of insanity with Horatio and the guard Marcellus in 1.5 to assure them of his fitness to rule as a future king capable of protecting the *"safety and health of this whole state"* (1.3). So, in the interim, they should not doubt his sanity or otherwise lose confidence in him, however *"strange or odd soe'er I bear myself"* (1.5).

Ophelia's father-commanded ending of her relationship with Hamlet provides the prince with the final element of his 'antic' ploy: to *"let belief take hold"* (1.1) that Ophelia's rejected love is the cause of *"the madness wherein now he raves"* (2.2). Hence, Hamlet's disheveled *"doublet all unbraced"* (2.1) visit to her closet, his teasing of Polonius (*"Have you a daughter?"*, 2.2), and his risqué banter at *The Murder of Gonzago* (*"Here's metal more attractive"*, 3.2).

But, on fearing she is responsible for the prince's madness and, with it, his murder of her father, Ophelia herself succumbs to insanity. In summary, I see Hamlet's antic disposition ploy as an example of the disaster-prone *"deep plots"* (5.2) about which the prince later speaks to Horatio.

Sample 2.3

The third sample response argues that the Hamlet's 'antic' behavior provides an emotional outlet for the prince to release his rage and, by so doing, enables him to cling to his sanity.

"But break, my heart, for I must hold my tongue", the disinherited prince declares in his first soliloquy of 1.2. When he decides shortly afterward to put on an *"antic disposition"* (1.5), I believe it is at least in part because such a talkative lover of *"words, words, words"* (2.2) cannot remain silent for very long.

Whatever Hamlet's motivation for his adopting *"antic disposition"* (1.5), it functions as a coping mechanism that helps the prince cling to his sanity amidst the *"sea of troubles"* (3.1) that engulf him. He taunts and vents his rage at those who serve the king and queen. Polonius, he calls a *"fishmonger"* (2.2); and Rosencrantz he insults as a toadying *"sponge"* (4.2). In effect, he pretends to be mad to prevent himself from collapsing into actual insanity.

I do not believe Hamlet's so-called madness is ever anything but an act. Horatio twice questions Hamlet's rashness: firstly, his desire to speak with the Ghost, and later to enter the fencing duel. But his trusted friend never doubts the prince's sanity. Certainly, Hamlet's sharp awareness of others' duplicity never deserts him.

I interpret the prince's opening question to Ophelia in 3.1 (*"Ha, ha! are you honest?"*) as an echo of his earlier query to Rosencrantz and Guildenstern (*"Were you not sent for? ... Come, come, deal justly with me"*, 2.2). Accordingly, I believe much if not all his verbal outburst is not for her ears but for the benefit of the *"seeing, unseen"* observers. By denying any relationship with her (*"I loved you not"*), I believe Hamlet's purpose is to shield Ophelia from any later accusation that she was a throne-seeking co-conspirator in the *"hot blood ... bitter business"* (3.2) action against King Claudius that may follow that evening's performance of *The Murder of Gonzago*.

14.3 – Hamlet's psychology: *"A kind of joy"*

Depression, passive-aggression, aboulomania (a pathological inability to make decisions), Post-Traumatic Stress Disorder—do any of these insights from the world of psychology help to illuminate why Prince Hamlet is the person he is? Or, to borrow Rosencrantz's question: *"Good my lord, what is your cause of distemper?"* (3.2)

Sample 3.1

As Claudius and Gertrude believe, is Hamlet depressed by the death of his father? Or is the prince's behavior what psychologists today would call a passive-aggressive protest against his disinheritance?

Hamlet's speech to his two old school friends in 2.2 (*"I have of late ... lost all my mirth"*) is often cited as evidence that the prince is in the grip of a deep and disabling depressive condition. Does the 'melancholy Dane' not bemoan that the world *"appears no other thing to me than a foul and pestilent congregation of vapours"*?

But Hamlet speaks these words only after discovering Rosencrantz and Guildenstern were *"sent for"* to spy on him. Moreover, the prince's claim to have listlessly *"forgone all / custom of exercises."* is contradicted by his later remark to Horatio in 5.2: *"since (Laertes) went into France, / I have been in continual (fencing) practise."* Hamlet's teasing of his opponent (*"Come, for the third, Laertes: you but dally"*) and success against Laertes (*"A hit, a very palpable hit"*) indeed suggest the prince has not neglected his fencing practice.

In the 1.2 court scene, the queen shares the king's diagnosis that Hamlet is suffering from *"obstinate condolement"* and *"unmanly grief."* It is only natural that the prince should mourn old King Hamlet's passing. But Hamlet never speaks of any fond memories of his father. Nor, in 5.1, does he visit his grave. The emotionally-blackmailing Ghost of 1.5 (*"If thou didst ever thy dear father love..."*) offers no expression of affection for his son. And the Ghost's complaint regarding his *"foul and most unnatural murder"* is that death has deprived him *"Of life, of crown, of queen"*—a list from which his only child is noticeably absent.

I would argue that Hamlet's *"inky cloak"* demeanor before the court, along with his surly responses to the king and queen, are not signs of depressive bereavement (*"I have that within which passeth show"*, 1.2). Rather, they are a form of personal protest against what has followed his father's death (*"That it should come to this!"*, 1.2).

Psychologists today apply the term passive-aggression to a pattern of negative and antagonistic behaviors displayed by a person unwilling or unable to confront authority figures directly. Hamlet's *"suits of woe"* (1.2) make clear his discontent while stopping short of openly challenging the legitimacy of Denmark's new king and queen.

Sample 3.2

Does Hamlet suffer from aboulomania: a paralyzing inability to make decisions, to the extent that it affects the sufferer's ability to think and function rationally?

Is Hamlet's reluctance to murder King Claudius at the command of the Ghost evidence that the prince suffers from a psychological condition that impairs his ability to make decisions? Are we to believe that if the prince were 'cured' of his supposed mental disability, he would immediately seek out Claudius and run him through with his sword?

In my opinion, it is not a defect in Hamlet's character that impairs him from following the Ghost's *"dread command"* (3.4): to assassinate Denmark's duly elected monarch and Queen Gertrude's new husband without evidence of guilt (*"grounds / More relative than this"*, 2.2). Instead, it is the impossible nature of his dilemma. For what mentally sane person, on finding themselves in Hamlet's situation, would not delay?

Because his uncle has committed a seemingly perfect crime that left behind neither witnesses nor evidence, old King Hamlet's son is without any form of legal remedy. Assuming the *"spirit that I have seen"* (2.2) is an *"honest ghost"* (1.5), the prince's only hope is for King Claudius to make a public confession of his crime, give up his crown, and seek forgiveness. It is to achieve exactly this outcome, of course, that Hamlet stages *The Murder of Gonzago*. For *"I* have heard / That guilty creatures sitting at a play ... have proclaimed their malefactions" (2.2).

As for the alternative option of disposing of the king as his uncle did the prince's father—through a murder disguised as an accident—and afterward replacing him on the throne, this is not a path Hamlet could follow without himself becoming another Claudius: a usurping villain in this life and a soul damned in the next. Afterward, might Hamlet too not struggle with a tormented conscience (*"O heavy burden"*, 3.1)? And like Claudius, could Hamlet find forgiveness only by giving up *"those effects for which I did the murder"* (3.3)?

In summary, I cannot accept the interpretation that the title character of *Hamlet* the play suffers from weakened willpower or pathological indecisiveness—a condition psychologists call aboulomania. Nor do I believe Shakespeare's purpose is to leave the audience with the simplistic lesson of 'Action good, delay bad.' For the impulsive Laertes behaves oppositely to Hamlet, and the play does not end well for him either.

Sample 3.3

Prince Hamlet: the artistic, scholarly intellectual—and the callous, near-sociopathic serial killer. Is Post-Traumatic Stress Disorder (PTSD), following his loss in childhood of the court jester and surrogate parent Yorick, an explanation for these dual and seemingly contradictory aspects of the prince's personality?

It is widely recognized that a deep shock or grief can leave a person so emotionally numb they lose temporarily both their sense of self and awareness of their surroundings. For example, in Shakespeare's *Romeo and Juliet*, the male lead laments to his Horatio-like friend, Benvolio: *"This is not Romeo ... I have lost myself. I am not here."* (1.1). Among the personality-modifying symptoms of experiencing a severe traumatic loss may be a long-term retreat from the real world into a safer, imaginary one.

Is Hamlet a victim of Post-Traumatic Stress Disorder (PTSD)? And is his make-believe refuge from reality the environment he so dearly loves: the theater? For there *"the adventurous knight / shall use his foil and target; the lover shall not / sigh gratis"* and *"the humourous man shall end his part / in peace"* (2.2). Certainly, the prince is never less like his caricature of the 'melancholy Dane' than when in the company of the Players. Their arrival to Elsinore is his happiest moment in the play; as Rosencrantz later remarks: *"there did seem in him a kind of joy / To hear of it"* (3.1). Indeed, the prince fancies he would find success in an alternative career of a playwright and actor: *"Would not this, sir ... get me a fellowship in a cry of players?"* (3.2).

Only in the 5.1 graveyard scene when he recalls the long-dead Yorick does Hamlet speak with a sense of genuine human connection. It is not difficult to imagine the roguish court jester substituting both for an often absent-at-war father (*"he hath borne me on his back a thousand times"*) and an emotionally distant, self-absorbed mother (*"those lips that I have kissed I know not how oft"*). Perhaps to the aged-seven only child, the loss of *"a fellow / of infinite jest, of most excellent fancy"* was the traumatic moment when *"Hamlet from himself be ta'en away"* (5.2).

In extreme cases, PTSD sufferers may lose the ability to distinguish between the real life and their imaginary one; in either world, everything is merely a series of *"actions that a man might play"* (1.2). Consequently, they may value the humanity of actual people as no greater than that of fictional characters. The result can be behaviors that appear at best lacking in empathy and at worst seem almost sociopathic. For example, the prince's sending to execution of his two old school friends so shocks Horatio that in his final *"All this I can truly deliver"* speech of 5.2 he will excuse the play's villain Claudius from any blame for it: *"He never gave commandment for their death."*

14.4 – Oedipal complex?: *"Incestuous sheets"*

Along with his belief that Shakespeare's plays were in reality written by Edward de Vere, the 17th Earl of Oxford, another of psychologist Sigmund Freud's theories was that Prince Hamlet was afflicted with something he termed an 'Oedipal complex.'

Is Prince Hamlet perversely obsessed with his mother's sexuality? Or does his concern at his uncle's and mother's conjugal relations have a more practical basis: that it might produce a rival heir whose birth would make permanent the prince's disinheritance?

Sample 4.1
The first sample response argues that Hamlet's wish to protect his already-thwarted inheritance from the birth of a rival heir is sufficient reason for his urging of his mother to shun Claudius' bed. No further psycho-sexual motivation is necessary to explain his actions.

"With most wicked speed to incestuous sheets" (1.2)—does Hamlet's reaction to Queen Gertrude's speedy remarriage reveal a perverse obsession with his mother's sexuality? Or is it evidence of an entirely practical concern by the prince for his future safety?

King Claudius' assurance to Hamlet that he is *"most immediate to our throne"* (1.2) is surely little comfort to his nephew; for that was the status *"The expectancy and rose of the fair state"* (3.1) prince enjoyed from the moment he was born. But what if the *"o'erhasty marriage"* (2.2) of his *"uncle-father and aunt-mother"* (2.2) produced a rival heir? Would the child of a living king not outrank the child of a dead one? We can assume the manipulative Claudius would deploy the *"witchcraft of his wit"* (1.5) to make it so.

One or more offspring conceived in what the Ghost calls the *"royal bed of Denmark"* (1.5) would present a grim prospect indeed for old King Hamlet's son. At best, he would be set to endure life-long house arrest at Elsinore in the *"cheer and comfort"* (1.2) of King Claudius' surveillance;

at worst, the prince would, like his father, be disposed of in some 'accident' contrived by his uncle to clear the way for his own hereditary line of succession. In my view, Hamlet's sense of self-preservation alone provides the prince with sufficient reason for urging his mother: *"go not to mine uncle's bed ... Confess yourself to heaven; / Repent what's past; avoid what is to come"* (3.4). Accordingly, there is no need to search for some psychosexual motive buried so deep in Hamlet's subconscious that no character in the play nor even the playwright himself is aware of it.

Sample 4.2

Sample response number two argues that adaptations of *Hamlet* which transform Shakespeare's 3.4 closet scene into a Freudian bedroom scene are unsupported by anything in the actual text of the play.

Hamlet productions that add a bed to the closet scene, feature a seductively dressed queen, and show son and mother kiss full on the lips owe everything to Freud's notion that the prince subconsciously desires to possess his mother sexually—and nothing to Shakespeare's actual play.

Firstly, there is no 'bedroom scene' in *Hamlet*. In 3.2, Rosencrantz says to the prince *"She desires to speak with you in her closet"* and Polonius tells the king: *"My lord, he's going to his mother's closet"* In 4.1, the king remarks: *"And from his mother's closet hath he dragged him (Polonius)."* Moreover, the 3.4 scene is described in the play's text as taking place in 'The Queen's closet.' According to the Merriam-Webster dictionary, a closet is "a monarch's or official's private chamber." And how likely is it the queen has a second *"royal bed of Denmark"* (1.5) in her closet in addition to the one in her bedroom?

Secondly, Hamlet's only directions to Gertrude in the 3.4 text of *"Sit you down"* and *"You shall not budge"* contain little hint of erotic interaction.

Thirdly, Hamlet resorts to using sexually charged language against his mother only after the following have left her unmoved: an accusation of murder (*"As kill a king"*); the dismissal of her remarriage as a loveless fraud (*"As false as dicers' oaths"*); moral disapproval (*"Heaven's face doth glow"*); and an appeal to her aesthetic judgement (*"Hyperion's curls … like mildewed ear"*). All of which leaves Gertrude in fear of her son's rage—but still puzzled as to its cause: *"Ay me, what act?"*

In summary, Hamlet's assault on her senses (*"Ha, have you eyes?"*) and sexuality (*"rank seat of an enseamed bed"*) is not the first approach of a subconsciously incestuous son to a teasingly seductive mother. Instead, it is his last resort in seeking to shame Gertrude into recognizing what he believes her former brother-in-law has made her (*"He hath … whored my mother"*, 5.2): a woman who has prostituted her body in exchange for retaining her status as queen.

Sample 4.3

Oedipus was a King of Thebes in Greek mythology who featured as the title character in the playwright Sophocles' 2,500-year-old tragedy, *Oedipus Rex*. Not knowing he was adopted, Oedipus married Jocasta, with neither groom nor bride realizing they were, in fact, son and mother.

Psychologist Sigmund Freud misapplied the term 'Oedipal complex' to describe a psychological development stage in which young boys sexually lust after their mothers. Moreover, because the son views the father as a rival for his mother's affection, he entertains murderous fantasies of disposing of him so that he may replace his father in his mother's bed.

Oedipus, of course, was troubled by no such desires; in fact, when he afterward discovered the truth about whom he had married, he blinded himself in shame. As for his equally shocked and distraught wife/mother Jocasta, she hanged herself with bedsheets.

Assuming that Freud's theorized 'Oedipal complex' condition actually exists, is there anything in the play to suggest Prince Hamlet suffers from it?

> According to psychologist Sigmund Freud and his followers, the reason for Hamlet's play-long hesitation in killing King Claudius is that he subconsciously identifies with his uncle. Why? Because Claudius has acted out in reality what the prince only dares to imagine in the repressed fantasies of his Freudian subconscious: he has removed the prince's father, and seduced and married Queen Gertrude. Accordingly, the prince cannot bring himself to murder Claudius—for in taking his uncle's life the prince would in effect be ending his own. At least, subconsciously.
>
> But Hamlet in act one is himself contemplating suicide (*"I do not set my life in a pin's fee"*, 1.5). Should that not make it more rather than less likely that the prince would murder an uncle who, in his Freudian subconscious, he supposedly imagines as a mirror of himself?
>
> In so far as the prince does harbor a fantasy about his parents' marriage, it is not to imagine himself as an incestuous interloper between father and mother; quite the contrary. His quest is poignant rather than perverse. It is to rescue his mother's soul (*"Confess yourself to heaven"*, 3.4) and condemn his uncle's (*"as damned and black / As hell, whereto it goes"*, 3.3). This suggests a son's longing to reunite in the afterlife the fractured-by-Claudius parental relationship he cherishes in his memory (*"so loving to my mother ... Why, she would hang on him"*, 1.2). Nothing could be less incestuous or 'oedipal' than a son wishing he could restore his father to his mother's side.

What of the suggestion that Hamlet identifies—in his Freudian subconscious—with his father-killing and mother-marrying uncle, Claudius? If that were true, one would expect the prince to imagine his uncle seduced his way into his mother's affections through some combination of personal charisma and sexual allure that the supposedly incestuous prince might fantasize about emulating. However, as *The Murder of Gonzago* demonstrates (*"The Poisoner woos the Queen with gifts"*, 3.2), Hamlet views Claudius' winning of his mother as an entirely mercenary or *"hire and salary"* (3.3) arrangement between two self-interested individuals.

As for the eventual killing of Claudius in 5.2, Freudians attach psychological significance to the fact that Hamlet can murder his uncle only after Gertrude is already dead. But the events of the final scene are adequately justified by dramatic necessity. For the prince must be provided with the rationale for dispatching his uncle in an act of spontaneous public justice rather than delayed private vengeance.

In summary, I cannot agree that Sigmund Freud's Oedipal complex theory, misnamed after Sophocles' Greek king who never suffered from it, adds anything to our understanding of Shakespeare's Danish prince and the title character of play which Freud believed was written by someone else.

14.5 – Ophelia's trauma: *"Divided from herself"*

Whatever the motive for and nature of Hamlet's *"antic disposition"* (1.5), there is no doubting the genuine trauma of Ophelia. Polonius' daughter has become an iconic representation of every powerless and voiceless young woman who is divided between her true self and the role she has been forced to play in order to conform to social expectations.

Sample 5.1
Did Hamlet's ploy of feigned madness have the unintended result of sending Ophelia into real insanity? Or was it her own participation in Elsinore's web of deception that led to her madness and suicide?

In 2.1, Ophelia fears her rejection of Hamlet has driven insane the prince on whom depends, in her brother's words, *"The safety and health of this whole state."* After Hamlet's *"doublet all unbraced"* visit to her closet and unaware of the prince's put-on *"antic disposition"* (1.5), Ophelia worries that Polonius' interpretation of Hamlet's behavior (*"Mad for thy love?"*) may be correct: *"My lord, ... truly, I do fear it."*

But Ophelia's downward descent only begins with her agreement to become part of Elsinore's world of deception. Under her father's direction, she participates in the *"'twere by accident"* meeting with Hamlet of 3.1 in order to discover, as Claudius explains to Gertrude, *"If't be th'affliction of his love or no / That thus he suffers for."*

Ophelia's opening remark to Hamlet suggests she misses him in her life: *"How does your honour for this many a day?"* After her humiliating exchange with the prince, it is Hamlet's apparent loss of reason (*"O, what a noble mind is here o'erthrown!"*) that causes Ophelia the most grief. For the same madness she mistakenly believed was caused by her rejection of him, she now sees as the explanation for his rejection of her.

Following Polonius' murder and Hamlet's exile, the uncertain and distressed Ophelia of the first three acts declines into the traumatized Ophelia of act four. Her mood of grief and sadness, combined with the passivity that characterized her life, culminates in Ophelia's surrender to *"self-slaughter"* (1.2). Despite her apparent suicide, she is laid to rest in a church graveyard, if only with *"maimed rites"* but along with other *"peace-parted souls"* (5.1).

Sample 5.2
The second sample response focuses on Ophelia's social isolation as a contributing factor to her mental collapse.

Along with the emotion-venting outlet of his *"antic disposition"* (1.5), Hamlet is sustained through his trials by two other factors. One is his sense of self-worth; as he reminds Rosencrantz, he is *"the son of a king"* (4.2). And, as is shown in the very first scene, he enjoys the loyalty of Horatio and the palace sentries. For it is not to the king but to the prince they report the Ghost's appearance, *"As needful in our loves, fitting our duty"* (1.1).

In contrast, Ophelia is entirely alone. With her brother absent in Paris and lacking a Horatio-like companion in whom to confide, it is to her meddlesome and manipulative father Polonius (*"What's the matter ... i'th'name of God?"*) that a clearly upset (*"affrighted"*) Ophelia turns in 2.1 with her report of Hamlet's wordless and disheveled (*"no hat upon his head"*) appearance in her closet.

After being subjected to Hamlet's abusive and self-contradictory rant—against women, men and himself—in the nunnery scene of 3.1, Ophelia next endures the humiliation of hearing the king dismiss *"neglected love"* as the *"something in (Hamlet's) soul"*, for *"his affections do not that way tend."* Her opinion unsought by her father (*"We heard it all"*), and holding her unreturned *"remembrances"*, the *"of ladies most deject and wretched"* Ophelia is left abandoned and uncomforted: *"O, woe is me."* Even Gertrude, the play's only other female character, will later refuse to offer her comfort in her distress: *"I will not speak with her ... What would she have?"* (4.5). With her only parent Polonius now interred in an unmarked grave (*"At his head a grass-green turf"*), and crushed by the weight of humiliation she has been forced to carry alone, Ophelia is finally broken by the manipulative world of Elsinore.

Sample 5.3
On seeing nothing in her future but disappointment, Ophelia makes the one decision about her life that is within her power: she ends it.

Ophelia's madness is also for her a form of liberation. In her trauma, she has not so much lost her powers of reason but is using them for the first time. But, for so long unaccustomed to communicating her true feelings, she must borrow from the symbolic language of flowers and popular ballads to express her clear understanding of her bleak situation in a world of corruption and betrayal.

As a spectator of Hamlet's adapted *The Murder of Gonzago*, she has *"heard it all"* (3.1). Her flower offerings carry specific accusatory messages for both Claudius and Gertrude. c, *let's have no words of this, but when they ask you what it means, say you this."*

She next recites a balled verse that expresses what has pushed her beyond the bounds of sanity: the maddening contradictions of her situation. In the song lyric of a naïve girl who is seduced by the promise of marriage only to be abandoned because she is no longer a virgin, Ophelia sees the impossibility of anything in her future but failure and disappointment: *"I cannot choose but weep."*

Ophelia makes the one decision about her existence that is within her power: she ends it. In her short and restricted life, Ophelia's inner but never-to-allowed-bloom nature was characterized by Hamlet as that of a *"nymph"* (3.1): a free-spirited, woodland-dwelling goddess associated—prophetically—with the element of water. In her manner of death, Gertrude describes her as a *"mermaid"* drawn back by nature to the water, *"like a creature native and indued / Unto that element"* (4.7).

14.6 – Conclusion: *"Cudgel thy brains no more"*

Is the Ghost really his father? Is Claudius a murderer? Was his mother an accomplice? Can he trust Ophelia with his knowledge of the Ghost? Or might she submissively yield up his secret to her domineering father, just as she later surrenders the prince's love letter (*"in obedience, hath my daughter shown me"*, 2.2). And should he take revenge or not? As for Ophelia, Hamlet's uncertainties are reflected in her doubting the sincerity of his *"almost all the holy vows of heaven"* (1.3) love for her.

Over the first three acts, the tormented grappling of Hamlet and Ophelia with their dilemmas is mirrored in Guildenstern's report of disputes between theater companies: *"O, there has been much throwing about of brains"* (2.2). At the play's end, however, the two characters accept their bleak fates by each surrendering to death: she, to the *"weeping brook"* (4.7); he, to Claudius' *"he shall not choose but fall"* (4.7) rigged fencing duel.

Sample 6.1
In an influential book published in 1969, Swiss-born psychiatrist Elizabeth Kübler-Ross introduced a five-stage conceptual model that outlined how sufferers typically process deep grief or loss, although not necessarily in strict sequence: denial, anger, bargaining, depression, and acceptance. This first sample conclusion suggests Hamlet passes through the first four stages to end the play in a state of fatalistic acceptance of his *"heaven ordinant"* (5.2) destiny.

> At the play's end, Hamlet arrives at the final and fifth stage of what eminent psychiatrist Elisabeth Kübler-Ross chronicled as the five stages of grief: acceptance.
>   The prince's response to the Ghost's accusations (*"O my prophetic soul. My uncle?"*, 1.5) reveals he already suspected Claudius of murdering his father. Yet Hamlet had still chosen to depart Elsinore and resume his life at Wittenberg. In this state of denial or avoidance, he resembles what the Ghost calls *"the fat weed / That roots itself in ease on Lethe wharf"* (1.5). Lethe was the river that

flowed through the afterworld of Hades; its waters caused forgetfulness of the past in those who drank from it.

For Hamlet, next comes the combination of anger and depression that is most deeply expressed in his second soliloquy: *"O, what a rogue and peasant slave am I! ..."* (2.2). Hamlet's scheme of using *The Murder of Gonzago* to uncover Claudius' guilt corresponds to his bargaining stage. But no matter what its outcome, it can never bring back to life his dead father and restore him to his mother's side. Hamlet, a Renaissance man of reason, tries and fails to reason his way through the dilemma with which *"providence"* (5.2) has presented him. But, to borrow the words of the gravedigger, the prince *"cudgel(s)"* his *"brains"* in vain (5.1).

Ophelia's *"self-slaughter"* (1.2) foreshadows Hamlet's suicidal return to Elsinore and with it his acceptance of his fate. As the prince must surely expect, the villainous Claudius has some life-ending *"exploit"* (4.7) prepared for him. As he confesses to Horatio: *"But thou wouldst not think how ill all's here about my heart. But it is no matter"* (5.2). Hamlet now accepts that the *"divinity that shapes our ends"* (5.2) will provide the circumstances for him to complete the task he has been fated to perform (*"To quit (Claudius) with this arm"*, 5.2)—but in a self-sacrificing and redeeming act of public justice rather than a sinful one of private revenge. Such is the acceptance of his fate the prince has embraced at the end of his tormented, play-long journey: *"for heaven hath pleased it so"* (3.4).

Sample 6.2

In the manipulative and maddening Denmark ruled over by King Claudius and Queen Gertrude, the only escape for Hamlet and Ophelia is through death. Here is the second sample conclusion.

"Still better, and worse"—Ophelia's deflecting response in 3.2 to Hamlet's risqué banter carries a poignant echo of the vows exchanged at a traditional marriage ceremony, and are met with his reply: *"So you must take your husbands."* But the play cannot end with the marriage of Hamlet and Ophelia because of the *"incestuous sheets"* (1.2) union of the prince's *"uncle-father and aunt-mother"* (2.2). that is celebrated at its beginning. Tragically, the play concludes instead with their double surrender to suicide: Ophelia to a *"muddy death"* in a *"weeping brook"* (4.7), Hamlet to Claudius' and Laertes' *"he shall not choose but fall"* (4.7) rigged fencing duel.

Her submission to her manipulative father, who in turns serves a corrupt king, costs Ophelia her sanity and leaves her with only one route of escape from the *"heartache / That ... flesh is heir to"* in this *"calamity of ... life"* (3.1). Her *"too too sullied flesh ... resolve(s) itself into a dew"* (1.2). In Elsinore's graveyard, she is at last free from a world that exploited and dismissed her: *"rest her soul, she's dead"* (5.1).

The Hamlet who returns to Denmark in act five has abandoned his *"antic disposition"* (1.5). He faces his adversary King Claudius without dissimulation (*"If his fitness speaks, mine is ready", 5.2*). He requests Horatio to tell his story, for the *"wounded name"* (5.2) Hamlet leaves behind of *"he that is mad and sent into England"* (5.1) is an incomplete version of his tragic tale.

Hamlet's last words to the dying Claudius—*"Follow my mother"* (5.2)—are those of a *"scourge and minister"* (3.4) wedding celebrant who extends forever in a hell of *"sulphurous and tormenting flames"* (1.5) the marriage that blocked his path to his father's throne and his hopes of sharing it with his *"fair Ophelia"* (3.1).

Sample 6.3
Deception is both a moral failing and a psychological burden. A type of multiple personality disorder is required of his subjects by King Claudius whose reign is itself a fraud.

When Claudius' remarks about his nephew that neither *"th'exterior nor the inward man / Resembles that it was"* (2.2), we are reminded that Elsinore is a place where there may be two possible answers to the question posed in the play's opening line: *"Who's there?"* The king's exterior pose of grieving brother, caring step-father and benevolent monarch conceals the true 'inward man': a murderous villain who poured poison into his sleeping brother's ear and then proceeds to poison the character his subjects.

Rosencrantz and Guildenstern, two formerly *"Good lads"* (2.2), are enlisted as spies. And *"fair Ophelia"* (3.1) is commanded to exploit her former relationship with the prince to uncover the source of Hamlet's *"turbulent and dangerous lunacy"* (3.1) which King Claudius fears may contain *"some danger"* (3.1).

After he manipulates Polonius' grieving and angry son into the rigged fencing duel, the king advises Laertes to *"keep close within your chamber"* (4.7). As it turns out, Claudius is correct to doubt Laertes' ability to keep their *"exploit"* (4.7) a secret. For as the duel of 5.2 progresses, we hear him admit in an aside: *"And yet it is almost against my conscience."*

In a country ruled over by a corrupt and all-powerful king, the only alternative to absolute obedience is to hide one's core identity or true self behind a false public mask. This motif of divided selves and fragmented identities is all-present throughout the play. In the first scene, when Horatio is asked about the Ghost by Marcellus: *"Is it not like the King?"*; Horatio replies: *"As thou art to thyself."* It is a response that suggests 'thou' and 'thyself' may be both different and the same. Gertrude's advice to Hamlet in the next scene of *"look like a friend on Denmark"* is met in 3.4 by his rejoinder of: *"Assume a virtue, if you have it not."* And before the nunnery scene of 3.1, Ophelia is advised on how to stage a most convincing performance for deceiving the prince. Hamlet's *"transformation"* is described by Claudius as having put the prince *"So much from th'understanding of himself"* (2.2). As for Ophelia's later breakdown, the king believes it to be the result of her becoming *"Divided from / herself and her fair judgment"* (4.5).

"Denmark's a prison" (2.2), Hamlet tells his two old school friends. But, as with any totalitarian regime, it is also an incubator of what psychologists call Dissociative Identity Disorder (DID): a condition that leaves sufferers with split personalities, who act differently according to which one happens to be dominant, and without a sense of which is their true identity.

At the play's end, it is Laertes' truth-revealing exposure (*"the King's to blame"*) that leads to Claudius' downfall. His corrupting and maddening reign depended on others becoming as false as he. But the 'real' Laertes is not a Claudius-like deceitful poisoner; instead, he is a basically honorable man. Laertes answers the call issued to the Ghost in the very first scene: *"stand, and unfold yourself."* In so doing, he follows the advice rather than the example of his father, Polonius: *"This above all: to thine ownself be true, / And it must follow, as the night the day, / Thou canst not then be false to any man"* (1.3).

Printed in Great Britain
by Amazon